PEBBLES FROM SULAIMAN'S MOUNTAIN

IFTIKHAR H. MALIK

DEDICATION

Dedicated to the Kalasha of Chitral and Sheedis of Balochistan.

Contents

- "The author seems to be the new David Lodge of the global scholarly community." *Karine Leno Ancellin: American academic in Greece.*

-"Iftikhar Malik's intellectual rigour and wealth of knowledge shines through his prose." *Sarvat Hasin: 'This Wide Night'; 'The Giant Dark'.*

- "Iftikhar Malik has spent an intellectually vibrant and productive lifetime in Western academia; is an avid traveller with a keen eye for the aesthetic and a scholar with deep and discerning appreciation for historical, political, and cultural discourses." *Osama Siddique: 'Snuffing Out the Moon'; 'Ghuroob e Shehr Ka Waqt'.*

-"Iftikhar writes with flair and much mastery of language of a milieu that he is familiar with. This brings the almost unknown world of academics, intelligent women, romantic interludes in a global setting." *Aquila Ismail: 'Of Martyrs and Marigolds'.*

-Protagonists remain "brave, passionate yet composed whereas diction resonates with truth but gently." *Shamsa Ghaznavi: Public intellectual.*

-"… intellectualism, academic culture, romance, humor and that precious joie de vivre … are the strands of what really is a story of history and human connection." *Mehr Husain, Literary Critic.*

Page Blank Intentionally

PREFACE

"Yes, and how many years must a mountain exist

Before it is washed to the sea?

And how many years can some people exist

Before they're allowed to be free?

Yes, and how many times can a man turn his head

And pretend that he just doesn't see?

The answer, my friend, is blowin' in the wind

The answer is blowin' in the wind."

(Lyrics by Bob Dylan in Richard Williams, *A Man called Alias,*
New York, 1992, 42.)

TURBAT

"Welcome to Turbat—*our* ancestral land—Miss Annette Sandeman," Gul held his English partner by her arm the moment Fokker aircraft stopped taxiing down the small runway surrounded by reddish-brown hills dotted with isolated clumps of palm trees often in the crevices as if shying away from human sight. These ancient trees lodged in those distant fissures, yet visible this crispy morning, stood still as if punctiliously observing the brunette from West Country, whose freckled face had already assumed a slightly tanned hue owing to a few days spent in Karachi. Back home in Salford—halfway between Bath and Bristol--intermittent April showers strove hard to flood the Avon, alerting her Anglo-Saxon sub-conscience of a stark contrast between these two distant lands that were otherwise intertwined peculiarly. Balochistan, the largest province of a new country and located to the west of the Indus, was avowedly brown, adamantly dry, and trenchantly daring yet no less observant as were the people back home in a starkly green and wet Englistan--quieter but no less alert. While emerging from a cooler aircraft, Anne felt a waft of dry, warm breeze on her arms, whereas her wavy locks dared sparkling brightness that never seemed to age, rather steadily gaining in heat as the day wore on. This being an early morning, the proverbial harshness of the desert terrain was still invisible behind the stolid dunes, standing watchful like the Chinese terracotta soldiers.

"Gul, it isn't as hot as I'd dreaded; on the contrary, the air feels uniquely clean and pristine." Anne promptly withdrew her arm from Gul's hand as she would occasionally in Bristol, where they had met a few years back in Joe's class on creative writing.

"Yes, don't let our sun cajole you since it gets vindictively hot as the day goes by, and in a short while here, you'll perhaps absorb the corpus of sunrays that otherwise requires an entire year in good old Somerset or Devonshire."

"But that still didn't deter great grandpa Sandeman from residing here without discarding his usual English attire, kitted with his pith helmet. Mind it, the tough Scot died here in Las Bela in 1892 after serving the Raj for four decades, virtually reigning

Balochistan, though one may proffer many questions about Sandemanism. You may have permanently tanned skin plus the advantage of being on the home ground, but never underestimate my resilience."

"Okay, *Baba*, I was just cautioning you in case our irreverent weather and rustic habitude tire you out. Unlike those tough Bristolians, Bathonians are somewhat spoiled and slightly on the fragile side. Mind it, Salford is nearer to Bath than to Bristol, though Keynsham takes that credit."

Before Anne could respond to my impish quip, we found ourselves sauntering into the small lounge meant for passengers, and amidst the small crowd gathered to receive new arrivals, we saw Anjum waving at us. Just behind my younger sister stood our parents, Shahnaz and Nauroz. Ammi was attired in her usual Balochi tunic and white linen shalwar whereas Abu Nauroz's white turban appeared to command over the small motley crowd eager to hug us and carry our suitcases. I was home with a woman, a degree, and two greying sideburns—all in the same order. Mother was over the moon, as I could amply detect through those brown teary eyes. In contrast, Dad, always subtle and diligently restrained on such occasions true to his lifetime in cities and bureaucracy, was mirthful and gave me a bear hug. At the same time, Anne remained intertwined with Ammi for a considerable time. Anjum looked exuberant and waited for her turn to share the joy of meeting Anne, with whom she had spoken a few times, sharing information about Baloch handicrafts, the stubborn landscape, especially its spectacular coast featuring Hingol Park-- the largest and unique of its kind in the country. Overheard on the phone, Anjum had obviously briefed Anne on coastal Balochistan, the land route taken by Alexander on his flight back to Macedonia along with 30,000 troops and faced with the heat and inclement weather while hemmed between cliffs and the Arabian Sea, half of his force perished on this 540-mile windswept journey. Now, a snake-like road traversed the heights and lows of this expanse, often cutting through rugged rocks where, if luck would have it, vigilant eyes could detect some solitary Marco Polo sheep—Markhor--alternating its satiated gaze between a stark blue sea and quaint brown topography. Cars, lorries, and camouflaged military trucks incessantly moved like ants on this highway, reputedly the most spectacular in South Asia. In fact, it headed towards Gwadar, which Pakistanis, with the nod and ample supply of Yuan from Beijing, were building up as a replica of their version of Dubai or even Muscat, both lying across the Gulf.

"How very sweet to have a Sandeman back in Balochistan! You look gorgeous, Anne, as if my elder brother in Karachi and his charming wife ensured proper acculturation and acclimatization for you."

"So splendid to see you, Anjum, Abu, and Ammi, and thanks for offering me this special honor by being at the airport. Never mind, a Sandeman reincarnate returns home. Our air hostess, Raheela, is also from Turbat."

I'd noticed the cabin crew passing by us, and Raheela, with a captivating smile, paused to share pleasantries. "Anne, Raheela was my class fellow at the university in Quetta and was always entranced by the idea of seeing the world from above."

"Anjum was the brainiest and naughtiest girl of our cohort, and we often wondered what kind of a special man would win over the heart of this immensely independent woman. Now, she is administering the entire Attock district up in the north. Yes, I travel across Pakistan with the national carrier and occasionally to Oman, Dubai, and Saudia, though I dutifully prefer coming back to Turbat."

"Raheela, Anne is from a historic family in England maintaining special associations with Balochistan since the nineteenth century. Remember, our residence hall was situated on Sandeman Road in Quetta. What a small world!" Anjum had already begun to steer the social wheel in her subtle way whereas I hugged Abu after touching Ammi's knees while absorbing her Arabic prayers on my return following another sojourn abroad.

"Anjum, I remember Gul visiting us occasionally with your parents, posing as a no-nonsense chap. Gul and Anne, we should catch up over tea next time I am in town for an extended weekend. Regards, Uncle Nauroz and Auntie Shahnaz! I got to go as we need to freshen up for the journey back to Karachi, which is due in half an hour."

"See you, Raheela, and safe travels," we all spoke at once in unison.

Winding through the suburban road, which appeared more like a country lane around Glastonbury and bordered by the orchards of palm and walnut trees, we headed towards our home in the town's western corner. Our ancestral place, now lived in by an uncle, was in the town center where a warren of narrow lanes and ever-multiplying shopping plazas surrounded the traditional abode called haveli, which displayed a mixture of old and new with grape vines and rose bushes hugging wooden beams that supported a thatched roof over the veranda. As is the case in such houses, the kitchen was perched on the other side of the compound, itself featuring berry and sheesham trees, so keenly knotted with my childhood. Our newer house was built some two decades back since Abu wanted a spacious, modern accommodation equipped with all the amenities, including a study, guest rooms, servant quarters, and a meticulously designed garden. This suburban neighborhood evolved in the 1990s when Baloch sardars, following one another, started sending their sons to premier schools in Lahore and Quetta, followed by comfortable jobs in public domains. Poorer and less educated families still sent their sons to Oman and, if possible, to Dubai, though Iran was comparatively well off and our Makran county bordered the land of Saadi and Hafiz; still, we preferred working and living across the Indus lands or beyond the Gulf.

While acquainting Anne with some spots linked with my childhood, Anjum, with a Master's in English from Lahore's prestigious Kinnaird and now a civil servant, assumed the role of an interlocutor displaying an unprecedented sense of ease. During the short drive, Abu's interjections were succinct and occasional, allowing Anne to surmise the people and places she was encountering for the first time, though I had briefed her copiously back in Bath. A major chunk of this arable land was our hereditary area featuring clumps of keekar, sheesham, mulberry, and palm trees traversed by water channels, though Anjum, quite smartly, avoided mentioning its ownership so as not to betray a modicum of feudatory pride. In fact, the land, other than being a mainstay for our mundane life, was the closest link with our roots, and despite owning a house in metropolitan Karachi's Defence, Abu, and even my brother identified Turbat as the actual home. In the open space, a toddler Anjum would join Mukhtar, Zahid, Raheem, and myself when we played marbles or some form of improvised cricket. Junior to me by two years, her being a girl did not matter for any of us, though her forays stopped soon as she joined the girls' school and we entered high school. In a sense, we were like other rural-tribal people since sedentary and even cosmopolitan pursuits never superseded our instinctive rootedness in this distant town, which even for many fellow urbane citizens, happened to be situated in a rather less privileged part of their country.

Somehow, I had assumed that Anne, in general, had a fair idea of our household, including Aunt Zahra—the housekeeper—who had been with us since her childhood because her parents virtually ran the place during the bygone era of my late paternal grandparents. The first person to welcome Anne home was, in fact, Zahra herself whose gracious smile and extended arms exhibited spontaneous warmth, imbibed with affection that comes only with long-term associations. They both were meeting for the first time while I, surreptitiously, tried to study Anne's face as she met the African member of my family. Anne, as always not to be alarmed or deterred by sudden encounters, hugged Zahra as if they had known each other for decades and, in response, received kisses on both her cheeks that had gained a deeper pink glow in our late morning sun.

"Salaam Aunt Zahra, so very nice to finally meet up with you. *Aap kaisay hain?*"

"*Waalaykum Salaam Baity, Humm theek hain. Aapko Khush Amdeed.*"

All of us standing aside were witnessing and even relishing this bonhomie where our de facto matriarch had already adopted a guest as if the later might have been a missing member of the Gichki family. Other than ensuring proper food on the table, Zahra monitored and mentored our guards, gardener, and driver, along with ensuring the quality of provisions often brought in by the hawkers specializing in their respective commodities. At times, I used to wonder at the extent of Zahra's energies given the fact that in addition to helping Ammi in the kitchen and other household chores, she fully ensured the smooth running of her own family, which for a while lived in a side quarter that my father purposefully built and where her two sons and a daughter grew up. Following their education in the local mosque and high school, Rustam and Arsalan went away their own ways—with the former working in Oman while the younger and muscular Arsalan joined the country's coast guards. Zeenat attended local schools in Turbat, though Anjum regularly coached her at home, and following her A-levels she left for Karachi to stay with my brother's family to continue her higher studies. Zeenat was industrious, well-read, and into athletics and, like Anjum, prepared for civil service, which she eventually joined, given her brilliant academic career. Aunt Zahra was a widow after losing Uncle Ahmad a few years back when his foot happened to hit a hidden mine somewhere between Turbat and the local military cantonment, probably planted by Baloch separatists waging a war against the Pakistani army to wrest control of their province. Our Baloch people are divided into three countries: Pakistan, Iran, and Afghanistan, with several tribes living in India's Rajasthan as well, though most of them live in Karachi—even outnumbering those who reside in Pakistan's otherwise largest province accounting for almost half of its territorial size. After Karachi, Quetta, Khuzdar, Turbat, Gwadar, and Dera Bugti, Las Bela, and Muscat hold visible Baloch communities divided into several tribes and significantly land dependent. Excepting some affluent chieftains—sardars—most Baloch are landless, whereas, with the arrival of education and jobs, one detects a semblance of a minuscule middle class which, owing to politicization, wrestles with the issues of identity, including those who desire to create an exclusive Baloch state called "the Greater Balochistan." Sandwiched between the enduring and certainly merciless clutches of sardari system and the ever-expansive tentacles of a younger state, some Baloch youth periodically resort to guns, and Ahmad, like his other numerous counterparts, accidentally found himself in this crossfire and proved one more stat in an ever-growing list of fatalities. Following her selection for civil service,

Zeenat was preparing herself to work in the country's foreign ministry before getting posted abroad as a diplomat and thus was unable to meet us here in Turbat.

Thanks to Zahra's meticulous efforts, Anne's room was bedecked with traditional curtains, wall hangings, and bed coverings crafted by local women specializing in knitting and weaving skills, including the purdah-style rug unique to our part of the world, unlike Bokhara's *feelpa* (elephant foot) or the Isfahani counterparts often beautified by amorous peacocks. I could gather right away that Anjum's own aesthetics played a significant role in furnishing this upper-floor room that lay between mine and hers, whereas our parents occupied the main floor, which included storage areas and a kitchen fronted by an open courtyard featuring flowerbeds watched over by some palms and eucalyptus trees. Given our climate, jasmine, and roses, when in bloom, especially during the summer months, are nature's generous concessions for rural Balochistan, otherwise embodying a testing, even harshly arid climate with very little rainfall though occasional showers can also cause deluge through flash floods when our rugged hills unleash torrents both to feed and flood our soil. Balochistan is unique for its gigantic size, yet smaller populace compared to other regions in the subcontinent. It is also exceptional for its brown open space characterized by low-lying hills often taking on a pinkish-orange hue contrasted with the shocking blues of the sea to its south. Traditional men, wearing their own style of turban seen nowhere else, sport beards and longish hair, and true to our desert's preference for camels over horses, pastoral lifestyles permeate the valleys where a wide variety of cacti feed our sheep, goats, and camels though for bovine species farmers scout for green fodder. Excepting the Kharan desert and coastal areas featuring granular sand and dunes, the soil in the rest of Balochistan is overwhelmingly rocky with sparse vegetation, and while flying over its extensive tracts, one only notices enormous, brown, and persistently stark spread that stretches all the way into eastern Iran and southern Afghanistan until one detects snow clad peaks of the Alburz and Hazarajat, but nowhere else in the entirety of Balochistan. Our colorful handicrafts, ornate textiles, and sturdy footwear reflect those unique environmental features of this land with fewer incentives for population explosion, keeping our atmosphere as primeval as ever, along with a discomfiting level of irately hot temperature.

Anne's new digs were, in fact, often occupied by Bahram and Shireen during their visits from Karachi, which weren't too frequent except for Eid or any other specific family engagement. Bahram was a civil servant employed by the central government in the revenue department while Shireen practised medicine at the Aga Khan Hospital, and both took turns in looking after their two children besides some regular help from an au pair. Living in the Defence and close to the sea, we stayed with them for a week before taking off for Turbat. Bahram was senior to me by five years, while Anjum followed me two years later. Bahram, like the other two siblings, gained his master's in politics from Lahore's Foreman Christian College, when Abu's job alternated between Islamabad and Lahore, though Bahram enjoyed living in the residence hall among a formative and no less joyous company of cosmopolitan class fellows. His competitive group of Punjabi, Baloch, and Pashtun students included careerists, often joined by a few Sindhi and Urdu-speaking friends, to whom Lahore meant a cherished venue for uppity civil service positions or, alternatively, future higher studies in some British university. In his early posting at Campbellpur, now called Attock, Bahram met Shireen, facilitated through some mutual friends, and they both ended up marrying each other. Shireen's versatility in languages like Hindko, Urdu, Pashto, and English coalesced well with Bahram's extrovert disposition, and their dates often took them to Kund where the blue of the Indus met the brown of the Kabul— vigilantly observed by a receding Punjab and a formidable Frontier. Shireen's parents, like many people from the upper Indus regions, came from a military background and professionalism on both sides was able to override the divergent forces of ethnicity and distance and helped the couple undertake marital vows. When on the phone with her mother, Shireen's Hindko resembled our Brahui, the native language of most Baloch and itself mighty older than Sanskrit, though Hindko, despite its Persianized vocabulary and Arabic script, claimed to be the true descendant of ancient Prakrit. Our visitors were often surprised by the multiplicity of languages spoken in our home, especially at the family gatherings with Zahra—the matriarch-- shifting between Brahui and Urdu, whereas the rest spoke latter or

"Perhaps it's too soon to ask, but Anne, how do you find Aunt Zahra being a part of the Gichki family?"

I threw this rather unsettling question at Anne after we both had partaken lunch, which, despite its apparent plainness, still manifested an elaborate spread. While sipping on some qahwa, deemed a digestive following a fuller meal, we both were lounging on the veranda, affording a vintage spot looking over the lawn and trees all the way to those dusty hills that I grew up watching and where Gichki lands touched the boundaries with those of Gashkoris—a fellow Baloch tribe and sometimes resolute rival over water resources and regional politics. Our underground waterways, called *karez*, caused occasional strains, manifestly overridden by sagacious elders.

"I'd heard about African communities inhabiting the coastal regions of the Gulf, Balochistan, and Western India, and Anjum had certainly mentioned Zahra as a member of the extended family. Without sounding presumptive, I do not see a Baloch equivalent of Mammy in Gone with the Wind in her. Of course, Zahra is not a slave, but frankly, her ancestors were, even possibly for some generations, though not as miserable as the chattel slaves in the American South."

"Quite right. The world blames Arabs, and then the Europeans for enslavement, yet several other societies like our Baloch, Gujaratis, and even the Khivans up in present-day Uzbekistan were slavers, as were the past empires all the way up to the Ottomans. Of course, most slaves happened to be Africans, given the comprehensive post-Columbus documentation, yet numberless underprivileged people, especially after the warfare, routinely fell victim to bondage. Our coastal areas including Jiwani, Gwadar, Las Bela, and certainly Karachi and further east in lower Sindh, people of African descent called Sheedis, make a visible presence in our social mosaic though their status within the Baloch social hierarchy remains ambivalent."

"Having lived in these Asian regions, other than their complexion, they must have retained some cultural norms further underpinned by spiritual linkage with Africa." Anne's knowledge of American legacies was not off the mark.

"Quite true. Though Omanis, or better to say the Sultanate of Muscat, with its empire extending all the way to Zanzibar and territorial possessions in and around Mombasa and coastal Somalia, shipped slaves across the Indian Ocean in recent centuries, yet slave trade predated our Omani cousins. Undoubtedly, Basra, Baghdad, Kuwait, Yemen, and Saudi Arabia—not to talk of North Africa—retain sizeable proportions of people of African origins, and they have been there for millennia. In fact, the earliest recorded and enduring slave rebellion, called Zind, went on for decades against the Abbasid caliphate in the later half of the ninth century. Slavery and racism went hand in hand, and despite some matrimonial alliances and proximities, color-based discrimination stays rife at all these places—even in Sudan, which is itself African by any definition—yet the ruling elite always looked down upon Darfuris though, in terms of creed, they all are Muslim. Zahra and her family may be very near to us, and Baloch nationalists fighting the Pakistani army may define Sheedis as fellow Baloch, but to every keen observer, social segregation is a pervasive reality, and poverty further exacerbates it. Sorry for this mini-lecture, fellow sojourner!"

"I like the term proximities, which to me is an apt description of parallel communities with fluid borders. Aunt Zahra owes her status because you, Baloch, are a traditional society, and here, the concept of honor includes even those who might not be related to you through kinship yet enjoy proximity with the families that they have been associated with for a long time. Her loyalty and age might have further earned her this elevated position. As you say, her children are grown up and financially better off, but she prefers staying with you and might even be lording over your siblings without any rebuke from the parents."

"Quite right, Anne. While growing up with Rustam and Arsalan, I would visit the same maulvi sahib for religious instruction along with attending the same primary school, though it was only on rare occasions that we ate together in our kitchen since Aunt Zahra cooked separately for her family in her own home. Her daughter, Zeenat, was like a younger sister to Anjum, who mentored her all through those formative years. Of course, our festivities and funerary rituals obliterated this distinction, which carried somewhat subtle acceptance on all sides. We three siblings moved to cities to study whereas Rustam and Arsalan couldn't, and after high school, entered the job market though Zeenat continued, and that too brilliantly. Our Sheedis still marry among themselves, as do the Baloch and the rest, whereas inclusivity, especially through marriage, is rare even in a multicultural city like Karachi. At places, I have heard them being called Habashees or Ethiopians, which again is a misnomer since their ancestors could have been from anywhere in Sub-Saharan Africa."

After tediously dilating on history and anthropology, I soon became aware of delivering a prolonged oratory and quickly queried Anne in case she needed to have a siesta—something quite normal in Turbat as an aftermath for a slightly early lunch.

"I guess I'm okay and never mind sharing this valuable information. Other than meeting your family, I wanted to learn about Balochistan and possibly its little-known aspects of history even beyond its borders. Not that I am seeking some Orientalist exotica or am eager to follow the footsteps of my senior ancestor; instead, it may help me in my writing given the fact that Joe always encouraged us to follow our nose, digging up newer realms and themes."

"Wish Joe were alive today since he would have been happy to see you here in the westernmost part of the subcontinent that he deeply cherished in his person and fiction."

"Gul, I know your family is exceptionally understanding of our close friendship, but not being a married couple could have its own hazards, so, frankly speaking, you will have to be more forthcoming in alerting me to the areas that may not be socially acceptable."

"To tell you the truth, being a foreign guest is a unique privilege here, yet it also comes with a tag. What it means is that some people may be too curious occasionally asking intrusive questions such as about marriage and children. My immediate family knows that we are very close to each other and possibly passing through a phase of gestation before we make up our minds in any possible direction. Never forget, here man-woman relationship like ours means marriage vetoing any premarital sex, though I am not suggesting for a moment that we are all strictly monogamous and acutely celibate until we get married."

"Gul, every society retains some preconceived notions, and Salford is no exception either since it is hemmed in between a lofty Bath and a self-conscious Bristol--both gullible to pomposity which may accrue not from the number of tourists and imperial outreach but simply as a reaction to the guilt owing to their share in that 'peculiar institution.'"

"Well, one can say the same about Turbat as it lies somewhere between Karachi and Quetta or lodged on the way to Zahedan, and our Gwadar resembles Keynsham and may assert itself emphatically as an emerging Dubai or just continue as a former market town. Never forget our past preoccupation with that peculiar institution whose direct proofs are our Sheedis, Aunt Zahra, and her family."

"Gul, as we charted out back in England, I want to visit Quetta and Fort Sandeman and, if possible, the border with Iran and certainly your new Dubai. Turbat affords us just that rare opportunity and proximity which is reassuringly solidified by the mentoring companionship of a Baloch, reputedly my spouse."

"Sure. We can begin with Koh-i-Murad this afternoon after a short round of Turbat itself. But a bit of siesta will do us no harm."

Our afternoon tea, slightly against the pervasive norms, was sugar-free or *pheeki,* which hakims recommend to those who have some health issues such as diabetes or erratic bowel movements. Zahra was used to this since we "city-returnees," among many other new habits, often avoided taking sugar, though they would mercilessly prey upon halwa and burfi. However, to her, tea was incomplete without sugar and buffalo's milk though qahwa would entail no milk but a good addition of cardamom seeds and fresh mint. Her favorite karak chai, a stronger, sugary version of milky tea, was always served with large, circular, and thick millet cakes cooked on the pan and layered with home-churned butter with a dash of honey. Of course, she would equally ensure a portion of cake rusk, which again was an alien addition but meant to satiate a certain urban palate. Anne dunked her millet bread like rusk but found it somehow challenging and instead opted for smaller bites swallowed down by tea.

Present-day Turbat prides itself on colleges, offices, a cantonment, and a Shahi Bazaar, which is an odd but no less interesting mixture of old and new shops. We came to Hamid Dashti's shop after a drive around the schools and some suburban areas featuring elaborate private residences neighboring the military cantonment, where the roads were certainly broad, tree-lined, and well-kept, with several houses sporting front gardens. Dashti, other than selling groceries, held a collection of books and magazines that attracted many literate Turbatis to converse with him on the latest works from Iran and Pakistan in Persian, Urdu, and English. Occasionally, Dashti contributed articles for newspapers in these two countries and attended periodic poetry recitals at private homes and academic institutions. Anne enjoyed talking to Dashti, who offered her two books on Baloch history and a small Urdu pamphlet on Zikris while refusing to accept any money; instead, he invited us to return for tea.

While heading towards the Kech River, I drove through the locality, mostly inhabited by Sheedis, flagging the multiculturalism of this border town. Of course, smaller hut-like mud houses with thatched roofs, almost non-existent lanes, and a starkly visible presence of donkeys and goats featured this neighborhood, which happened to be the poorest, with most men and women either working at the Baloch households or simply laboring in the local bazaar unless they were away in Karachi or Gwadar. Aunt Zahra's brother and family came forward to welcome us all three as we sat down on the charpoys covered with traditional Baloch kilims to be served with qahwa and pakoras, freshly made by Nuzhat, Zahra's niece and an undergraduate student at the college specializing in humanities. Anne enjoyed talking to Nuzhat, and among other subjects, they both zeroed in on Jane Austen and Nadeem Aslam since Nuzhat wanted to teach English literature after an MA from Quetta. Anjum and I felt proud to see her speak so confidently and clearly with a native

English speaker whom she was meeting for the first time. Her parents and younger siblings were even more pleased with Nuzhat's ease and sociability.

For me, the astonishing surprise was that Anne had never mentioned her grasp of Nadeem Aslam's fiction, though she was familiar with the works of Bapsi Sidhwa, Sara Suleri, Kamila Shamsi, and Mohsin Hamid as she was at home with some known Indian fiction writers in English.

"Anne, it never dawned on me that you had read Aslam, our shy novelist who reputedly goes about only in the dark and isn't a sociable soul at all yet seems to know the inner vibes of human psychology."

"Well, Aslam is intriguingly subtle and political in his own way as he bludgeons the contemporary geopolitics of this part of the world, especially after 9/11. I thought you remembered meeting him at a literary festival in Bath some time back, Gul!"

"Oh, yes, now that you remind me, we did accompany him and Pankaj Mishra to Patisserie Valerie, right across the Guild Hall. He was mostly smiling but avowedly reticent in conversation, though Pankaj was quite forthcoming. From one of his interviews, I gathered that it took him five years to complete the first chapter of one of his novels. Must be a diehard perfectionist."

"Kamila had a prior engagement that day, but somehow, in passing, you were able to mention her mother's *Hybrid Tapestries,* which you view as a pioneering study of English writings by South Asian Muslim writers, including a fair number of women. I won't mind meeting Muneeza Shamsie next time we're in Karachi."

"I have read *Maps for Lovers* by Nadeem Aslam, and this romantic fiction remains one of my favorites," Nuzhat interjected at the right time. "I have read Mishra's articles in the *Guardian* and watched a few of his interviews, and he impresses me with his courage and diligence, and like most of us, he wasn't born with a silver spoon."

"Nuzhat, perhaps Karachi will be a better option for your postgraduate studies, and we can certainly ask Bahram and Shireen to introduce you to local literary circles." I tried my best not to sound patronizing, and Nuzhat knew it since, as a toddler, she used to spend quite some time at our place, and frequently, I found her moving around in our study, touching books, especially those with bright colors. She was a true disciple of her older and successful cousin, Zeenat.

"I can certainly think about the university in Karachi or such other institution as my Baba wants me to be a professor like you, and, in the same vein, Mother is not in a hurry to marry me off." She said with a chuckle as we begged our leave to move on to our next destination. Anjum and Anne were wrapped in close hugs by Nuzhat and her Mum while Baba put his affectionate hands on their heads. After promising to come back for a breakfast of parathas, home-churned buttermilk, and cooked spinach and mustard leaves, we headed towards Koh-e-Murad—the mountain of hope and mysterious supplications.

BRISTOL

You'd have to be slightly eccentric to like Joe Williams. He wasn't a typical varsity tutor; rather, he was informal, austere, and immensely warm-hearted. With boundless energy, a knack for cooking, and a deep fondness for India and all things Indian, Joe loved to talk—and there was no end to the topics he'd cover, nor were two hours ever sufficient for his weekly interactive class. He taught us a postgraduate course in travel writing within the English department at Bristol. A group of twelve students of varied backgrounds and ages followed Joe each Tuesday through the winding corridors of the building that housed history, politics, and anthropology. More often than not, we ended up at the Hawthorns for lunch. Although we were only a stone's throw from Whiteladies Road, Joe avoided Brown's, either due to its haughtiness or simply because it wasn't affiliated with the university. Besides, even the name of the road put him off, as Joe often sneered at this peculiar English habit of clinging to old names, especially when they hinted at snobbery or a colonial past.

Not religious himself, Joe sometimes discussed his Welsh heritage, sprinkled with a bit of Jewish ancestry, and often criticized the bingo chain Mecca for its insensitivity in sticking with that name.

"What else can you expect from an establishment interested only in emptying the pockets and purses of elderly pensioners and the unemployed?" he'd say. "It's in the same league as those Atlantic City, Reno, and Las Vegas casinos, busing in excited, hopeful one-night gamblers, each dreaming of becoming a millionaire. On the way back, they've lost their week's savings, quarreling among themselves over trivialities. Another week gone. And soon, they're back on those casino buses, laughing with their pals. Woes of ugly capitalism!"

We tended to agree with Joe, who had, in fact, been an insider during his college days, having worked for a few summers in casino kitchens hidden away from the boardwalk, often facing the grim urban squalor neighboring those ornate casinos. Joe occasionally mentioned his short stint at Gonzaga University in Spokane, in the northwestern United States, where he attended a summer course on American literature and gained a reputation as an oddity. His exceptional height, deep-set glasses, thick brown hair, and seductive accent made him a novelty, popular among Northwestern women. Joe also spoke of his travels around the state, describing snow-clad mountains, a vast desert, the Columbia Gorge, and the rainforests stretching to the coast near Seattle.

It was at Gonzaga, established by Italian Jesuits decades ago, that Joe met Anila, a Bengali Indian student pursuing a postgraduate degree in American literature. With her long, shiny black hair, almond eyes, and coppery skin, Anila soon outshone her American classmates, developing an intimacy with the visiting Anglo-Welshman. This relationship sparked Joe's interest in Indian literature, philosophy, and even some ascetic elements of Hinduism. Years later, following several visits to India and brief reunions with Anila—now an academic in Calcutta—Joe published two travel-laced novels that landed him the teaching job at Bristol. Like several other colleagues, Joe was paid on an hourly basis, which was insufficient for a married man with two sons. Fortunately, he had inherited part of a mansion on Marlborough Road in Bath, adjacent to the Royal Crescent and almost encircled by Victoria Park, which somewhat solidified his financial position—though not permanently. Realistically, it was his wife, Emma, whose steady job at the Royal United Hospital chiefly supported the household.

In the following weeks, we would learn that Joe was driven by an insatiable curiosity. Beyond his attachment to Anila, his quest for truth, adventure, and something inexplicable led him deep into everything Indian: from the Baul minstrels to the Punjabi Sikhs, spicy cuisine, and the ancient booksellers in Lucknow. His fascination with the imambaras and palaces of Lucknow was boundless, as the city itself had been a literary hub during a bygone Nawabi era, although Joe himself was no admirer of the Raj. He could recall the names of the booksellers in Lucknow whose crammed shops held volumes in nearly every major language of the subcontinent. Despite the chaotic environment, they could still retrieve any requested tome from beneath the piles.

During their heyday, Joe's parents circulated among the upper-crust Bathonians, whose predecessors in the long eighteenth century prided themselves on creating a "polite society" far from the humdrum of London and the imperial exploits of Bristol. Many built grand mansions or magnificent crescents on scenic vantage points in the city, and, among other aristocratic customs, they patronized the arts. Life-size portraits decorated their homes, although some of these artworks later ended up in local galleries. This period coincided with Bath becoming a hub of splendid Georgian architecture, as its hot sulfur springs attracted visitors from far and wide for medicinal purposes. Naturally, some streets near the Abbey, Roman Baths, and Avon River housed working women in lower-quality accommodations, giving Bath a dual character: known for its art, fashion, architecture, and affluent patrons, yet home to a less glamorous side—something not widely recognized outside Somerset.

Long after our graduation, we learned that Joe decried his father's pompous demeanor, as he imposed strict upper-middle-class morals on Joe and his two siblings, where manners and appearances took precedence over substance and informality. Joe often shared photos of his late parents, who, until their final years, maintained an old-fashioned lifestyle—much to the disgust of a rebellious Joe, the youngest in the family, who was heavily influenced by countercultural literature and music. His exposure to 1970s America further fueled his defiance, while India offered him an alternative intellectual and cultural world.

Joe's class opened a window onto a wider world for me, a world I'd been blind to given that my previous studies and travels were limited to the North Atlantic, punctuated only by brief holidays in Spain, Italy, and Dubai. His teachings removed the mental blinkers I had worn for so long, which had made my perspectives stubbornly provincial. I was familiar with the classics, semi-classics, and more recent literary works, many of which conveyed a sense of self-sufficiency—not by intent but by content. With the dissident voices of the 1960s, figures like Ginsberg, Chomsky, Said, Rushdie, Ghose, Kureishi, and Arundhati Roy were challenging Eurocentrism, inspiring a generation of nonconformists like Joe. His rebellion wasn't solely against his parents' pomposity or their life in a listed Georgian mansion in Bath; it was also a fierce rejection of mediocrity that thrived on class, color, and creed—not necessarily in that order.

Unlike our idealized view of universities, Joe saw them as structured hierarchies that often served the status quo. Despite vocal elements, they generally resisted dissent or any radical departure from a middle-of-the-road stance. Joe's popularity and outspoken nature proved to be his undoing. Without a tenure-track position, he remained on a paltry, wage-like salary. Universities needed academics like Joe to broaden their curriculum to include distant, unfamiliar regions like India and Africa, but they were hesitant to disturb senior colleagues devoted to the established literary canon.

Joe thrived in his classes, which sometimes extended to the stairs, the union café, or even his home in Bath. He had sold his portion of the Marlborough mansion to his brother and instead bought a modest terraced house in Oldfield Park, a neighborhood popular with students and wage-earners, far from the Georgian mansions and famed crescents. We never asked Joe about Anila, although they had shared a few rendezvous in Bengal during his later visits, until distance and circumstance ended their relationship. However, their connection had profoundly transformed Joe. Despite his varied literary accomplishments, he was at heart an "Indian," more at ease with folk singers, sadhus, eccentric Jewish bakers, and elderly bookworms than with self-important Anglo-Saxon literati.

When Joe invited us to his home—which happened three times over the two semesters we spent with him—we were treated to dal, chapatis, boiled rice, chutney, and a selection of vegetable dishes, often bhajis, all prepared by Joe himself. Emma, despite her full-time job, would sometimes help by baking a special cake. They had met in Bristol at a time when Joe's visits to India had begun to wane, and Emma was completing her postgraduate work in sociology at the university. Introduced by mutual friends at a party at the Smugglers' Bar, a folksy pub between Queen Square and the Harbour, they formed a bond. Although Joe liked Bristol, his roots in Bath, coupled with Emma's job, ultimately anchored him to his hometown. Emma adored Joe for his unconventional lifestyle and contrarian views, which would have marked him as an atypical man. Their two redheaded sons and two Labradors kept life busy, yet Joe continued writing, all the while hoping for a stable teaching position in the area to support both his literary and financial needs.

However, Peter, the head of his department, thwarted Joe's aspirations, keeping him on a contract without the prospect of tenure, plagued by his own insecurities and jealousies. With no proper office and crowded, sometimes loud tutorials, Joe often met with his students at Nero's Café or the Hawthorns. The latter, conveniently located on Woodland Road and exuding an informal ambiance, was a mutual favorite, despite the lively eateries on nearby Park Row and College Green.

Joe's class included a motley of students, predominantly mature and British, with a clear majority aspiring to be writers—some struggling and a few even with manuscripts awaiting a literary agent to connect them with a publisher. The internet had facilitated faster communication within and beyond our class, but, even long before Covid, we seemed to be losing human contact and face-to-face socialization. This was where Joe's willingness to discuss new and old literary works, his own experiences with agents and publishers, and his travels on shoestring budgets drew nearly a full house to these café sessions. It was here that I spoke with Gul a few times, especially when we explored subcontinental themes and authors, reassessing the postcolonial analyses of writers from Rudyard Kipling to William Dalrymple.

In his early twenties, Gul, with a dark, curly mop of hair atop his sinewy, medium build, was neither a passive listener nor someone who monopolized discussions; instead, he knew just when to pause or interject. After a few initial sessions, where Joe led with his acerbic humor and boundless energy, early reticence melted away. Informality, peppered with light humor, became the norm. One night after a hearty meal at Joe's, where we had all contributed in one way or another, Gul and I walked from Moorland Road in Oldfield Park to Weston, across the Avon, to catch our X39 bus back to Bristol. It was late October, with a slight nip in the air and a darker night, and since it was the weekend, we noticed undergraduates from Bath's two universities heading toward the town center. Bath, a favorite of wealthy pensioners, received a sizeable number of day-trippers from London, Oxford, and Bristol, but by early evening, it settled into a quiet calm—unlike Bristol, which always bustled with activity, especially around the university and near the Harbor, where several bars and eateries made it a hotspot for pub crawling, particularly on weekends.

"Anne, will you be going all the way to the main coach station in Bristol, or are you dropping off somewhere along the way?" Gul asked, his tone friendly yet unobtrusive.

"You might be surprised to know I'm not a Bristolian; I actually live in a small town between Bath and Bristol, so I'll be getting off soon after we're on the bus. Where do you live, if I may ask, Gul?"

"I share a rooming house near Temple Meads—in fact, Totterdown—a neighborhood known for student housing and a distinctly proletarian vibe. It reminds me a bit of my native land back in Balochistan."

"I'm not the typical student myself; I still live with my mother, though I plan to move to Bristol at some point once I find my bearings at the university and perhaps a part-time job. Totterdown is actually on my route to Bristol, just before Temple Meads."

"Well, I'm not strictly a literary type, unlike most in the class, since I study sociology. But my interest in English literary writings on India and the ongoing debate on post-colonialism led me to enroll in Joe's course. I enjoy his knowledge, enthusiasm, and informality."

"After my PPE at St. Hugh's in Oxford, I returned to Salford to spend more time with my mother, and along the way, I decided to pursue a postgraduate degree in creative writing at Bristol."

"I've only visited Oxford briefly, though I graduated from University College London before moving to Bristol. So I might qualify as a West Country chap, if not a permanent resident."

We soon boarded the bus, which, at this hour, had fewer passengers, giving us some privacy to continue our conversation and even exchange contact information for future meetups. After leaving Bath, the bus passed by the country pub, The Globe Inn, its masthead displaying a brown fox—a familiar sight on my journeys between my hometown, Bath, and Oxford.

"There's a medieval village called Newton St. Loe on that hilltop behind the trees—it's hidden from view now. It's a quaint place with stone houses and country lanes, and it even hosts the headquarters of the Duchy of Cornwall," I said to Gul, trying not to sound like a tour guide.

"I've heard of the village and the university nearby. I actually considered applying for their postgraduate program but chose Bristol instead. Not a bad choice, I suppose!" he replied with a mischievous wink.

"I'll be getting off at the next stop, which happens to be near two pubs, though there are several along the Avon. I might sound like a bit of a pub connoisseur, don't you think, Gul?"

"Not at all—and if you were, what's wrong with that? I enjoy the informality and coziness of a traditional pub myself. It's a good place to reflect on Marcuse and Giddens over a pint of local ale. How far is your house from the bus stop? Not to question your physical vigor, but in case you'd like an escort this time of night!"

"Thank you, Gul, but it's just a few doors down. Salford's a safe town. See you next week!"

Mother was not far from our door, and soon after settling on the sofa, I began recounting my rendezvous with Joe, Emma, and the rest, though I refrained from mentioning the ride home with Gul. Father, after spending his summer in Salford, had returned to his job in Dubai, where he'd been working as a military advisor for the past few years since retiring from his British regiment. The previous winter, the three of us had a family reunion in Dubai for two weeks, and the organized life, apparent prosperity, immense consumerism, and sunny, sandy beaches lingered in my memory—especially those early morning cycle rides and occasional evening drinks at lively spots. The Emiratis looked after Dad well, and he enjoyed the warm climate with all the perks of a Western expatriate, though he sometimes reflected on the other Dubai, populated by Asian and African blue-collar workers and unskilled laborers, whose existence in this "dreamland" often meant hardships and testing circumstances, compounded by exploitative middlemen and traffickers.

Dad had spent most of his military career at Salisbury, Sandhurst, and Bristol before settling in the West Country. This move was more Mother's decision than his, bringing a Scotsman to settle near Bath due to her job in the university library and her fondness for the Georgian city. Susanne, a Dane, had met Dad at a party while studying information technology at the University of Glasgow, which turned into a serious love affair and ultimately prevented Susanne from returning to Denmark. They married in both Glasgow and Odense before a job offer from Bath led to their relocation. Both adored the Roman city and its increasingly famous university at Claverton. I came along within a year, though I would prove to be the only junior Sandeman on this side of the borders.

Susanne Sandeman—unlike the stereotypical Scandinavian blonde—had dark hair and deep brown eyes, partly owing to an Ashkenazi strand in the family. She occasionally traveled to Denmark, in addition to her annual visits to Scotland, and was especially close to one of her uncles, a writer with a stupendous book collection. In his youth, Frederic had traveled through India and encountered eminent writers like Mulk Raj Anand and R.K. Narayan. These novelists' stories, which depicted the lives of ordinary Indians with a superb diction, expressed both hope and hardship during times of transition. While Anand, who attended Cambridge, was widely traveled and well-known, Narayan, almost a centenarian and a Tamil, spent most of his life in southern India, creating the fictional town of Malgudi. Susanne's uncle frequently mentioned Narayan, a significant influence in her decision to focus on the Indian novelist for her MA thesis, which I had the chance to read during my own years at St. Hugh's. Though Susanne was modest about her research, I had nothing but deep admiration for her diligence and professionalism. I occasionally nudged her to publish a paper or two derived from her thesis, but she shied away, perhaps feeling she wasn't "academic enough" and uncertain about her language skills, despite her exceptional proficiency.

Our house in Salford was named Malgudi—much to the bafflement of our visitors—and beyond that, I chose to study literature partly because of the interest inherited from my mother's side. In a way, this could explain my innate desire to become a novelist, which led to my selection of Joe's module at Bristol. Bristol had launched its creative writing program in the 1990s, following a trend at universities like East Anglia, which began under the tutelage of writers like Malcolm Bradbury. This new discipline quickly became popular, providing comfortable employment opportunities to the satisfaction of university administrators. The publishing industry's growth, the rise of literature festivals, the accessibility of printed works through technology, and teaching opportunities in Asia fueled the mushrooming of creative writing instruction, with established authors holding academic chairs. With Fay Weldon, Teresa Hadley, Steve May, and several others, we aspired to be flag bearers in the West Country. Interestingly, many tutors and students were women, including a fair number of fresh graduates. Our first doctoral graduate was a woman, now a prominent fiction writer in Britain, and we had teachers—again mostly female— who specialized in children's books, environmental literature, comics, and poetics. Peter, Richard, Joe, and several adjunct faculty focused on specific genres like American literature, criticism, drama, and suspense, though we notably lacked representation from Afro-Asian specializations, as Anglo-Saxon prominence prevailed. In that sense, Joe was both a norm and an exception—a bohemian whose vocal enthusiasm and informal camaraderie with students raised eyebrows on St. Michael's Hill.

Bristol was always a city on the move, with a multi-layered cultural depth. There were frequent calls to bring down the statue of Edward Colston, an eighteenth-century slave trader who had become a benefactor through donations to schools and a music hall. Bristol saw repeated protests and petitions to rename parts of the urban landscape linked to slavery and plantation culture, becoming one of the earliest cities in Britain to elect an Afro-Caribbean mayor. Our campus was also often in the spotlight, due to the imposing Wills Memorial Building, which housed an elaborate art collection on the Empire, funded in part by questionable endowments.

I recall visiting the British Empire and Commonwealth Museum near Temple Meads with Dad in 2003. He pointed out an old map of India, showing me Quetta, Kandahar, Las Bela, and Fort Sandeman. The town of Fort Sandeman, named after his great-grandfather—the colonial agent for all of Balochistan in the late nineteenth century—was strategically located, ensuring collaboration from Baloch and Pashtun tribes in this far western expanse of the subcontinent.

"Grandpa was a tough soldier with a keen sense for human traits, especially of tribal people. He was a 'practicing anthropologist,' you might say, who used both 'stick and smile' in his dealings with the chieftains, especially during the Second Anglo-Afghan War from 1878-80. He spoke the local languages, knew complex family connections and feuds, and, through guns and gifts, managed to pacify the tribes. In his heart, he was fond of this arid land and its turbaned, bearded inhabitants—and even died among them in Las Bela, though it was somewhat premature." Dad gave us this insight into our family's connection with Balochistan.

"You showed us his photographs, diaries, and correspondence back in Scotland, Dad!" I said, with a hazy yet instinctive desire to revive the senior Sandeman through some fictional, if not biographical, account.

"Oh yes, quite a few of them. He was a towering figure with a handlebar mustache, radiating an aura that was impossible to ignore, especially in his regimental uniform. His early biographers praised his toughness and diplomacy in what they called the 'pacification of the tribes.' But in recent times, given the criticism of Empire, historians have raised issues with his policies. Maybe, at some point, you could pen his biography," Dad said, his voice carrying a tone of confidence, and Mum seemed to share his sentiment.

"It's odd that they changed the names of these cities in the 1970s: Fort Sandeman is now called Zhob, a name that better reflects local traditions and a bit of historical rewriting. But, as I understand, Jacobabad remains Jacobabad due to some sort of spiritual status granted to John Jacob, who, like Robert Sandeman, is buried there. Jacob's descendants were reportedly well received in Pakistan during the previous decade, as the late colonial official is venerated as a saint by some locals in Sindh. They also changed the name of Fort Munro, a citadel built by Robert Sandeman in the 1860s and named after a fellow commissioner of a nearby Baloch district in Punjab. However, there are still schools and landmarks in Quetta that carry Grandpa's name. Don't forget, those are some of the hottest places on earth."

"I would love to visit those towns, especially Fort Sandeman where your—our great-grandfather—spent most of his life. Maybe then I could write something about him." I blurted out, my desire evident, pleasing my parents as we moved toward the dining room.

"Perhaps we could all visit Balochistan—especially during the winter months, if there's such a thing as winter in that part of the world," Mother said, concerned about the climate, subconsciously comparing it to her native Denmark and now Britain.

By 2008, only a few years after our visit to the British Commonwealth and Empire Museum, it had closed down, with its holdings and heritage sent to London or placed in storage in the city. This decision was made due to its consistent failure to attract a steady number of visitors, leaving a bitter taste in Bristol; even Bath and Exeter were disappointed by its closure. Meanwhile, life continued around Temple Meads; cyclists between Bath and Bristol passed by the site, now flanked by new apartment towers, and the freshers at Bristol's two universities remained clueless about this lost chapter, though many of them actively protested the presence of Colston's statue.

Joe wasn't overly enthusiastic about the museum, despite his appreciation for art. He admired the portraits in the Holburne Museum dating from the Mughal and Raj eras, yet wasn't fond of Bath's crescents or Beckford's Tower, which he saw as being built on "seedy" colonial wealth from plantations and the colonies.

"I wouldn't dismiss these Georgian buildings outright; without them, Bath wouldn't be Bath as we know it. Perhaps I'm a loyal Bathonian," he mused, "though I don't have many cherished memories from my own early years in our Marlborough house. My best times were walking Terry, our dog, in Victoria Park, or sometimes heading up the road to check on the elderly residents of Sion Hill."

"What about Bristol, Joe?" Gul interjected during one of our sessions at the Hawthorns in early November.

"Many people don't realize that Bristol has more Georgian buildings than Bath, though Bath has monopolized the recognition. As you might have seen when you visited my neighborhood, we don't have the grand crescents on our side, but the road to Claverton and the university has charming stone houses, with a location on the slopes that lends them an unmatched opulence. Bath prides itself on some lovely squares, though nothing like Queen Square in Bristol. Then there's the Harbour, Clifton, Brunel's Suspension Bridge, Colston's statue, and Pero's Bridge—all holding their own against the Royal Crescent, Jane Austen's Centre, the Abbey, and the Circus in Bath. As a blue-blooded Bathonian, I still hold my city unrivaled, miles ahead of the rest. Never mind this self-infatuation," he added with a laugh.

"Is Pero's Bridge an attempt at political correctness or a gesture of belated guilt, Joe? I hope I don't sound too skeptical," I asked, genuinely curious.

"Both, really, Anne. But bear in mind that 2007 marked the bicentennial of the abolition of the slave trade in Britain, the same time the Empire Museum closed." Joe's words brought back my own memories of that era.

"Pero Jones was an intriguing figure, I think. He came here— or rather, was brought here—from the West Indies in 1783 to serve the family of George Pinney, a planter and trader who also kept a slave girl as a domestic. Pero is thought to have passed away in 1798, and perhaps there's a dissertation on him somewhere, gathering dust, just waiting to be brought to public attention."

"Why do people keep fastening padlocks onto this pedestrian bridge instead of leaving it as it is?" Richard Nightingale asked, clearly bothered by the unusual custom.

"Rich, I suppose we mortals are always afraid of being forgotten, and lovers are no exception. So young couples—many of them from our university, or just tourists—take part in this ongoing spectacle. I only hope these locks don't end up weighing down the bridge and pulling it into the harbor! Just kidding, of course. But Paul Boateng, the former Labour Minister who inaugurated this bridge in 1999, might do well to recruit volunteers to free it from this ever-growing bondage. Remember, a lock represents not only security but is also a symbol of slavery and bondage." Joe's family, with its Welsh, English, and Jewish lineage, only emphasized their English identity—much like their Victorian ancestors who saw themselves as New Romans.

Today, we live in an England where this smorgasbord of ethnic and cultural boundaries, especially in the cities, is gradually undergoing a 'chutnification,' eroding the formerly rigid boundaries of community and tradition.

"In our part of the world, trees at Sufi shrines, especially in rural areas, often accumulate colorful rags left as offerings. Most of these people are poor and needy, suffering from illnesses or other misfortunes, seeking saintly intercession. There might be lovers among those visitors too, leaving their mementos. Graffiti could be yet another medium of memorialization." Gul seemed to be broadening our discussion.

"Building on what Gul suggested, can we say that the otherwise publicity-shy artist, Banksy, is leaving his politicized footprints through his artwork?" Joe was spot on.

"Definitely, with an impactful sense of sardonic humor. Like his latest sketch just below the second-floor window of a house on Park Row, which looks as if someone's hanging from the windowsill." Like everyone else in the group, I'd noticed this piece in the university area, especially since academia and the media were raising concerns about the prevalence of mental illness among university students. Banksy was certainly popular on campuses, particularly after painting critical pieces in the

Walled-Off Hotel, right next to the Israeli Wall cutting across the West Bank.

After our extended session, everyone filed out of the café, while Gul and I volunteered to clear the tables, giving us a chance to pick up where we'd left off the previous week on the bus.

"Anne, what're your plans for Friday evening?"

"Haven't made any. What's up?"

"I'd like to impress you with my cooking skills—if that's not too bold a challenge for your palate!"

"Well, I hate being judgmental before I try something. I'm sure it'll be more flavorful than my bland pasta or omelets."

"Is 7 p.m. okay? I can meet you at the Temple Meads stop for the X39. My place is just ten minutes away in Totterdown."

TOTTERDOWN & OXFORD

I could have disembarked the X39 near Totterdown, on this side of the Avon, but I continued to Temple Meads, where I knew Gul awaited me. Totterdown is the reverse of posh, well-known Clifton: it's low-profile, a bit congested, and reputedly rough, yet popular with students and modest wage earners. Close to the train station and not far from Georgian Bristol and the university, this hilly township sits along the main road connecting the city to Keynsham, Salford, and Bath. For a small-town girl like me, it was still an unfamiliar world, and besides enjoying an evening with my host, I hoped to get a feel for the area.

"Thanks for coming over Gul. It's a bit wet out now. Hope you didn't have to wait too long!" I was genuinely appreciative of his gesture.

"No problem at all; it's good to get some fresh air. I'm used to the rain—it took some time to adjust after arriving from a hot, dry climate." Gul sounded upbeat.

As we walked toward his place, we crossed the old bridge and took a sharp right at the traffic signal. We skirted a small park and climbed what appeared to be a modest hill. After a few more streets, descents, and turns, we stopped in front of a terraced house in a lane of similar dwellings, all compact and without the front gardens I was used to in Salford. Our conversation, light and informal, ranged from the weather to his neighborhood and Bristol's diverse culture. Gul again mildly warned me that his food might be a bit spicy, which only made me feel more eager.

"Forgive my naivety, Anne. I should have checked if there were any dishes or ingredients you'd prefer to avoid!"

"Don't worry, I'm not fussy. I don't have any allergies and can handle almost anything—even if it's spicy. Actually, I think I've developed a craving for hot food. I used to visit Hussain's Kabob Van in Oxford's City Centre at least once or twice a week for a late snack. Often, I'd go on my own on a rickety bike, but sometimes, friends from St. Hugh's would join me, eager to devour doner kebabs smothered in chutney and red onions. When I moved out of college accommodations in my final year, I chose digs in Cowley to be closer to all those ethnic food spots." My response seemed to reassure Gul, as a relaxed smile appeared on his face.

His house had a reasonably spacious front room, part of which doubled as a kitchen and dining area. It was pleasant and orderly—unlike some of the shared student residences I'd seen, including my own back in Oxford. His three housemates weren't around, either occupied elsewhere or perhaps giving us the privacy that such an evening warranted.

Our evening began with an Italian red, toasted pita, and hummus as we toasted to a new phase in our careers. Gul seemed pleased with his choice of Bristol for postgraduate studies, and I had no regrets about my own decision.

"I do miss the hustle and bustle of London, especially the British Library and the cafés and bookshops in Bloomsbury. Bristol is quieter, a slower pace. It offers more privacy, which helps me focus on my work," Gul said thoughtfully.

"I suppose it's natural to miss the place where we had our first college experiences. London is definitely lively, and I sometimes miss Oxford and its quaint traditions. But, to be honest, I've outgrown many of those undergraduate habits."

"Anne, being an undergraduate allows you certain liberties and idiosyncrasies; it's part of growing up. Partying, keeping odd hours, or devouring late-night kebabs after a night out—these are phases, or, if you'll allow me to say, prerequisites for gaining maturity. For international students, there's an added layer—political discussions about issues back home, debates on the role of religion or its absence in one's life, all creating a kind of contested socialization."

"Is it a privilege or a drag being an international student, if I may be blunt, Gul?"

"It can be both, Anne, depending on one's background and personal choices. Some students become completely 'ethnicized' or even 'ghettoized.' Some may become religiously zealous, while others radically distance themselves from it all. I've known students who spent all their time in labs, taking breaks only for prayers. And then there are those whose main focus is merry-making. There are also a few who manage to find a workable balance in their lifestyles."

"Yes, as a sociologist, you wouldn't miss that, Gul. Politics and religion are major socializers, but they can also divide or spoil relationships. As you say, it depends on variables like age, subject area, class, and even gender, if I may add."

"Anne, I was going to use the word moderate for my third category of people—those who aim for a balanced lifestyle away from ideological divides—but it's too qualitative and a bit loaded, given the geopolitics."

"I get that. But it's not a clear-cut clash of cultures. We all go through adjustments in new places and eventually find our footing. Maybe, it would be a learning curve for me to live somewhere entirely different from England, to experience a culture completely removed from this Anglo-Saxon certainty."

"Despite our justified urge for decolonization, I don't think you can entirely escape one hegemony or another. If it's not Anglo-Saxon, it might be French or Russian, and now there's the rising influence of China. Outside of these, many non-Arab Muslims, like myself, experience an Arab hegemony since our faith is deeply Arabized in its content and contours, though it claims universality in creed. … But I'm keeping you busy in conversation while you must be starving. Let me heat up the dishes, and we'll continue this over dinner."

Topping up our goblets with a Tuscan red, Gul went to the kitchen while I followed to set the table. A unique blend of herbal fragrance and meaty aroma filled the dining room. The meal included bhuna lamb, spinach with tomatoes, grilled chicken kebabs, boiled rice with chickpeas, and naan, with raita and mango pickle on the side in case I wanted to add more spice or mellow my portion.

"I buy ingredients, especially meat, from Easton, while the naan comes from the Indian place near my neighborhood, next to the King's Arms—so the punters don't have to walk far for curry after a few pints," Gul remarked with a sense of humor that matched the relaxed atmosphere he had created for the evening. "Sorry if the food's lacking in any way; I often call my younger sister, Anjum, back home to get tips on seasoning, temperature, and timing—especially for dishes like pulao. Still, I can't cook like her or Mum."

I was devouring the food eagerly, piling it high on my plate and scooping it with naan. "Don't be silly, Gul! It's lush and so sumptuous that I've already polished off half my plate in minutes. I was starving, yes, but it's the way you've prepared these dishes so meticulously."

"You folks are very polite and generous with compliments, whereas my family back home would still find faults in my cooking. Men aren't trusted much with food preparation—it might be a universal truth. Though, funnily enough, most chefs here are men. I remember seeing graffiti back in Lahore on a beer glass that read: 'Only two things wrong with men: everything they say, everything they do.'"

"Gul, I can't vouch for that graffiti—though maybe I'll ask Banksy for his opinion!" I laughed. "Honestly, though, regardless of this 'equality mantra,' there are talented and well-meaning people of every gender. Coming back to your dishes, I should probably improve my skills beyond pasta and noodles, though you know how popular they are with students."

"Anne, I mostly live on pasta, noodles, pizza, and soup, with the occasional Pakistani dish when I make the trip to Easton. I like visiting Easton; it keeps me connected to South Asian and African cultures. Easton is quite the opposite of Clifton or Brandon Hill and different from Totterdown with its rich cultural diversity."

"Maybe it's just my ignorance or laziness, but I've never ventured into Easton, even though I live only a few miles down the road. I guess I'm overdue for a visit," I admitted.

Sensing a hint of guilt, Gul remarked, "You'll have time to explore Easton once you're settled in Bristol. I made a good choice buying a second-hand hybrid bike—it's great for exploring this cycle-friendly city at my own pace."

"I used to cycle in Oxford, even late at night, often without lights or a helmet. But in Salford, I haven't kept it up. Though we have broad, mostly empty streets, plus the Avon towpath, which has some of the most scenic spots in Somerset. I rarely go there, though. What a shame, Gul!"

Without realizing it, I lightly placed my hand on his wrist. He didn't seem to mind; instead, a gentle smile spread across his face, as if he appreciated the spontaneity.

"No need to feel bad, Anne. Maybe we can explore Easton, Avon Gorge, and the towpath together. I hear the Two-Tunnels route is open for pedestrians and cyclists now. We could add cycling beneath Bath to our itinerary." Gul's reassuring tone was just one of the qualities that distinguished him from other men in my life. He had a quiet maturity, free of empty bravado. At the Royal High School in Bath, a girls-only institution with no chance to meet boys, I had dated a couple of boyfriends in Oxford, one after the other, trying to make up for lost time with my lack of early experience.

Boris was an Etonian, intelligent yet unscrupulous and flamboyant. Grant, from St. Edmund Hall, was restrained and somewhat shy. Boris had been quick to claim my virginity after a late-night party at Balliol, which I rather gleefully accepted, viewing it as a way to begin a new chapter by "tasting the forbidden fruit." Besides, I felt I had to do it—everyone else "had done it." We'd just celebrated a successful debate at the Union Society, where our full-house event on the British Empire saw the expected defeat of the motion to defend it. The evening continued in Boris's room overlooking St. Giles, with champagne corks popping after our victory and late-night pizza bites. Boris and I had been dating since we'd met at the Union during my second year. Our first class together had been on the Romans; aside from their history, I was interested in the classics, while Boris, a diehard Thatcherite with a romantic notion of European grandeur, sought out what he called the "glorified European past."

Grant, in contrast, came from a banking family rooted in Henley-on-Thames. Boris's reckless escapades and knack for bed-hopping eventually brought me closer to Grant, and we shared a quieter, more intellectual companionship. We enjoyed meeting at the café in Blackwell's or cycling to The Perch, across the meadows from Oxford. Yet his academic intensity was offset by a certain passivity, and after six months we drifted apart. Physical encounters were infrequent, with me often taking the initiative. In the end, I had no more energy for experimentation. The final rush of essays, tutorials, Union events, and Collections consumed my remaining time at Oxford.

Now, without any of that exoticism or bravado, Gul seemed to evoke a different kind of attraction, one tempered by mutual restraint and perhaps a budding connection beneath the surface.

Gul, while topping up my goblet, encouraged me to refill my plate, which I obligingly did. The evening had taken on a delightfully familiar feeling, as if we'd known each other for ages and our mutual fondness had only grown over time.

"Gul, your food is so sumptuous that I don't mind indulging myself in such a gluttonous way," I blurted out, spearing a lamb cube with my fork while tearing a piece of naan, soaking it in chutney.

"So, my cooking meets your approval! Anjum back home would be doubly pleased that her phone tutoring paid off, and her brother isn't spending all his time on the screen or discussing Baloch politics with other Pakistanis."

"Gul, since you mentioned Balochistan, I have to tell you about my own connection with your homeland. My great-great-grandfather lived and worked most of his life in Balochistan. I've seen some of his memorabilia—pictures, postcards, maps, and correspondence."

"Anne, honestly, I had a hunch. From Joe's first class when you introduced yourself as Anne Sandeman, I thought there might be a connection, but I didn't want to jump to conclusions. What a marvelous coincidence! Here's to the Sandemans and to Balochistan!" he toasted.

"To Balochistan, and to my Scottish ancestor—though who knows how well those Victorian colonists fare in modern perspectives, let alone in the decades to come. But let's not get into semantics now, Gul. Here's to you!"

Just as our glasses clinked, the front door opened, and a bearded, middle-aged man with spectacles and a well-worn leather valise stepped in.

"Good evening, folks. Hope I'm not intruding—I just need to grab something from the fridge," he said as he headed to the kitchen. Gul quickly interjected.

"This is Professor John Gallagher, a historian at Bath Spa University and my housemate. John, this is Anne Sandeman, a fellow graduate student at Bristol."

I stood up, extending my hand toward him. "Pleased to meet you, Professor Gallagher. I think we're practically neighbors; I live in Salford, just near Newton St. Loe."

"Thank you, Anne—please, call me John. So, you're from Salford or nearby, unless you're strictly from Bath itself?"

"Yes, I'm from Salford, John," I replied, adjusting to the first-name basis with a hint of reservation.

"I pass through Salford six times a week on the bus, occasionally more if I'm around for open days or graduations. You two go on with your meal; I'll be out of your way in a minute. Just need to warm up this nominally Mediterranean concoction."

John took out his spaghetti from the fridge, gathering his salad ingredients. Gul invited him to join us, topping off a glass of the Tuscan red as he did.

"Gul, the food looks sublime. Are you both sure I'm not intruding?"

"Not at all. Please, join us," we both assured him in unison, and John joined us with a smile.

"How was the open day at the university, John?" Gul asked, handing him a fresh plate.

"Thank you for this sumptuous meal—I really needed it after today! I spent the day at Newton Park, responding to the usual questions from parents, already charmed by Bath's beauty and history. And with the campus looking lovely in the warm sun, the cows and sheep obligingly staying out of the way on the hillsides, the visitors seemed well and truly enticed. Forgive my rustic description, Anne," he added with a chuckle.

"Not at all, John. I can only imagine the routine questions from prospective students and their families. Newton Park is truly scenic, especially with those two lakes. Capability Brown left his mark there, much like he did at Blenheim."

"Yes, Capability Brown and his team did well under pressure from their employers, just like their counterparts overseas did in the colonies, especially in Africa," he replied. "I was supposed to be in Leicester this weekend, but we rotate on these events. I'm sure the managers are pleased to see, as they put it, 'more bums on seats.' What are you studying, Anne?"

"I'm studying literature, with a particular interest in American and Afro-Asian works. What are your areas of teaching, John?"

"As you might guess, I teach British history overseas, with a focus on the Empire, along with modules on Ireland and revolutions since 1789," John said, while helping himself to some kebabs, rice, curry, and chutney. Gul waited for a moment before interjecting.

"John's book on the British Empire has been translated into several languages. It's a powerful rebuttal to what Niall Ferguson and other apologists have been promoting so aggressively."

"Sorry for jumping ahead, John, but do you by any chance lean toward Marxist historiography in your view of Britain's international role?" I asked, following Gul's introduction.

"Yes, to an extent, though in this work I focus less on class and more on the violence inflicted in India, Ireland, Africa, and the West Indies. It's Orwellian, really—colonists expanding their reach through gunpowder and greed. And, in many ways, the Americans inherited and extended this trajectory. But I'll leave Marx and Mao to rest in peace; I don't want to spoil this lovely evening or distract from Gul's magnificent cooking, though he's the least qualified proletarian I know!" John added with a mischievous smile, winking at Gul.

"Thank you for the lovely meal, and it was a pleasure to meet you, Anne. I'll be off to my room. See you around."

"John, I have some bread and butter pudding in the oven for dessert. You're more than welcome to stay, if you'd like," Gul offered, glancing at me for approval.

"Absolutely, John. I'll second what Gul said," I added.

"Very tempting, indeed, but I'll head to my room for now. Thank you again," John replied, retreating upstairs as Gul and I finished dessert with some black Americano.

"John's an interesting academic—perhaps another contrarian like our Joe, but in a different league from the average Oxford dons. I wouldn't mind meeting him again," I remarked.

"Perhaps I should've mentioned him earlier, but since he's rarely here on weekends, I didn't think to do so. John's focus on history is unique, especially in these times of nationalist discourses across emerging nation-states. He's a serious scholar, and, as you saw, instinctively down-to-earth and informal."

"I imagine someone like him doesn't get much media attention, and I doubt conservative institutions here would embrace his work. I wonder if he knows about my colonial ancestors!" I mused.

"John chose Totterdown over more upscale areas, and I've never seen him in formal attire—just jeans. He uses public transport to commute to Bath and Leicester, and when he meets neighbors, it's usually at our local pub rather than fancy restaurants. He makes his own food with simple ingredients. He really does live by his beliefs. You're right; he reminds me of Joe. Perhaps we could introduce them sometime. More coffee, Anne?"

"No, thanks, Gul. It's nearly ten, and I should head to the bus. I really enjoyed the evening, though."

Gul walked me to the bus stop, and soon I was settled on the X390, which took a detour through Keynsham to bring passengers closer to their homes in this market town.

When I got back, Mum was up, reading, and we talked about my evening over a glass of sherry. I described Gul as a knowledgeable, polite, and hospitable person who had gone out of his way to make me feel comfortable and let me enjoy the evening. Mum had a general knowledge of Balochistan; she knew that the Baloch and Pashtuns, both trans-Indus communities, were distinct ethnic groups, known for their traditional hospitality but also their sensitivity to honor. I mentioned that Gul's family was middle-class and well-placed in a young country, which seemed to sit well with her, though I was careful not to hint at any growing intimacy between us. At some point, I shifted our conversation to John Gallagher. She recognized his name, recalling his reputation for defying long-held academic orthodoxies.

Without pressing about my plans for accommodation in Bristol, I casually mentioned that it might soon become a reality, as I had already visited a couple of affordable, convenient places. We agreed to visit them together, and I suggested setting up appointments for the next morning so Susanne could take leave from her job.

00000

Tuesday afternoon suited me best since, after Joe's class, I could scout for accommodation with Susanne without missing the after-class session with Joe. I noticed I was being more talkative in the group and, without mentioning my Totterdown meal, I referred to some of John Gallagher's critical work, as I had skimmed through his volume on the Empire and a few articles, thanks to online library access. Gallagher held George Orwell in high regard, condemned British policies in Ireland, especially around the Easter Uprising, and denounced colonialism in the tradition of the Chartists and later socialists. His work extended to critiquing U.S. militarist policies in Palestine, highlighting the Anglo-American support for Zionism, which must have ruffled feathers within and outside Britain. Joe, aware of Professor Gallagher but unfamiliar with his works, was eager for my input.

"Professor Gallagher is a committed Marxist, and in this post-Cold War era of American primacy and 'Fukuyamian' optimism, he may be one of the few remaining leftist voices in academia addressing macro issues linked to contemporary geopolitics. He seems to follow the contrarian tradition in British society, from

Chartism to today's Socialist Workers Party. My guess is that he's a committed Trotskyite, with no sympathy for Stalinism," I explained.

"Does anyone else want to add to what Anne has shared so persuasively, and with such authority?" Joe's praise was typical, with his trademark touch of admiration. I noticed Gul raising his hand.

"Building on what Anne said, I should add that John Gallagher and I share accommodation in Totterdown, and he's certainly a renowned historian in the tradition of E.P. Thompson and Eric Hobsbawm. I've read his book on the Empire, and in my view, it's one of the most incisive and openly critical works of its kind. For John, the world is already Orwellian, and he argues that 9/11 provided an excuse for North Atlantic powers to reestablish unilateral hegemony over the rest."

The group was visibly intrigued, realizing that Gul shared a house with someone of Gallagher's intellectual stature, and often engaged in debates with him.

"How does Gallagher come across in social settings?" Joe asked, curiosity clear on his face, echoed by the rest of the group.

"He's a down-to-earth, approachable person, though he avoids too many grassroots contacts since he's busy writing and publishing. His work keeps him occupied at Newton Park, and on weekends, he joins his family in Leicester. I'm lucky to have him as a housemate, and the two other students from the University of the West of England are equally thrilled by his presence. He's always accumulating books as a well-known reviewer, and authors must be delighted by his intellectual engagement."

"Gul, could you invite him to spend some time with us? If Gallagher is open to it, we'd be happy to support and coordinate as a group," Joe suggested enthusiastically, eager for the chance to host John in the class.

"I'd be glad to bring it up with him and keep everyone posted. Would this event be a formal lecture, a casual meet-up with snacks, or even an informal meal?" Gul asked.

The group leaned toward an informal gathering where John could discuss his research, followed by a Q&A—all with some food. There was a brief debate between having snacks or a buffet meal, but consensus ultimately leaned toward a buffet, with everyone looking to Joe. Gul added,

"If John agrees to join us, I can check the possibility of renting the community center in Totterdown, and I don't mind offering our small kitchen for food prep—though I'll need permission from my housemates."

Julia, Elisabeth, Katherine, Joe, and the rest of the class cheered Gul on, and we left it at that.

00000

Two significant developments took place in early November that year: I moved into a rented accommodation near Cabot Circus, and John agreed to forego his weekly commute to Leicester to spend a Friday evening with our class. My new place was shared with two graduate students and a senior nurse, offering more space and convenience with nearby markets, bus routes, and cycle paths. Depending on my schedule, I could walk or cycle to Woodland Road or even up to Clifton. Moving into my own place also facilitated my new part-time job as an editorial assistant at the BBC studios on Whiteladies Road, a ten-minute walk from the university's main campus. My 20-hour weekly role involved working with producers on David Attenborough's nature series— a dream role, especially in this elegant area of the city, which often reminded me of those elaborate red-brick houses in North Oxford dating from the Victorian era, though here, grand stone mansions lined tree-filled boulevards, surrounded by manicured lawns.

Just a fortnight later, we all gathered at Gul's house to help him and Joe prepare for the evening with John. The meal featured mainly vegetarian dishes, along with minced meat kebabs Gul had mixed with herbs and spices before grilling on medium heat. I helped with the chickpea rice, while Katherine, Julie, Elisabeth, Alfred, and Steve handled the salad and baked two enormous fruit cakes. For naans, Gul arranged a delivery from the local Indian restaurant, ensuring they'd arrive fresh and hot just before dinner. Other classmates managed the room setup and carried drinks, crockery, and cutlery to the venue. Joe brought extra pots and pans, while Deewan Mishra of the local Indian restaurant generously lent us plates, glasses, and cutlery. Joe also made daal and mixed vegetable dishes, using recipes Anila had shared with him years back in Spokane, though we all knew not to mention that town unless we wanted Joe to drift off into fond recollections (and a bit of chastising of Uncle Sam).

John joined us at the community center after returning from Newton Park, where we all gathered in a semi-circle to hear him speak, with Joe acting as the moderator. Gul had invited his two housemates, Ross and Albert—humanities students at UWE— who were already aware of John's work. Joe and John greeted each other warmly, as if they'd been acquainted for years, an interaction that felt slightly un-English but fitting, given their shared outlooks.

"John, welcome to our clan, and thank you for spending time with us instead of making the commute home. We've already invaded your kitchen and premises to establish our hegemony," Joe joked.

"No problem, Joe. I've heard quite a bit about you and your group from Gul, who occasionally supplies me with meat and spices and has been tutoring me on the -stans that we and the Russians can't seem to stop interfering with, now with the Chinese joining in," John replied, with a twinkle in his eye.

Joe invited everyone to introduce themselves as drinks and appetizers—salsa, olives, and pita bites—were passed around.

"John, how did you bring together Ireland, Orwell, and the Chartists in your work, leading to so many influential publications?" Joe asked to start the discussion.

"I was born into a working-class family and started as a schoolteacher in Hull, where I connected with a few activists and gradually became involved in leftist politics. My spouse shares a similar background and is also an academic. From early on, I became a critic of organized violence—the kind our country committed in the name of 'civilizing missions' across oceans: in Asia, Africa, Australia, the Americas, and next door in Ireland.

Orwell, who came from a colonial background and was born in Burma, saw it firsthand. His experiences in the Spanish Civil War disillusioned him with totalitarianism," John explained.

Joe continued: "In Britain, when we discuss India, we tend to have two contrasting views: one of a helpless subcontinent and another of a vibrant, exotic India. How does this compare to Britain's view of Africa?"

"India helped Britain discover both its strengths and weaknesses and contributed to defining 'Britishness' as a unified identity beyond regional and ethnic differences. Losing the North American colonies made Britain look elsewhere—India, Australia, and Africa—giving it a sense of renewed greatness. India fascinated us, and it still does, with its customs, pluralism, and surprising absence of resentment, considering the colonial past. The English language, democratic principles, and administrative structures remain deeply rooted in South Asia, even after seven decades. In Bristol, we're confronted with another aspect of the Empire—slave trade and plantation culture, woven into the city's fabric. Liverpool has managed to engage with its history to some extent, but here in Bristol, and even in Bath, there's still a reticence."

Julie was the first to speak up after John's comments. "John, if I may ask—teaching in the West Country to mostly younger students from the same region, do you see a lot of curiosity when you raise these issues?"

"Certainly, Julie. In the initial weeks, students fresh out of high school go through various adjustments, and I try to avoid being a demagogue. Still, my reputation, so to speak, often precedes me. Some students continue to challenge me until their final semester, but they still come back on graduation day to get photos with me and their parents, and I end up writing reference letters for them long after they've left Newton Park. And this was all happening even before academics started calling for the decolonization of humanities. You're a sharp group and open to engaging with challenging perspectives as long as they're backed by archival evidence and intellectual rigor," John replied.

I decided to test John a bit, throwing out a teaser: "John, historical developments are never purely black or white—there's plenty of grey. The Empire was a violent institution that left behind brittle legacies, but it must have brought some benefits, whether from goodwill or self-interest, especially in areas like education, health, and infrastructure."

"I don't dismiss those developments, and they're certainly significant, but they were all steeped in self-interest and driven by hierarchical views of the people being ruled," John responded. Steve then asked about Ireland's unique role in the British Empire.

"Quite unique," John observed, "and binary as well. Ireland was perhaps the first organized colony, the 'first frontier.' Over time, it became a junior partner in Empire-building, supplying men, material, and eventually missionaries. Still, I appreciate the early cosmopolitan influence of the Irish Home Rule Leaguers."

Elisabeth was curious about the role of women in the Empire: "Were British women—or memsahibs—agents or instruments of the colonial enterprise? And I don't just mean housewives, but missionaries and those who wrote back home or even published books!"

"It's difficult to generalize, as there was a clear class system among British expatriates in the colonies. However, women were largely expected to strengthen the Empire, which was mostly seen as a male paradigm. Margaret MacMillan's biographical work focuses on European women—primarily British women in India. There are now recent works by Indian women historians filling this gap in modern history. Interestingly, some non-European female visitors, like the American writer Katherine Mayo, fully supported the Raj."

At this point, Joe invited everyone to dinner. Gul had just received freshly baked naans from Mishra, and the rest of the dishes were set on the table, along with beverages. Out of respect, we let John serve himself first. Clad in jeans, he was the least formal person at the table, yet he answered questions with patience even during the meal. With the spicy food, ample wine, and beer, the evening unfolded effortlessly. Joe and Gul joined the others with their plates, while I made small talk with my classmates, who all appreciated John's accessibility and intellectual depth.

Dessert and coffee were served toward the end, allowing for another mini session with John. This time, Joe asked him to summarize his latest research, followed by a final Q&A, including those who hadn't yet had a chance to speak. Joe leaned back, allowing us to engage directly with John, who shared his insights without a hint of self-righteousness. I couldn't help but marvel at how Joe and John, from distinct backgrounds, shared a similar academic ethos and might be serving as role models for generations of students like us.

We invited both teachers to cut the cakes, and I helped Julie and Elisabeth serve slices, while Richard and Katherine poured us coffee. It was certainly late by the time we finished, with everyone pitching in to clean and carry crockery, cutlery, drinks, and leftover food back to Gul's kitchen. Not much remained, as everyone had enjoyed each dish thoroughly, especially the naans and kebabs.

As we prepared to depart, fully satisfied, Joe thanked John on our behalf and extended an invitation to join us next time at the Hawthorns—our favorite spot up the hill on the other side of the Avon. We all joined Julie in a round of applause for Gul, grateful for facilitating such a memorable evening that everyone enjoyed to the fullest.

LAHORE & EYAM

After everyone had gone back to their places, I lay in bed, reflecting on the evening in all its aspects: the discussions with John, the quality and quantity of food, and the overall collegial ambiance that made it feel as if Totterdown had been taken over by our varsity clan. Everything had gone perfectly, with my classmates savoring the occasion to the fullest. John, by choosing to spend the evening with us rather than returning to his family and with his remarkable ability to put everyone at ease, was truly the highlight, with Joe not far behind. Without Joe's enthusiasm and input, achieving such spontaneous conviviality might have proved elusive. While John had retired early to his room, I found my own body clock stalled. I felt no exhaustion, despite such a busy, though truly memorable, day.

Gradually, I understood the true source of my restlessness. I yearned for Anne—to hold her close and let my fingers weave through her thick, lush auburn hair that framed her deep brown eyes, which sparkled with a captivating charm that stirred even my otherwise rugged heart. Years of diligent work at private schools under my father's strict but benevolent guidance, followed by a self-absorbed stint at UCL, had made me a somewhat practical person. Yet, I couldn't deny my past flings in Lahore and London. My outings in Lahore with Naveena had been platonic, with only the occasional kiss behind trees or hand-holding in Gulberg's cafes, but in the process, I memorized a full spectrum of romantic Urdu poetry, occasionally dipping into Keats and Shelley. To impress Naveena, I discovered poets like Ghalib, Mohani, Faiz, and Shakir on a deeper level. She was a city girl with a slim frame and graceful poise, seemingly fascinated by a man from the rugged mountains, but, despite my teenage longing, she held back, cautious of the unknown.

Naveena was clever, pursuing a bachelor's in fine arts, with a background at Lahore's prestigious Grammar School and a well-off family behind her, yet she was filled with a deep sense of humor and modesty that set her apart from other girls in her Kinnaird circle. We'd met at a debate at Lahore College for Women, where students from metropolitan institutions competed.

Despite some initial awkwardness, I hadn't done too badly, much to my own surprise, winning first prize in the declamation contest. The topic had been "Men have failed, so Women should rule," a contemporary euphemism that may sound a bit dated now.

"Congratulations to the Kinnaird team," I called to Naveena with a mischievous smile.

"Thanks. We did our bit, but GC was way ahead. Credit to you guys." Naveena was warm, and I knew I wasn't too far off the mark.

"Hey, I'm Gulbaz Baloch from Turbat. First prize should have gone to you, not just because the motion was overwhelmingly carried but because I was honestly a bit shaky at the start."

"I'm Naveena, from around here. I didn't notice any shakiness; I thought your oratory was spot-on, with the right moves at the right time."

Chuffed, I replied with an air of nonchalance, "Our job's done; why not have a cup of tea at the café if you're free?"

"Sure. The organizers are still busy with the chief guest and VIPs, and I'm dying for a hot chocolate."

"Thanks, Naveena. There are a couple of chairs in that corner. I'll go get our drinks while you grab those seats; otherwise, we'll be left standing in the crowd." I quickly made my way to the canteen and returned a few minutes later with a tray holding our drinks and two slices of carrot cake. "I thought we could use a bit of sugar after a tense but exhilarating afternoon."

Naveena appreciated the thought and asked about my subjects, which came as a bit of a surprise to her, considering that most students gravitated toward law or the sciences, while I was pursuing the humanities.

"Well, it's not that I underestimate the importance of medicine or engineering, nor am I against young people choosing military careers for the glamour. But I want to work with people, on the people, and for the people. Humanities is my way," I explained.

"That's very Lincolnian, but I'm with you on this," she replied. "My own passion for visual arts comes from a concern for people, animals, and the environment. After Kinnaird, I might just end up in your neighborhood—the National College of Arts. From the 'pen tribe' to the 'brush tribe,' I must say. Anyway, I need to go; I see Zarifa waiting for me." Naveena finished off her cake and washed it down with a quick gulp of hot chocolate. "Thanks for your hospitality, Gulbaz."

"The pleasure's mutual, Naveena. How about meeting up in a week, same time, same place? We could get another 'studenty' bite!" I wasn't about to let her go without securing our next meet-up—not too soon, but not too far away, either. The planner in me had momentarily replaced the debater.

Her affirmative response led to several outings in Lahore's parks, Gulberg cafes, and the Old City, each one bringing us closer. At first, we discussed our studies, then novels and poetry, with occasional mentions of history and politics. We both avoided religion, a mutual decision stemming from our shared disillusionment with ultra-orthodoxy and the violence it often entailed. Though both from relatively comfortable families, we still championed causes dear to most idealistic college students: land reform, women's empowerment, a ban on consanguine marriages, and even purdah.

One night, as we enjoyed kebabs, baba ghanoush, and vegetarian haandi at Cuckoo's in the Old City, with the Mughal Mosque and Lahore Fort shimmering under a full moon, I posed a question to Naveena:

"We seem to agree on so many progressive reforms for our society. Do you think we're just being idealists, ahead of our time, or maybe just play-acting at ideology?"

"Whatever it is, I don't mind," she replied. "Without ideals and a concern for the world, life would feel monotonous—the usual nine-to-five cycle. Gul, we have a long road ahead, but we need to ensure the little spark in us doesn't die out." Her words were both inspiring and mesmerizing. "I may not have grand ideals, but I want to explore myself and the world around me. What I like about you—beyond intelligence—is your humility, something rare in our society's upper echelons. A kind and attentive soul in a princely body. I feel lucky to have gone to that debate."

My words brought a smile to her face, and I took her hand under the table, away from the curious eyes of other diners. She didn't pull away from my soft grip, and we both sensed that our paths had drawn closer. Still, it was too early to commit ourselves to a full relationship—not because we were undergraduates and emotionally immature, but because we each needed time to find our own way in the world.

We held hands whenever we could, kept phone calls brief, and preferred meeting in person a couple of times each month, usually followed by long walks and tea. It's not that we weren't physically attracted to each other, but our joy in simply being together made our platonic closeness even more fulfilling. Perhaps, in some ways, we were old souls. Once, we ventured into the Lahore Museum on our way to the National College of Arts to be overwhelmed by the Indus heritage as we saw the human size statues of a brooding Buddha, temple carvings and material artifacts from Mohenjo Daro, Taxila and Harappa. A curator explained that countless seals from the ancient Indus cities remained undeciphered, holding secrets of the past. But the Gandhara collection, with its majestic images of Buddha, impressed us most—symbols of a regal yet otherworldly presence.

"Gandhara linked us with India and Central Asia in powerful ways, especially under Ashoka and later Kanishka," I explained, sharing a bit of historical context.

"It was from here that Buddhism spread to East Asia, and the Brahma faith evolved into what we call Hinduism as it traveled east to the valleys of the Ganges and Yamuna," Naveena added thoughtfully.

"I wonder why we Baloch are often seen as outsiders when we're clearly part of the Indus Valley heritage. But it seems to be a trend here to trace origins to the west or north—something that just adds to the complex identity struggles," I said, feeling a twinge of indignation.

"Maybe this is a point for debate in our institutions, but it's interesting how so many people across three continents trace their roots to the so-called 'Old World.' Only Native Americans seem to reject the Bering Strait theory, and Australian Aboriginals are often lumped into the 'greater India' category," she observed, putting identity issues into a larger context.

After passing by Kim's Bookshop, we decided to grab some chaat from a vendor between the museum and the arts college—our destination, where a young artist had invited us for tea. She had already gained a reputation for her sketches of historic buildings in the Old City.

00000

I met Lisa in the library at UCL, where she worked part-time and where I was a regular visitor, especially in my first few weeks. She studied archaeology and was looking forward to a class trip to Turkey while earning extra money as a part-time assistant in the library. Our initial smiles gradually turned into greetings, until, in my second term, I saw her in the cafeteria during lunch. It was rush hour, and the only seat available was the one across from her.

"Hello again, Lisa, nice to see you here! I'd always thought—naively, perhaps—that librarians never ate, living only on lofty ideas that drifted down from the bookshelves."

"I usually bring my own sandwich—a real one, not a lofty one—but I was lazy this morning and came here. It's a chicken panini with Mediterranean veggies. What about you?"

"I've got a roast beef sandwich to keep up my protein intake. Like you, I usually bring my lunch, but today I needed a break from tuna and corn. I'm Gul, an international student studying humanities."

"Good to meet you, Gul. I'm studying archaeology," she replied.

"Any particular focus?"

"Not yet. Just covering the basics until I get some field experience with a team—depends on all kinds of factors. I'm going on a short trip to Turkey with a group from UCL and keeping my options open. Have you been to that part of the world?"

"I spent ten days in Turkey on my way to London from Pakistan. My cousin works at the embassy in Ankara, and we traveled to Izmir, with a short stopover in Istanbul. It's a beautiful country with a fascinating history, straddling three continents. I'm sure you'll enjoy it. Where are you headed?"

"We're going to a site about sixty miles from Konya, in the heart of Anatolia."

Lisa didn't seem in a hurry, as her shift at the library didn't start until two, so we lingered over lunch. By the end, we'd made plans to meet at the British Library the following week to visit a new exhibition on Chopin and have tea.

"Chopin's life was short and sad, but undeniably remarkable. He had admirers everywhere, though he was plagued by health issues that ultimately cut his life short," Lisa said, with a touch of sadness, as we wandered through the displays.

"He found a companion in George Sand in France, and for his health, they moved to Majorca. But Chopin missed his piano, which he'd left in Paris. Sand arranged for it to be transported to the island at the cost of three hundred francs. She, her two children, and Chopin lived in a farmhouse, but his health continued to decline even as his fame spread. He accomplished so much in his short life but never enjoyed good health." I paused, worried I was rambling, but Lisa was listening intently. "Have you heard the story about his heart?" she asked.

"During a tour of Britain, Chopin fell seriously ill and returned to Paris, where his sister cared for him, though he never recovered from tuberculosis. He died in 1849, just 39. She preserved his heart in a jar of alcohol and sent it back to Poland, where it was kept in a church. During WWII, it was moved to a secure location," I explained. "Chopin supported Polish independence from Russia, faced prejudice in Austria, and found France more welcoming. In those conservative times, Britain was cautious about Polish independence."

"Thanks for sharing, Gul. With 2010 being his bicentennial, this visit to the British Library seems like a fitting tribute. I appreciate you suggesting it," she said, touching my arm as we moved toward the café near the towering shelves of embossed tomes and gazetteers.

"I came here last term for an exhibit on Omar Khayyam and his translations in the West, particularly Edward Fitzgerald's. It was a glimpse into the period when Persian classics sparked a renaissance across the Muslim world, right before the Crusades. During that visit, I heard about this upcoming Chopin exhibit."

"What got you interested in Chopin?" Lisa asked.

"Well, my father's a fan of classical music, both Western and Eastern, and Chopin is one of his favorites. He's an academic, so I grew up around discussions of the Romantic era—figures like Chopin, Sand, Hugo, Keats, Byron, and Shelley were all names I heard early on. For a while, I even thought George Sand was a man, like George Eliot," I admitted.

Lisa had to get to her desk soon, so we walked back to UCL's main building, with its marble facade and massive Greek columns. We planned to meet the following Friday for drinks at a local pub. She headed into the library, and I went back to my room on Gower Street to finish an essay on Sir William Jones and his work on Indo-Islamic classics. The more I researched, the more complex he seemed—a polymath with a knack for inquiry who pioneered themes that later Orientalists, many of them colonial historians and anthropologists, would take to new heights—or lows.

Taking intermittent breaks from writing, I reflected on my encounters with Lisa, who radiated a natural spontaneity, vigor, and sincerity. She was neither the typical academic nor a superficial fun-seeker but someone with a genuine bohemian spirit. Spending time with her boosted my confidence; she seemed so authentic and open to exploring the world without the imaginary barriers people often build around themselves to guard against insecurities. I was careful not to idealize her, but there was a raw, invigorating Freudian energy that made me feel as if my slumbering youth had finally come of age.

Reaffirming our loyalty to Jeremy Bentham, the founder of our college some two centuries ago, we walked into the pub named after him, just around the corner from the main campus. It was nestled among high-rises, safely removed from the bustle of Oxford Street and the nearby Euston train station. A relatively small setup featuring Bentham's portrait on its sign, our local was crowded with punters—mostly couples and a few groups. Being a Friday, both the pub and the pavement outside were packed, with pints clinking and everyone chattering away, seemingly oblivious to how anyone could hear each other in the din. Perhaps it was more a matter of reading each other's lips and expressions than relying on sound. We squeezed ourselves in by the bar, holding our drinks and hoping to find seats. Like everyone else, our words remained mostly inaudible until our faces drew closer.

"To you, Lisa," I toasted, lifting my pint of ale.

"To you, Gul," she replied, raising her gin and tonic, "and of course, to Jeremy Bentham and Chopin."

"Bentham was the benefactor who, two centuries ago, bought the first building with a hundred pounds to start our college. Life without a purpose is an empty shell, as we discussed the other day." I hesitated slightly, feeling self-conscious about my philosophical tone, but Lisa was attentive.

"I wonder if Chopin and JB ever crossed paths in London!" Lisa mused.

"I'm afraid not—Bentham died in 1832, and Chopin didn't visit Britain until over a decade later," I replied, resisting any hint of triumphalism, then added, "But JB's legacy lives on; his preserved body is still in that cabinet in the Wilkins Building. And though they say he participates ceremonially in College Council meetings, it's mostly a rumor." I had read this tidbit in the Encyclopaedia Britannica but still preferred to imagine his body wheeled into meetings.

"In appearance, Bentham reminds me a bit of Benjamin Franklin—big head, observant eyes, and sparse, long hair," Lisa remarked, quite accurately.

"Very true; they may have met during Franklin's time in London. I believe Mahatma Gandhi studied at UCL as well, drawn by Bentham's utilitarianism and UCL's openness to admitting students from the colonies," I said, hoping it would interest Lisa and lend a touch of authenticity.

"Gandhi is still present in spirit at Tavistock Square, not far from one of his mentors, and both people and pigeons enjoy free access to the Mahatma. I often go there for lunch, especially on my vegetarian days." We laughed, picturing the garlanded statue of Gandhi with pigeons perched on his head, and others scurrying around accepting crumbs from visitors.

A couple vacated a corner table, which we quickly claimed, thanking our good fortune. Taking turns, Lisa fetched drinks from the bar, emphasizing her assertive sense of reciprocity. With better acoustics here, we could finally talk without straining.

"Gul, educate me on Balochistan. My knowledge is embarrassingly basic, though I tried to look up some information—using the usual sources, you know!"

"Balochistan is a vast, mostly arid region spanning parts of Pakistan, Iran, and Afghanistan. In Pakistan alone, it covers almost half the country's landmass. It's mostly rocky deserts with scattered shrubs, though certain valleys around my hometown, Turbat, have palm groves and mulberry trees. Water is cherished, and with such high temperatures and scarce rainfall, our ancestors created underground channels called karez to survive. The land is harsh and unyielding, but the pristine air and striking landscapes are unmatched. The coast along the Arabian Sea has its own rugged beauty. My town is close to the Iranian border. My family has held onto ancestral lands for generations, but education and careers have shifted our lives. Karachi, Dubai, Quetta, Muscat, and Lahore are now popular destinations, though our hearts remain attached to the endless desert. My father, recently retired as a senior civil servant, now manages our land. My older brother and his wife live in Karachi, and my younger sister is considering higher studies in the UK or joining the civil service. Hope that's enough to start!"

"Thanks for sharing, Gul. I'm an urbanite at heart—everyone says Oxford is a 'city,' though Cambridge remains a 'town.' My parents, both academics, are originally from Derbyshire, though I grew up in the South-East, going to Oxford High. My dad teaches Philosophy at Exeter College, and my mom curates Renaissance art at the Ashmolean. I chose archaeology because it's a bit of a blend of their worlds. UCL attracted me for its academic reputation—and because I wanted to experience living in the heart of London."

"I plan to visit Oxford soon, but I've heard the Peak District in Derbyshire is one of the most beautiful parts of England. Does your family still go there often?"

"My father inherited a home in Bakewell, right in the heart of the Peak District. Some of my mother's relatives live in Eyam, a village known for the plague outbreak of 1665-66. It draws visitors from far and wide. Besides the breathtaking landscape, the area has such a rich history, though the influx of tourists in summer can turn villages like Bakewell into car parks. Thankfully, most visitors are respectful and help keep the district's natural beauty intact."

"It reminds me of the Lake District, famous for its scenery and overrun with tourists, though the Peak District might attract more British visitors. In Balochistan, the heat and dust discourage tourists unless they're particularly adventurous, but in Pakistan's northern areas, climate change and the influx of tourists have strained the landscape. Newly built roads through the Karakorams and Hindu Kush bring more travelers, and interaction between the locals and visitors is both evolving and somewhat predictable," I added, reflecting on the complex but often familiar dynamics of tourism.

We left the JB, still abuzz with punters, and stepped out into the calm of the streets, with Lisa leaning into me—not from the effects of two modest drinks, but because of the shared warmth between us. Sometimes, that inner pull takes over, guiding bodies in a rare harmony that people call intimacy or serendipity. Feeling peckish, I remembered a spicy pizza in the freezer I'd saved for a late-night snack. Lisa wasn't in a hurry to head back to her place on Bunning Way, across from King's Cross, where a taxi would be wiser at this hour to avoid a walk past the rowdy crowd near the Northern Line station.

The shared kitchen was empty when we started on our pizza, aided by a bottle of Bordeaux that had been patiently aging beside my bookshelf, waiting for a special occasion. And tonight, I could think of no better reason to open it. Once we'd finished our snacks, we took our glasses and retired to my room. Sitting beside each other, holding hands, we shared a spontaneous kiss, and things deepened. Our lips met in a quiet fervor, hands exploring in their own rhythm, tracing and discovering as our bodies grew receptive to each sensation. We clung to each other like climbers hanging onto a rope on a sheer ascent, and a few minutes later, amidst Lisa's soft murmurs and my own excitement, I said a tender farewell to my long-held bachelorhood.

"Gul, that was exhilarating; why the mischievous smile?"

"Just because, in this 'epochal post-virginity phase,' I feel as if I've grown by decades—though I'm probably a bit of a latecomer!"

"Honestly, your moves this evening suggested otherwise. Still, I did have a few doubts—but all beautifully dispelled. I love being with you—your strong, hairy arms around me. They feel like they're protecting me, celebrating me, and quenching something that's been building   since you talked about Chopin the other day. Just a little confession I thought was due," she teased.

"That's wonderful, Lisa. Let's make this night ours—no interruptions, just us."

"I couldn't agree more. I wouldn't mind resting my head on your shoulder, not caring if either of us drifts off. This night belongs to us. JB must be smiling, though I'm not so sure about your Gandhi, with his fondness for abstention!"

I wasn't sure how long we stayed, nestled like spoons, my face buried in her red hair and my hands clasped around her freckled shoulders. But before long, our bodies reawakened, exploring each other with a passion that soon turned tempestuous. Our eagerness grew in waves, until we were transported to a raw, instinctual state—a moment both recreational and, thankfully, far from any procreative intentions.

We continued to meet intermittently—not just on weekends, but sometimes midweek too. Though our connection was intense, we never missed classes or let our studies slip. Life remained a well-paced routine, but far from the dull linearity it had been before that evening in Bloomsbury. A smile crept onto my face every time I passed Bentham's cabinet, thinking he must be pleased with the connections his college facilitated. Surely, his spirit was savoring the mingling of diverse minds—and hearts.

The Christmas break took us in different directions, but before my flight home, I managed a day trip to Oxford, where Lisa treated me to a romantic lunch on the Ashmolean's rooftop. We strolled around the Bodleian and ended the day at the Turf Tavern, enjoying drinks with hands and knees teasing under the table, making plans for a hiking trip in the Peak District during Easter break.

00000

Lying in bed, reminiscing about my friendship with Lisa, I found myself missing her unfettered presence. Her friendship was free from clichés or hang-ups, a refreshing contrast to Anne, who, while not difficult, carried a slightly more formal air that made me desire her nearness even more. I sensed that Anne wasn't as detached as I'd once thought; I felt she might respond if I dared to make a move. Lisa, though, was altogether different—especially during our trip to the Peak District, which not only marked a high point in our relationship but also brought a touch of realism to our buoyant companionship.

The weather was still on the cool side, with a pale sun struggling through a thick fog as a tentative English spring arrived, accompanied by a riot of cherry and rose blossoms. Emerging from Lisa's flat in north London that April morning, I packed my rucksack, fleece, flask, and hiking boots into her car's boot, where her own gear—trekking poles, goggles, and trainers—were already stashed. Soon, her compact BMW was heading north on the M1 towards Sheffield. We'd planned to stay in Eyam, where

64

Lisa's aunt, Mary, a retired teacher, had left her house key with a neighbor before heading to Oxford for Easter break.

By now, Lisa's parents knew about our friendship, and we'd had dinner together during one of their visits to London. We chose Colbeh, a cozy Persian restaurant with an informal vibe, set apart from the bustling shawarma joints on Edgware Road. Over authentic Persian dishes, we talked about our studies, future research, and British politics in the Middle East. I found the Hammersleys amicable, with no hint of suspicion or snobbery. They seemed pleased about our friendship, which, like us, they viewed as something meaningful yet uncommitted. Though they hoped Lisa would establish herself professionally before any serious commitments, they were liberal enough to accept our friendship and didn't bat an eye at the prospect of her forming close connections at university.

Aunt Mary's cottage, made of mellow stone, was on Church Street in Eyam and was one of the preserved "plague cottages," with a history dating back nearly four centuries to the Black Death. According to village lore, afflicted residents quarantined themselves to prevent the spread of disease, and people from neighboring villages would bring provisions, leaving them at a distance. Our visit to the nearby church and museum was a humbling experience, a reminder of how death had once stalked this beautiful, secluded village in a stunning landscape of rolling hills, green meadows, and hidden brooks.

With tea flasks, cucumber sandwiches, and flapjacks, we decided to walk up the narrow road behind Eyam, passing quiet houses hidden among towering trees and lush hedges. We continued to the youth hostel, which buzzed with hikers and bikers, some of whom were regular visitors to the area, eager to share tales of their adventures. After studying the local trail maps, we exited and headed up a path that left the paved road, winding through woods and offering a fabulous view of Eyam below. After passing a stone wall, we took a narrow, winding trail that eventually led us to a waterfall bordered by ancient trees. Seeking privacy, we settled behind blackberry bushes, Lisa unwrapping the sandwiches while I poured tea. Feeling both tired and exhilarated, we relaxed, compressed together on the blanket. Our affection soon turned into a moment of intimacy, as the seclusion and natural surroundings stirred something instinctive, evoking a joy that felt timeless and essential, as if satisfying an innate thirst.

Later, while walking further down the path, we encountered a group of cows surrounding a fallen calf. To avoid any risk of agitating them, we took a small detour and soon met a farmer on a tractor headed toward the calf. Back on the main road, we turned left and soon arrived at Mary's house. Lisa's mother had grown up in this historic cottage, and after her marriage, her sister Mary had lived here, later becoming involved in the local church and museum. The cottage was beautifully furnished, reflecting Mary's taste for antiques, with dark wooden beams, vintage stoves, and tapestries on the walls. We prepared a simple pasta meal with an improvised seasoning, finishing with a blissful apple crumble.

That dimly lit evening, Mary's LPs from the Seventies kept us company. The soulful voices of Barbra Streisand, Helen Reddy, Linda Ronstadt, and Carly Simon serenaded our friendship in this atmospheric corner of England, where mist and stillness ruled, and the occasional hoot of a distant owl echoed through the silence.

We had planned our main hike for Saturday, and it proved to be a busy day with a steady stream of day-trippers converging on the open area by Edale's village hall. Situated in Derbyshire, Kinder Scout, the highest point in the district and the southern end of the Pennine Way, demands a mix of focused determination and physical resilience—something one doesn't fully grasp until halfway up, when the climb over scattered, often slick boulders begins to test one's resolve. The early part of the trail is paved with slabs, allowing for a gradual ascent. Without trees, the view opens up to sweeping panoramas of heather-covered slopes and peaks, dotted with sheep grazing among the purple expanse. Down in the valleys by the streams, there are villages, each with roots reaching back to the Stone Age, now shaped by a history of landlords and a populace once reliant on sheep herding, farming, and eventually mining.

About halfway through, in a fenced-off area that looked like grazing land, we encountered a herd of shaggy cows with calves, all watched over by a large white bull who brayed menacingly at us, holding his ground. This formidable beast, presumably the father of the calves, seemed primed for yet another spring season. We avoided eye contact and kept a steady grip on our trekking poles as we made our way past him, relieved to find ourselves on the other side of a wooden gate.

Our lunch break was welcome and revitalizing, but the second leg of the hike was even more strenuous, with the food pulling energy toward digestion. Despite our longing and apprehension for the peak, we kept pushing on. Finally, sweaty and exhilarated, we reached the summit—a massive rock protruding over the void, offering superb views of valleys, hillsides, a water reservoir, and small farmhouses nestled among the foliage. Surrounded by other triumphant hikers, a sense of achievement set in, but we soon began our descent, choosing a different route that proved even more challenging, with steep drops and an uneven path that tested our endurance further. Even Lisa, whose legs had been moving with enviable rhythm, found herself stymied by sudden descents, made worse by swarms of midges swarming near puddles and thickets.

"It's as if these midges and ants knew exactly where to ambush us, Gul," Lisa remarked, irritated. "We didn't see them on the way up!"

"My ears, neck, and arms are under siege," I grumbled. "And here I thought they'd go for you, with all that talk about your sensitive skin. But no—they're utterly indiscriminate."

"I see other hikers battling them too. We should've brought repellent. We're paying for our blasé attitude now," she said, quite right.

"Did you notice some hikers with large packs? They must be camping near the summit or doing night hikes," I suggested.

"Maybe, and at least they won't have to contend with these midges," Lisa replied.

Near ground level, the descent became easier, leading us back to a well-traveled trail alongside Grinds Brook, now swollen into a swift-flowing stream. We'd nearly completed the loop back to Edale, our toes sore, arms red, and heads itchy, but no less exhilarated by our hard-won achievement. The village pub was filled with hikers savoring pints and hefty meals, so we joined the crowd at the Old Nags Head.

By the time we returned to Eyam, night had fallen, and we were utterly exhausted. After half-hearted showers, we fell into bed, too sore to move. It was only when sunlight filled the room around midday that we managed to rise, making coffee and toast, though even that felt like an uphill struggle. Despite our physical stiffness, we still craved each other's presence, and soon we found ourselves entwined, sharing a closeness that felt like the natural continuation of our hike. There was a growing sense of ease on Lisa's face as she surrendered to the moment, her movements filled with warmth and joy. In that quiet intimacy, we reached a blissful peak together, our entangled bodies filled with shared exhilaration.

The Peak District had marked the high point in our friendship, but like our hike, I sensed a foreboding in the distance that came to pass after our return to Bloomsbury. Exams, job commitments, and the summer break took us on separate paths, a growing distance that became a chasm by the time the autumn semester began. I left for a summer job in Vancouver, while Lisa went to Çatalhöyük, the ancient site near Konya. For a while, we stayed connected over the phone and email, but a coolness crept in. After two weeks at a dig site in Beyşehir, Lisa went to New Zealand for a job at a camp, reconnecting with an old school friend. Meanwhile, on my return to London, I worked long hours at the British Museum, saving up to ease Abu's financial burden, as Anjum was now studying in Lahore.

Our relationship, though deeply intimate and filled with mutual adoration, had always carried a transitory nature. We hadn't rushed things or been driven solely by physical attraction; it was more a blend of fun, companionship, and shared experiences that brought us together. But when we moved away from Gower Street, the relationship faded, lacking the depth to withstand the distance. It wasn't that we were irresponsible—perhaps just unconsciously "post-modern," embracing the fleeting nature of things without labeling it as such.

In contrast, my friendship with Naveena, while platonic and tinged with adolescent infatuation, proved surprisingly enduring. Back home, cross-gender friendships aren't as easily sustained unless they lead to marriage. Social norms place heavy emphasis on chastity, particularly for women, and assume that youth are prone to impulsive choices, warranting parental oversight. Although some clandestine liaisons do occur, especially in metropolitan settings, most young people abide by these boundaries. Naveena and I shared an emotional bond but kept things respectful and restrained, knowing that we had limited freedom within societal expectations. Saying goodbye to her before leaving for London had been painful, but we'd both talked about our dreams of studying abroad and knew this was the next chapter. Months later, she left for Hamilton College in upstate New York, where she studied English and literature, growing into the writer I once admired as an orator. She was awarded the Arnold Raphael scholarship, named after the former U.S. ambassador to Pakistan, who died in a plane crash near Bahawalpur in 1988. Though we drifted into separate lives, our friendship held on through sporadic contact. In a way, our bond had already transcended the teenage phase we once shared.

In a similar way, I thought I could maintain a redefined friendship with Lisa, but we drifted back to being acquaintances. Longevity in relationships of this kind, I realized, is often a fantasy—a beautiful one, but still fleeting. Yet memories of such connections linger, refusing to dissolve. Looking back, I see these experiences as essential for growth, even if they demanded a "pound of flesh," leaving me a bit more introverted and work-focused.

Reflecting on my years at UCL, I remembered Lisa's warmth and spontaneity, though I knew she had moved on, settling into a steady relationship with her old school friend, now working with her in the British Museum's Egyptian section. For me, that relationship had helped me mature, shifting my focus more toward work and academic goals. And now, in Bristol, I found myself once again yearning for closeness—when, right then, I heard a knock at the door. It was Anne.

THE CABOT CIRCUS

Following our session with Joe at the Hawthorns, as I hurried back to my department on Woodland Road, I heard Anne calling out to me.

"Hey Gul, I enjoyed every bit of our Totterdown venture last Friday. I know Joe and the class have already given their heartfelt appreciation, but I wanted to reiterate mine. It was my second visit to your place, and now it's my turn for some reciprocity."

"The pleasure was mutual. What's on your mind, Anne?"

"I'm inviting you over to my digs for a meal. I've been reinventing myself as a chef after those Cowley years. How does this Friday sound if you're free?"

"That's very thoughtful of you, Anne. I think I can make it. Should I bring anything?"

"No, just come as you are, Gul. Everyone's already impressed by your cooking and organizational skills. See you at seven. I'm planning to invite a couple of classmates from other departments—I think you'll enjoy chatting with them. I need to rush now to meet my tutor for another course."

"Yes, I've got an appointment too, Anne. Looking forward to catching up!"

I arrived at Anne's place with a bouquet of flowers and a bottle of Bordeaux. I had cycled over and, as I locked my hybrid bike near the entrance, I retrieved the provisions from its panniers. Seeing two other bikes already secured to the racks, I felt comfortable hitching mine next to them. Anne welcomed me at the entrance with a warm hug and led me through a narrow corridor into the living room. Her place was more spacious and tidier than our Totterdown residence. Yet, like most student accommodations, it exuded an informal, cozy atmosphere devoid of any pretense of luxury.

Anne's two other guests, Samuel and Jackie, had arrived a few minutes before me. They stood to shake hands as Anne introduced us. "Sam is studying politics with a focus on Islam-related themes, while Jackie is reading intellectual history. Gul, originally from Balochistan in Pakistan, is studying sociology."

After the introductions, we settled in and engaged in small talk, gradually branching into broader intellectual and recreational topics. As usual, Anne steered the conversation into more challenging waters.

"Thatcher and Reagan handed our societies, including higher education, over to market forces. Now it seems IT, through AI and social media, is taking the wheel. I'm curious, Jackie, or any of you, do you find its impact overwhelming?"

I waited for my turn as the others shared their thoughts.

"I find it quite useful for accessing source materials, which cuts down my library visits. But I do have serious concerns about the quality and reliability of the information overload," Jackie said, hitting the proverbial nail on the head.

Sam added, "We're witnessing the decline of print culture, although the middle and lower classes now have more avenues for expressing themselves, which affects politics. Still, this new form of socialization might reinforce the isolation that modern individuals face."

"I agree with both Jackie and Sam," I said, making sure I didn't sound overly skeptical. "It's a mixed bag, and there's no turning back to the life we once knew, whether in higher education or politics. Like how our generation sees typewriters and dial phones only in museums or movies, future generations might have an entirely different concept of a book—primarily electronic, like PDFs. Politically, communication may become easier for parties and governments, but socialization could evolve into fewer face-to-face interactions, making the individual fully modern." I emphasized 'modern' with air quotes.

Anne, ferrying our drinks, picked up on this point and looked intrigued. "I thought only post-modernists had issues with modernity. But maybe Westernization is still the main culprit in the postcolonial world."

"Yes, at times, modernity may appear only skin-deep, but it remains a significant variable. Japan, China, and some Southeast

Asian nations seem to navigate it without issue, and the same could be said for Latin American countries, where the dominant groups often trace their origins to Europe," I added, concerned that I might be implying modernity posed unique challenges for Muslim societies.

"I worry about modernity when I see all kinds of dislocations, violence enabled by modern weapons, and the uprooting of indigenous peoples. And mind you, we're talking about millions," Jackie said, framing modernity as predominantly European or Western in nature.

Sam interjected, "The debate over modernity isn't just limited to the post-colonial world; it's a significant preoccupation in the West too. Just a few years ago, we saw John Gray and Francis Wheen clashing over it. Let's not forget that totalitarian regimes, including fascism, are products of modernity gone awry."

"This is a fascinating topic that deserves deeper exploration. Gray and Wheen have already laid the groundwork, but for now, dinner is ready," Anne said with her characteristic smile. "Come on, everyone, let's move to the dining table."

An enormous salad bowl brimming with fresh greens, buckwheat that tasted like couscous, kiwi, corn, and avocado topped with smoked salmon awaited us. Slices of ciabatta, ready to be spread with hummus and salsa, were neatly arranged. The main dishes included a lamb and herb casserole, falafels sprinkled with coriander surrounding a rice platter garnished with fried onions, and a basket of toasted pita. For those avoiding meat, Anne had thoughtfully prepared a colorful mirepoix of sautéed vegetables in soy sauce.

"I cycled to Easton this morning to buy fresh mutton from an Asian butcher. That neighborhood is such a vibrant, multi-ethnic mosaic, unlike the more pompous Georgian Bristol," Anne noted, sparking a response from Jackie, whose academic focus aligned with these themes.

"I've been there twice," Jackie said. "It's a lively, multilingual community. I should visit more often. Where do you shop, Gul?"

"I go to Easton occasionally, mainly for meat but also for herbs, fruits, and vegetables. Places like Easton, Luton, Southall, Slough, and Bradford have reshaped Britain from within. These communities are living remnants of Britain's imperial history," I replied, hoping my forthrightness hadn't struck a nerve.

"Like the Empire, modernity is a complex and controversial paradigm, yet it remains a reality. I wonder if Professor John Gallagher shares that view," Anne said, broadening the conversation.

"Jackie, Sam, John is a professor of history at Bath Spa University and my housemate in Totterdown. He's an avowed Marxist and a fierce critic of the Empire. Regarding your question, Anne, I'm sure he'd be skeptical of any uncritical celebration of modernity, especially when tied to Western dominance. But he might also argue that without the exploitation of imperialism, the Industrial Revolution would have been an illusion."

Sam, who had watched Niall Ferguson's series and other documentaries, remarked that discussing the Empire's positive aspects was no longer taboo. Still, he acknowledged that historians like John Gallagher, Olivette Otele, Hakim Adi, David Olusoga, Eric Hobsbawm, and Victor Kiernan kept the debate alive, ensuring it would remain provocative for years to come. Jackie predicted that the discourse would intensify, driven by decolonial studies and demands to remove statues of figures like Colston.

Sam queried me about the relationship between modernity and Islam, which I believed was a matter beyond resolution, at least in our lifetime. "There are three views on this, Sam. Firstly, some believe that Islam, when confronted with different cultures and conflicts throughout history, has reinvented itself and is not a static paradigm. The second opinion group argues that Europe-led modernity disconnected Muslims from their golden era, and the way forward is to return to the past rather than imitate Western ways. The third view considers modernity a universal heritage, aligning closely with Gray's premises. This group goes a step further by suggesting that Muslims, like the Chinese and other East Asian nations, should embrace modernist norms and institutions to overcome debilitating vulnerabilities. Here, science, democracy, industrialization, gender rights, and freedom of expression are the desired goals, which naturally aggrieve the second opinion group, including Salafis and other puritanical factions. As long as the majority of Muslims remain suspicious of Western hegemonies—both past and present—including colonialism and direct interventions, nostalgia and confusion will continue to take their toll. I hope I didn't bore you and everyone else with this monologue!"

Sam was the first to respond. "I agree with you about this significant split among the Muslim elite, though the Diaspora may be slightly different, particularly the younger generations. The historiography I've read on reconstructing Islamic discourses is mostly produced by scholars based in the West, given the restrictions back home. Universities, media, and think tanks here facilitate critical Muslims in making their viewpoints heard. But political Islam, as I see it today, follows a variable trajectory; the revivalists seeking a comeback through democratic means are thinning out compared to those who pursue radical actions, including the use of force."

Anne, who had been replenishing our plates and glasses, interjected, "Who are some of these people who, as you say, are the flag bearers of such perspectives?"

"I don't know all of them," Sam admitted, "but most are academics, primarily migrant scholars, though some converts are also joining these debates. They remain divided between Syncretists and Salafists. I can think of Khaled Abou El Fadl, Amina Wadud, Ziauddin Sardar, Leila Ahmed, and Asma Barlas. I'd also place the late Professor Fazlur Rahman in Gul's first category. I hope those names are enough for now, Anne. There are many more, but I'd need to study them further."

"I guess in Britain and the West in general, Muslims are often grouped into two categories: purists and syncretists, which overlooks the pluralities among them," I added. "Most of them, anyway, are subjected to a geopolitical lens that indirectly empowers the extremists who, like the Neo-Cons, view the world in stark black-and-white terms with no shades of grey. Emphasizing oppressed women or the supposed loss of critical thinking among Muslims may not carry as much weight in the future. It's a superficial reading of a complex situation, and it reeks of exclusive subjectivity."

Anne, while serving her expertly baked apple pie, connected this discussion to our earlier conversation. "I think viewing Enlightenment as a divide between 'us' and 'them' is overly simplistic. The Huntingtonian premise, followed by the rushed post-9/11 analyses, reinforced this binary, which is why I find Wheen's arguments condescending and exclusionary. It's like saying, 'The Chinese may have taken our technical knowledge, but only our enlightened values can free them from robotic conformity.'"

As I helped clear the table, I realized I hadn't been as helpful to our host as I should have been during our meal. Taking the soiled dishes to the sink, I planned to replace them with coffee cups while Anne operated the percolator, allowing me to lean in and say quietly, "Anne, the food was wonderful, as you could tell by how we devoured it. The lively discussion added the perfect intellectual touch to this lovely evening. Thank you!" Without thinking, I lightly pinched her wrist and winked, receiving a spontaneous, mischievous smile in return.

With the table set for dessert and coffee, the conversation continued. The apple crumble, topped with a rich layer of cream, had its anticipated effect, invigorating us all for another round of discussion. Jackie, curious as ever, asked how plural societies in the past managed to coexist. Anne and I agreed that traditional societies relied on local structures and hierarchies to manage their diverse populations, though not always successfully, leaving many underprivileged groups, such as slaves and religious minorities, outside the safety net.

"Without unconditionally defending traditional communities," I said, "consider our system back home, where unwavering obedience to the sardar ensures basic needs like shelter and a sense of security. In contrast, Anne, that role has been taken over by the Westphalian state, which, more than technology and the rise of the middle class, is the biggest threat to traditional norms."

"The state," Anne added, "operates like an octopus, drawing in various groups and becoming a battleground. By its very nature and evolution, the state opposes multiculturalism, acting as a leveller by design. Nationalism, wielded selectively by those in power, turns into a tool of control and coercion, often in the name of demographic majorities. Afghanistan and Japan are unique examples: in Afghanistan, tradition remains strong even in the capital, while Japan, the epitome of modernity and Westernization, still bows to certain traditional conventions, making it a conservative society but one vastly different from Afghanistan."

"You're right, Anne. Kowtowing to the emperor is replicated at various levels down the hierarchies in Japan," Sam opined. "Afghanistan is a self-confessed traditional society, which is why the Taliban have shown such resilient staying power—something all those preachers of modernism and rights-based regimes cannot sufficiently fathom."

Jackie shifted gears by drawing our attention to a changing Britain, where the Empire, more than the industrial revolution and migration, had facilitated multiculturalism. France's experience, however, was radically different. "I attended a few lectures at the centre on Priory Street, but the most impressive so far was by Professor Bhiku Parekh. Despite stringent reservations by Tories like David Cameron, he argues that promoting multiculturalism benefits everyone."

"I was present at that lecture," I interjected, "which allowed me to trace the gradualist origin that defies the viewpoint that communal clustering results from ethnicity alone. Even France, with its emphasis on laïcité, hasn't found a roadmap for its banlieues." I felt I was on point, reinforcing the idea that economic factors play a central role in creating gated and ghettoized communities—not just in Britain but everywhere.

Sam, who had been quiet for a while, raised a valid point after clearing his dessert bowl. "I wonder how the Germans and Scandinavians will handle this issue. Will they follow France's assimilationist model or pursue the British paradigm of 'muddling through pluralities?'"

Anne responded, expanding the conversation with North American case studies. "The United States takes great pride in being a land of immigrants, underpinning its pluralism. But it still hasn't been able to resolve its color-based classifications, which become even sharper when combined with class factors. Canada and Australia might resemble Britain, yet the world is still searching for the best possible sociological model before we can think of a one-size-fits-all approach."

Jackie, in her exuberance, pointed out that most of what we had discussed fell within the parameters of sociology. Sam and I took an international approach, while Anne focused on the multiple factors driving systemic approaches in various states. It was past midnight, but being a Friday night, no one—including our host—seemed in a rush. As Jackie and Sam prepared to leave, unlocking their bikes and fixing the lights, I volunteered to help Anne wash the dishes and cutlery. She accepted reluctantly, both of us seeking an excuse to linger a bit longer.

Anne invited me for a shot of port after a joyous yet slightly strenuous day. She felt jubilant over the quality of the discussion and how the evening had unfolded. Coincidentally, her three housemates were away for the entire weekend. We settled on the large living room sofa and began reviewing some of the topics we had discussed earlier.

"Anne, without sounding patronizing, this was a quality exchange of views, and I'm really impressed by the calibre of your friends. A person is known by the company they keep, and I envy you."

Smiling, Anne replied, "I'm blessed when it comes to friends. And my company right now isn't bad at all, I reckon." We both giggled as her right arm slipped around my upper back, gradually pulling me closer. The adoration between us was mutual, though it had taken time and effort from both sides. This evening felt like the beginning of a new phase in our lives.

"Gul, sometimes I'm overawed by your intellectual grasp, fortified by maturity. How did all this come about?"

"As Saadi, the medieval sage, once expressed, it is impactful associations that transform even ordinary soil into fragrant musk. In one of his poems, he speaks of a piece of scented clay that intoxicates the onlooker, merely because it has been in the company of roses for some time. I'm just a learner and don't claim the elevated status you attribute to me, Anne."

"I've heard of his name; tell me more about Saadi."

"To many of us, Saadi is an invisible influence, passed down through generations by our grandparents. His ethical precepts are shared through lucid stories about humans and animals, each parable ending with a moral that resonates deeply. He lived and endured the Mongol onslaught on the Muslim regions and traveled through India, Syria, and the Arabian Peninsula, composing poems and stories in classical Persian. Simple in his habits yet sharp of mind, Saadi shunned ostentation and frivolity, urging a life filled with kindness, honesty, and humility. My maternal grandfather's generation read his works in school. I wonder how many people still read him in today's Iran—let alone in the subcontinent!"

"I've heard bits and pieces about Khayyam, and scholars like Rumi and Saadi must be towering figures in Muslim heritage. Compared to our Classics at Oxbridge, your universities could benefit from focusing on such intellectuals," Anne said with conviction.

"Yes, that would be true decolonization of syllabi and subjects, if post-colonial societies took it seriously. It might lessen our ingrained sense of inferiority to the West—and now the Far East too." Realizing that my thoughts might cloud the mood of the evening, I added, "But Khayyam is exceptional. His quatrains are unmatched—simple in form but rich in substance. They speak of mortality while urging us to savor life's beauty before our time ends. And I must remember good old Khayyam as we watch the world go by at this dawn." I pulled Anne gently, holding her arms until our eyes met, iris to iris. There was no need for effort; Anne willingly softened in my embrace as I traced her lips, which responded with an inviting warmth. We took our time, letting our fingers, tongues, arms, and bodies move in harmony, instinctively aware of those places and gestures that awaken primal desires. It wasn't mere physical longing but an urge for nirvana—or wisaal, as the eastern sages would say—a celebration of mental and physical unity, not just self-gratification.

We made our way to Anne's bedroom, our movements synchronized to Carly Simon's voice. Our shared energy became a chorus of rhythm, desire, and release, until Simon's "You're So Vain" made us burst into laughter.

"Is Carly attributing that vanity to you, Gul? Maybe not—you're more grounded, like Khayyam, without losing the romantic touch."

"I wouldn't call myself vain, though my single-mindedness might suggest otherwise. I do have moments of withdrawal when I seem lost in thought. But you, Anne, are far from vain."

"I'm just a small-town girl from the West Country, with some colonial ancestry and Danish features. Like you, I try to stay grounded, to be 'normal.' You understand, Gul?"

"In some ways, I do. But I'm no authority on defining others. I take people as I find them. Your Oxford background, unlike that of many, has made you approachable, not wrapped in the snobbery that often comes with an Oxbridge pedigree."

"Your family's strong traditions, stability, and exposure to diverse cultures could have instilled arrogance, yet you remain grounded. You're an enigma, Gul—an Oriental mystery, if my colonial roots can voice that."

"I hope those roots don't imply that a 'brown' local cohabiting with a 'white' colonial results in both becoming colonized, erasing centuries of hierarchy. Let's toast to that realization, Anne. Where's our port?"

She didn't take long to return with two filled glasses. We clinked them together and let the sheet slip away as our bodies intertwined, limbs moving as if racing time itself. The dawn lingered near Cabot Circus as I reflected on my journey to Bristol. Anne shuffled through her CDs until Helen Reddy's "Somewhere in the Night" began playing, perfectly complementing our experience.

"This is cheeky, Anne. With Reddy singing this romantic song, it feels like she's narrating our moment. Did you know she started performing again after a long hiatus?"

"Her early hits, like 'I Am Woman,' resonated with feminists and even made it into American textbooks. But 'Somewhere in the Night' captures a woman's love beautifully—and it can go both ways."

"Absolutely. It's marvelously expressed, and her unique, slightly nasal voice adds to the charm."

"How do you find Baez, Gul?"

"I like her anti-war and anti-establishment songs, particularly for their connection to the civil rights movement and the Vietnam War. But my favorite is 'Diamonds and Rust.' I may not have blue eyes like robin's eggs or need to call on a dial phone from a crummy hotel in Washington Square, but I still resonate with the sentiments behind those words, Anne. I wish I could compose something like that just for you—only for you!"

"How very thoughtful, Gul. I cherish your sentiment, which I can feel deep inside me, and words may never fully capture its intensity." Anne, sharp and honest as ever, continued, "Apparently, Joan wrote that song for Bob Dylan. They were lovers in the 1960s—an exceptional couple in extraordinary times. No wonder my parents and their generation are so nostalgic for that decade. When asked, they always say you had to be there, at Woodstock, protesting in the streets, or abandoning it all for something new. Some of them might have regrets, especially those who got tangled up with Maharishi."

"True enough; he was a master manipulator—a wolf in sheep's clothing—who preyed on the vulnerable, especially women, while amassing a fleet of luxury cars."

"He must have been quite the seducer, or maybe people were so disillusioned with materialism and monotony that they fell for a charlatan like him. He passed away a few years back at 90. A reincarnated Rasputin."

"People often attribute sexual prowess to eating meat, like our hunting ancestors did, but in this case, a vegetarian kept up his orgies without pause."

"Someone else consumed some meat earlier this evening and didn't take long to crave more flesh."

"That's true. That casserole took over, and it's still in control. You'd better watch out. The host wasn't far behind in enjoying that feast either. Thinking about it now, that was indulgent—but not as much as what I'm holding and savoring at this moment." We both laughed like teenagers, sneaking away for a playful conversation.

The sun peeked persistently through a narrow slit between the curtains, urging us to wake up. Down at the Circus, Saturday shoppers bustled about, gripping their provisions while mothers pushed buggies with playful toddlers squinting at their ice cream cones. I stumbled across the floor and realized it was nearly eleven. I rushed to the shower, wrapping myself in a white sheet that felt animated and eager for a hearty breakfast. "This shower is king-sized, and I wouldn't mind some company, Anne."

She had been up since I started navigating her en-suite and now I could see her sleepy brown eyes tracking me through the glass door. Soon, she joined me, and scrubbing each other with soapy gel took on its own momentum until the water turned lukewarm. We emerged, wrapped in towels, our hair tousled into playful curls—hers wavy and long, mine somehow still shiny and thick. Drying myself by the window, the sun shone directly on my face, reinvigorating me with warmth and energy.

"Hey, Madam Colonial, how about a Lahori breakfast at a South Asian place in Easton? I think we deserve a generous brunch."

"I'm all for it, Rustic Tribal! Let me put on some trousers before venturing into Tribalistan with a mischievous Stani." We both burst into laughter at this spontaneous characterization.

St. Mark's Street bustled with Bristol's seamless vitality and diversity, though it lacked the Georgian and Victorian architecture found near the Harbour, particularly in Clifton. On weekends, the street came alive with small shops, grocery stores, and ethnic restaurants, its narrow pavements crowded with daytime shoppers. By night, its clubs and bars filled up with university students out for dates or parties. Although Bath residents might boast about their city's self-sufficiency, it wasn't uncommon to find them enjoying Bristol's nightlife.

Winding our way through the aromatic blend of croissants, paninis, kebabs, and garlic bread, we finally reached a small, informal-looking eatery. Pancake-like breads were being fried in a large wok beside two deep pans filled with cooked chickpeas and halvah, emitting a fragrant steam. We took our seats, and Anne left the ordering to me.

"Six puris, a plate of halvah, two servings of chole with garlic, and two salted lassis," I told the adolescent waiter, likely the owner's son who was doing A-levels. "Also, bring two steaming naans, and keep the chilies, coriander, and ginger slices on a separate plate. Oh, and a plate of nihari with the naans. We've heard so much about your Lahori naashta."

"Sir, would you like it on the hotter side, or would you prefer a milder version for both of you?"

"Milder, please, and don't sprinkle garam masala on our savory dishes. We'll add it ourselves."

The steaming, aromatic food captured Anne's attention immediately. She may have tried some of these dishes back in Oxford, but here, they were part of a complete, authentic Desi breakfast. "Does desi mean native? Hopefully, it's not a derogatory term, Gul?" she asked.

"It depends on the context, but it literally means anything or anyone from the subcontinent, so it's unique to that part of the world. The antonym is wilayati, which means European, often specifically English, and sometimes it's gendered as gora or gori, referring to a white person. Time to eat, Gori Ma'am."

Anne quickly got the hang of making morsels of puris filled with chickpea curry. Soon, she was adding chillies and ginger, tempered by small sips of lassi. She tried the nihari with naan, her fingers diving into the brown, coriander-speckled broth. I watched her figure out the tender lamb shank, separating the meat effortlessly and sliding it into pieces of naan that soaked up the curry. Though she was sweating, she ate voraciously, her fingers deftly maneuvering through the deep bowls while our forks and knives remained untouched.

After finishing the spicy dishes, we turned to the halvah, which required a few more puris to fully enjoy. I ordered two glasses of sugarless karak chai—milky tea brewed with live tea leaves, cardamom seeds, and full-cream milk—to complement the halvah, rich with raisins, almonds, pistachios, and coconut shreds. The tea, brewed in a boiling pan, was meant as a strong finisher.

The meal was delicious, and we left nothing in the bowls or on the plates. I could sense Anne's desire for another glass of tea, so I offered to join her. Just then, our cups arrived, accompanied by four gulab jamuns floating in hot, sugary syrup. Ignoring any thought of calorie counts or sugar intake, we filled ourselves to the brim and wondered how we'd manage the bike ride back to our lodgings.

We slowly made our way out of the restaurant and strolled along the street, passing by a butcher, an ironmonger, and small kiosks selling mobile phones and accessories. Eventually, we reached the newly built Friday Mosque.

"I'm not planning to take you inside yet to recite the Kalima, Colonial Ma'am. Given my sins, converting someone might be the perfect way to have them forgiven and save two lives at once. What do you think of that?"

"Well, your Allah must be laughing at your fantastic algorithm. He already has a billion or more believers and probably isn't eager to increase the numbers, lest he annoy Moses, Jesus, Buddha, Krishna, and the other gurus who made their own promises. For what it's worth, my room wasn't far from the central mosque in Cowley on Manzil Way. On Fridays, I occasionally walked through the throngs of worshippers in Oxtown. So, maybe this ma'am already has a claim to being a believer. Tread carefully, Desi Sahib."

"That's hilarious, Gori Sahiba. So, no rush to take you inside the mosque yet!"

"I need to go back and work on my English assignment. What's your plan, Gul?"

"Honestly, after all that food, I won't last long at my computer finishing Joe's half-done essay. I might just hit the sack, and you should probably do the same, Anne."

"Thanks for the lavish desi breakfast. See you soon, Gul."

NEWTON ST. LOE

Our relationship encompassed many facets, oscillating between the platonic and the physical. With its intellectual undertones and occasional outdoor pastimes, it refused to become monotonous or wither away like so many transient pursuits. Gul and I grew close gradually, maintaining our respective discretion while continually discovering new commonalities, often as small, delightful surprises. This dynamic was born of a sense of maturity and stability that one acquires during postgraduate life, aided by living away from dorms and the comforts of home-cooked meals. Relationships formed during the turbulent undergraduate years often give way to more profound, stable bonds that may carry enduring strands. Some people choose to become loners, channeling all their energy into their careers, and references to past encounters may evoke only a fleeting smile. While the sentimentalization of first love, as folk tales suggest, never truly leaves one's memory, not every physical closeness equates to love. Some individuals nurture platonic love without the need for physical intimacy, though dismissing physical attraction in such relationships can be unwarranted. Ultimately, human relationships in all their forms are complex, defying simple explanations. People who once vowed to die for each other may later pass by with no trace of sentiment or nostalgia, while others never seem to reach that point of mysterious saturation in their affection.

Gul entered my life—and I his—at a time when I felt ready to embrace and sustain intimacy, free from fears of its impermanence or the threat of monotony. I had a job with promising prospects in a beautiful city where I pursued my passion as an emerging author, taking vibrant courses and living independently. Like Joe and a few others in the department, I sought to write through personal exploration—traveling and meeting interesting people rather than being confined to a chair and a screen. The BBC allowed me flexible hours, and the office environment was stimulating, filled with colleagues who shared my interests in outdoor activities. These experiences enhanced my writing and even earned me the admiration of David Attenborough. He appreciated my growing interest in traditional societies and, with his deep connection to the natural world, recognized the intrinsic link between humans and the animal kingdom. He particularly valued cultures that upheld ancient customs, which had safeguarded many species now endangered by modernity's relentless advance. This is not to imply that he dismissed the value of technology; on the contrary, he acknowledged how it made conservation efforts more impactful, bringing his vivid nature programs into millions of homes.

Balancing work and study kept me fully engaged, both illuminating a secure and fulfilling future. On weekends, I unwound with Gul, whose intellectual and physical vigor proved both stimulating and supportive. Despite our vastly different cultural and geographical backgrounds, any initial sense of strangeness between us quickly dissipated. Our casual relationship did not encroach upon our personal commitments, like meeting academic deadlines or socializing within our growing community. Gul was deeply involved in his academic career, working on a multidisciplinary project on trans-Indus societies that brought together anthropologists, political scientists, and historians and was generously funded by the European Union's Horizon program. The grant provided him with a comfortable financial assistantship and an on-campus office space. In addition to organizing seminars for faculty, visiting scholars, and Bristol's postgraduate community, Gul worked on a database sourced from texts in English, Pashto, Persian, and Urdu. This endeavor aligned perfectly with his research on Balochistan's history and society during the British Raj, focusing on how part of the region came to be known as British Balochistan with Quetta as its center.

The demarcation of borders that the British began with Persia and Afghanistan culminated in 1893 with the establishment of the Durand Line, placing British Indian territories on the eastern side. The British strategy of co-opting Baloch and Pashtun leaders, often with grants and imperial honors, maintained internal peace, while a similar approach with the Qajars and later the Pahlavis secured British influence in Persia, especially after the discovery of oil. Although the rulers of Kabul resisted British hegemony from the 1830s to the 1920s, they failed to fundamentally alter the geopolitical reality dominated by imperial interests. Baloch sardars, Pashtun khans, and Afghan royals sometimes aided rebellious clerics in their fights against the firangis, but such disturbances were often quelled through financial incentives and the British policy of blood and iron. The term "Mad Mullahs" became a common British label for Muslim clerics who waged guerrilla warfare in the mountainous border region, mainly on the Indian side, although the British were also wary of the rising power of the Shi'i clergy in Persia, who, like Catholics, followed senior priests known as ayatollahs in Qom and Najaf.

The Russians, and later the Germans, posed significant security concerns for the British in Delhi, Peshawar, and Quetta, but vigilant colonial officials stationed in Tehran, Meshed, Baghdad, and Kandahar safeguarded British geopolitical interests. They relied on local alliances and the formidable Indian Army, which they touted as the largest voluntary force of its kind. Gul, with his roots in the region and academic immersion, was ideally suited to coordinate the EU project. He understood the expectations of the funders in Brussels, who had the tacit support of officials in London and Washington. Our discussions on the research plan's scope enriched my understanding of the geopolitical history and societal complexities of the Baloch, Pashtun, and Persian communities, all shaped by the Great Game that had thrust them into the geopolitical spotlight, and now brought them back into focus after 9/11.

Not particularly fond of discussing imperial legacies and their blood-soaked recurrences in our time, we still found it impossible to detach ourselves from analyzing them. The interplay of internal and external forces kept masses trapped in blind alleys, extinguishing any hope for a better future. Gul often anguished over the human predicament, though he didn't attribute it solely to external forces. Yet he never surrendered his optimism, which I appreciated for steering the project away from geopolitical reductionism.

With the summer semester over and a brief respite from academic routines, we decided to cycle to Bath along the towpath, which ran close to the Avon and occasionally parallel to the railway tracks. Much of this paved path, now popular with cyclists and pedestrians, had once been railway tracks, especially near Bath, complete with tunnels once used by trains traveling between

Bristol and Weymouth. Though the tracks were long gone, the tunnels had remained locked and neglected until environmentalists and cycling enthusiasts campaigned to make them usable for residents.

Gul and I often met on weekends for discussions and cooking sessions, spending time at his place in Totterdown or mine. Weather permitting, we cycled around the city or picnicked in the Avon Gorge, west of Brunel's Suspension Bridge. There, we'd spread our sandwiches and tea on a blanket, positioned slightly away from the trails and grazing fields, which were often dotted with herds of cows overseen by fierce-looking bulls protective of their calves. One weekend, while in Totterdown, Gul suggested a visit to Arnos Vale Cemetery, a short walk from his house. He wanted me to see the resting place of Ram Mohun Roy, a Bengali Hindu reformer who had died in 1833 while visiting Bristol. With no cremation facilities in Britain at the time, Roy was buried under a structure styled like an Indian canopy.

As we walked through the main entrance, the shrine-like red stone grave came into view, with biographical details inscribed on marble slabs. Joe had mentioned Roy in one of his lectures while discussing the Bengali intellectual renaissance, where Roy was an early pioneer, paving the way for figures like Tagore and Chatterji, who later shattered colonial stereotypes about Indian intellectual inferiority.

"On my way to the university, I often pass by Roy's statue facing the city hall," Gul said as we stood by the grave. "It's an impressive and uncontroversial piece. Perhaps we could have tea and cake at College Green nearby, in Roy's company?"

"Not a bad idea—to sit with a learned man while being served tea by another," I teased, nudging Gul's knuckle.

"Funny how history immortalizes certain people. A written word, a sketch, a statue—they open up whole new vistas for reflection."

"True, but that immortality can just as easily be for terrible acts, which unfortunately abound in history."

"Agreed. I didn't claim that history records only the humane. It's just as much a spotlight on our worst deeds. History is memorialization—or vice versa, Ms. Sandeman, if I may say so!"

"I'm with you on that, Mr. Baloch. But let me cross the street for a moment; I see some bouquets in that corner shop window."

"Thoughtful of you, Anne. Flowers will brighten the spirit of a fellow Stani who was ahead of his time."

"Someone talking about the soul—must be Saadi or Rumi whispering in a modern Baloch's ear."

"He was a versatile man, our Brahmin buried here. Most of his work was in the language of Saadi and Rumi. His newspaper, published in Calcutta, was in Persian, and Roy had a strong command of Arabic and Urdu."

After leaving the flowers at his grave, we exited through the grand entrance and turned left on the pavement. The bright, sunny afternoon was alive with cars and cyclists passing by until we found ourselves in Gul's kitchen. "Why don't we take our baguettes and tea flask to Roy's statue in College Green?" I suggested as Gul handed me cheddar slices, pickles, and spinach leaves from the refrigerator.

"Sure, we can dedicate this sunny Saturday to Roy. I'm sure he wouldn't mind the chicken slices in your sandwiches. I read somewhere that some Bengali Brahmins weren't strict vegetarians. I wonder what Roy's Unitarian friends fed him, especially when his health was failing."

After locking our bikes at the racks, we strolled over to Roy's statue, which depicted him with a contemplative smile under a hood that resembled a blend of a scholar's mortarboard and a French beret. Gul broke the silence: "What a contrast between these two figures: Colston and Roy. Only three hundred meters apart on their pedestals, yet worlds apart in every other way. One was a slaver of countless Africans, the other a reformer who fought against widow-burning and child marriage."

"Niall Ferguson and my great-grandfather would likely use Roy as proof that the Empire wasn't wholly brutal or directionless."

"Yes, but what would they say about Colston or that chap in Oxford—I mean Cecil Rhodes—who brazenly disparaged African cultures and dehumanized people as kafirs?"

"I see your point, Gul. But alongside those perpetrators, there were still humane and tender souls who saved lives in whatever way they could, whether driven by moral conviction or some worn-out sense of duty."

Taking a bite of his sandwich and giving me a playful wink, Gul replied, "As we were discussing earlier, history isn't unilinear, nor is it just a chaotic patchwork of chronicles. It's fundamentally human, embodying both our refinements and absurdities. But I don't believe every chronicler is neutral—not even John, or Ferguson, Biggar, Dalrymple, Gopal, and the others. They all come with their own ideological biases, though that's not to dismiss their scholarship."

"You sound like an Oxbridge don. I can already picture you teaching there or at McGill in a few years, while I'll probably still be working on my first book. Maybe you could take me along like those women travelers in howdahs, carried by camels across the vast deserts of Balochistan."

"That's a poetic image, Anne, but you won't need a Stani to accompany you on your literary journey. Your maturity, anchored in wisdom and originality, holds the promise that many would envy. Keep journeying, fellow traveler, and find your own masthead. You are your own Saadi, while I am searching for my Khayyam."

"What did I put in these sandwiches that we're suddenly talking like old philosophers before our time?"

"It's the camaraderie, spurred on by a beautiful day that I wish wouldn't end so soon, Anne."

"I have an idea: how about we work on our own today, and if tomorrow is as lovely, we meet by Pero's Bridge late morning with our bikes, sandwiches, and drinks and head to Bath on the towpath!"

"Why not start from Totterdown or Cabot Circus instead?"

"Absolutely not, or we'll end up circling each other endlessly, pausing only for stray thoughts. Besides, I don't trust your intentions, especially after dusk."

"Very clever, but it's not just me burning the midnight oil, Anne. We should return to our studies like diligent students before our next rendezvous."

And with that, we went our separate ways after a warm bear hug.

Our bikes, freshly washed and tuned to their gleaming best, carried us along the paved trail that wove around small city parks nestled beside Sixties-era apartment towers, disused factories, and a series of overhead bridges. I led most of the way, familiar with the path that climbed a gentle slope parallel to the railway tracks stretching toward Lawrence Hill and the Parkway. After about twenty minutes, we reached the entrance of the dimly lit Staple Hill Tunnel, where occasional drips from above added to the cool, damp atmosphere. The tunnel, located in Bristol's Kingswood area, once belonged to the Midland Railway, which connected Bristol with Bath and beyond. Inside, the temperature dropped sharply, but with our steady cycling and layered clothing, we were comfortably warm.

Building on our momentum and bypassing green spaces, we soon found ourselves in open countryside. After navigating a wooded reserve, we arrived at the abandoned Warmley station, where a tempting tea stall beckoned us to stop and refuel. This popular halfway point on the towpath was teeming with cyclists of all ages and accents. The flat route, lined with trees and hedges, was kind to our legs, although Gul noticed that my thighs and shins had turned a pinkish hue, and with the sun now at its peak, I could see my skin taking on a light tan.

We sat on what was once the station platform, munching on blueberry muffins and sipping steaming tea. Gul's eyes twinkled with curiosity, prompting me to laugh and playfully chide him: "We're in public, Gul, and I can read your mischievous mind. Behave, or I'll sprinkle some icy water on your head."

"Don't even think about it, Anne. Let me savor these moments. I won't touch you, at least not here. But you are a stunning blend of Scotland and Denmark, with a brightness that even your great-grandfather must have admired from the Sulaiman Mountain. You shine in the evening glow, but in broad daylight, you're even more beautiful and alluring," Gul said, struggling to rein in his words and desires.

"Gul, you're alert and sharp as ever. But keep in mind, we're only halfway there, and I promise the landscape will open up once we pass Bitton. After that, we'll be in my territory—Salford— where you'll need to be on your best behavior. The Avon can be unforgiving to careless intruders."

"I promise to be on my best behavior, especially as we enter Sandeman country."

Bitton was bustling with railway enthusiasts who operated the tracks they had restored over the years, along with vintage steam engines. The station itself was a tribute to the Victorian era when railways were in their prime, and its preserved engines and carriages were rare relics of the second industrial revolution. We paused to watch a whistling steam train filled with eager young and old passengers. The uniformed driver and crew were ready to depart for the final station just before Salford, which overlooked the river. We pedaled alongside the train as it moved on an elevated section, flanked by expansive, sun-drenched fields where horses, cows, and bulls grazed peacefully, oblivious to human activity.

Somerset, in all its verdant splendor, soon ushered us into the outskirts of Salford. The Bird in Hand, a local pub that was a favorite stop for cyclists and hikers during the day and a lively gathering spot for locals from Salford and Kelston in the evenings, stood proudly between the towpath and the town, separated by the river and the railway tracks. Gul cast an eager look at the pub's packed beer garden, but we chose to move on, as it was already full and still a bit early for drinks. We both avoided alcohol during the day.

"My parents live about two hundred yards up from the pub and only visit in the evenings," I said.

"They live in a picturesque village, and I completely understand their preference. Imagine hundreds of cyclists stopping here to drain a few kegs, their adrenaline pumping," Gul said, with a deliberate Freudian slip that made me laugh.

A few yards further along, we paused on a bridge.

"Gul, this is where I used to come as a child with friends and our mums. We'd slip through the bushes for a dip in the river, followed by a picnic. Of course, they never let us jump from this bridge—it's too high. Further west, there are more bathing spots and water mills until you reach Kelston, one of the most scenic villages in the county, though not as famous as Newton St. Loe or Glastonbury."

"Kelston sits gracefully by the river, watched over by Roundhill. It's a beautiful landscape in the heart of rural England."

"Wait until you see Newton St. Loe and John's university. But let's keep going; we're getting closer to Bath. With this pace, we can even check out the Two-Tunnels Greenway, which has been recently restored by volunteers from the Sustrans charity."

Crossing the bridge again, we saw the city of Bath perched on the hills ahead. Leaving behind another pub, the Blue Dolphin, we crossed the Avon on a pedestrian bridge, following signs for the cycle route.

"Anne, this place looks familiar. Isn't this where Joe lives?" Gul asked.

"Yes, this is Oldfield Park. In about a mile, get ready for our first tunnel. It's shorter but well-lit."

Classical music, playing at a low volume, welcomed us as we entered the tunnel. We had to be watchful of pedestrians with buggies and dogs until we emerged into a short, green area that cradled us before we resumed our ride through the second, longer tunnel. This tunnel, like the first, was smooth and pleasantly cool. It took about twenty minutes to navigate before we reached the open space on the other side, where the hilly terrain, shaded by spruces and oaks, quickened our pace as we descended into Midford. We continued for a bit longer until we found a secluded grassy patch for our picnic.

The sandwiches, with their assortment of fillings, never tasted so delicious, and we devoured them eagerly before reaching for the fruit in the panniers. Lying beside each other under the watchful sun, we soon fell into a deep sleep as if we hadn't rested in days. It must have been over forty minutes before I woke up and gently shook Gul while holding a cup of tea and some biscuits for him.

"Get up, sport. Time to start our return journey with a short visit to the city."

"How long did we sleep, Anne? I felt like I was lost somewhere in those hills near Turbat, riding my Abu's horse."

"About three-quarters of an hour, Gul. We can't afford to laze around, or our bodies will lose their pedal power."

Bath was bustling with tourists and shoppers, making little room for two sweaty stragglers. Still, we found an ice cream vendor near the Roman Baths and enjoyed our treat while watching the rapids below the Pulteney Bridge. Soon, it was time to rejoin the towpath for our eighteen-mile return journey. We paused at Bitton to enjoy freshly brewed tea and fruit cakes, though the platforms and the old reception area were still packed with visitors.

"I don't think we'll be up for cooking or doing much else once we're back in Bristol. How about eating out?" I suggested.

"Definitely. We could go to our local in Totterdown or head to Easton for a Lahori-style spread. Pizza could also be a good option," Gul said as we left Bitton's tea cabin, a former train carriage converted into a café.

"Let's decide where to go once we're back in Bristol." I kept our destination vague, leaning toward Totterdown for a nightcap, especially since my shift at the BBC wouldn't start until early Monday afternoon.

"You could shower at my place. It's not as sleek as yours, but it gets the job done," Gul said, his tone laced with persuasive warmth.

The Staple Hill Tunnel was wider but not as well-maintained as the ones in Bath, and there was no music echoing from its rustic walls. Still, it served its purpose, facilitating our return to Bristol. Our legs, accustomed to the cycling, had gained their own momentum, and the bikes rolled steadily all the way to Temple Meads. This time, I followed Gul and didn't mind taking the left turn near the train station instead of crossing the river to Cabot Circus.

The shower, as Gul had promised, was forceful, and I lingered for quite some time before stepping out into his room, refreshed and wrapped in a towel. Gul, recharged and content from our day's adventure, was jubilant as we settled down with pizzas and garlic bread from a local takeout. Not satisfied with just our hearty meal, Gul brought out slices of cheesecake that we polished off with coffee while snuggled under the duvet. Life felt luxurious as Gul gently rubbed my back while I lay on my stomach, his fingers tracing the contours of my responsive, willingly resigned body. I felt his hands move over my thighs and shins, spreading a delightful warmth until I couldn't hold back any longer. Turning around, I wrapped my arms around him, finding a natural rhythm as I massaged his taut back muscles. Our bodies entwined in a series of twists and turns that lasted late into the night until sleep eventually claimed us both.

It was still early morning when I heard John close the door behind him as he left for his morning routine. I ventured downstairs to make two cups of black coffee, leaving a smiling Gul in bed. Soon, I was on my bike, heading toward Cabot Circus to start the new week.

Weeks turned into semesters and eventually years as we reached the culmination of our academic pursuits, fortified by coursework that enhanced our understanding and honed our pedagogical skills. From the second year onward, the focus shifted to intensive research. Gul and I no longer shared courses after Joe's module but continued to meet for coffee during the week or occasional weekend meals, never tiring of each other's company. His EU project introduced him to the political economy of his region, then called Af-Pak, necessitating extensive fieldwork in both countries and a visit from Turbat into Iran. He spent an entire semester traveling and gathering data, staying with his brother in Karachi, old classmates in Lahore and Islamabad, and making occasional visits to Turbat and Quetta for family reunions.

During Gul's absence, I had the opportunity to travel across the Mississippi and the Sahel region in Africa with Attenborough and his team, which not only added to my professional experience but also allowed me more time to delve into the works of Arthur Miller and Tennessee Williams—two literary titans whose styles and themes would form the backbone of my doctoral research.

Mum was aware of my deep, and no less intimate, friendship with Gul and might have hinted at it to Dad during his periodic visits to Salford. Early in my move to Bristol, the four of us gathered for afternoon tea at the Hawthorns. The meeting went smoothly, and my parents found Gul to be both amiable and respectful. Their perception of a spark between us was confirmed when they invited us for a Friday evening meal at the Globe Inn in Newton St. Loe. Dad and Gul had an engaging discussion about Robert Sandeman and his legacy, as well as Pakistan's efforts to develop Gwadar as their own Dubai. Gul also learned more about the African and Asian blue-collar workforce in the UAE, though both men expressed concern about the stark divide between unskilled laborers and Western expatriates, who were treated far better and often pampered by local standards. Except for Dad, we all enjoyed Italian red wine with our meals, while Dad preferred two pints of Bath ale known as Gem. The evening unfolded naturally, enriched by the traditional décor of the 17th-century country pub. Gul's words of gratitude to my parents were steeped in traditional respect and warmth.

After dinner, I suggested a brief tour of the village, and we filed into my car so that Gul could get a glimpse of the stone-built hamlet tucked behind sentinel hills and ancient trees. Newton St. Loe's quiet homes and farms looked mysterious under the rare starry night, with occasional light peeking through drowsy windows. The giant trees stood motionless as I navigated the narrow lanes with care, while Dad provided a running commentary about the Duchy, Prince Charles, and the adjacent university. Gul expressed interest in returning during the day and visiting John, who had extended an invitation for lunch at his university café in reciprocity for the evening he spent with us in Totterdown.

Gul and I returned to Newton St. Loe on a sunny weekday, taking a day off from our studies and work to visit John. Before meeting him, we explored the village, its churchyard, and the small square where an elderly woman ran a combined corner shop and post office. She explained that all residents were long-term tenants of the Duchy. Besides caring for horses, cows, and sheep, they tended fields and woods across the royal estate, while the university managed its own affairs as a tenant. We saw a royal flag fluttering over a larger mansion—the estate's headquarters—while the rest of the village exuded an enchanting medieval ambiance, steeped in silence. The houses were built entirely of local white sandstone, which also appeared in the walls, pavements, and the square where an ancient birch tree stood sentinel. Beyond a small nursery and the horses, rolling hills dotted with shaggy brown bulls and grazing sheep stretched toward the horizon, creating a scene of idyllic rural beauty.

After wandering around the lakes designed by Capability Brown, John guided us through the Italian gardens and into the university's student union, which faced a medieval castle. We joined two of his colleagues on their lunch break as students drifted by with trays. John treated us to panini sandwiches and salads, while he opted for moussaka. Our conversation included William Reeves, a Gothic literature expert, and Gavin Edwardes, an American literature specialist who had spent years studying and teaching in the U.S. before returning to Somerset and settling in the charming village of Lacock. Meeting these scholars, who shared my literary interests and provided informal mentoring, proved valuable to my research over the next few months. Gul enjoyed the openness and spontaneity of the gathering, contributing confidently to a discussion that touched on authors from Jane Austen and Bram Stoker to George Orwell, John Steinbeck, Joyce Carol Oates, and William Styron. John's witty remarks about "bourgeois pen pushers" added humor to the conversation.

On the way back to Bristol after an invigorating day at Newton Park, we decided to celebrate at the Globe Inn, recalling our previous visit there. This time, the pub was lively even in the late afternoon. Although John couldn't join us due to a class, we toasted his hospitality and scholarship with gin glasses, and Gul promised to pass along our thanks to him that evening. As we recapped the lunchtime conversation, I mentioned my curiosity about Bill Reeves and his research on Freemasonry. His tweedy attire and demeanor reminded me of Oxbridge dons, while Gavin, with his informal charm and knowledge of American literature and art, embodied a certain class of writers. Of course, our John, with his Trotskyite leanings and sharp wit, was a star in his own right, balancing humor with rigorous archival research. Away from the more renowned academic hubs of the South-East, these scholars held their own with confidence.

We raised our glasses to them and to our own friendship: "To a West Country colonial!"

"And here's to a Stani rascal!"

BATH

As toddlers attending a pre-nursery in Turbat, our teacher, who taught us the Quran and prayers in Arabic, often repeated one of his favorite Urdu sayings, which, in translation, went: "Travel is surely the means to success." Back then, our idea of travel was limited to neighboring villages within the district of Kech, either on horseback or riding on the pillion of Grandfather's bike. Longer journeys meant noisy, smoke-belching coaches heading to Quetta or further east to Karachi. Stories of people returning from pilgrimages to Mecca or retiring from military service in Oman conjured hazy yet fascinating images of distant lands across the vast, bubbling blues of the Gulf. We knew, in a way, that places like Dubai and Muscat were 'mini Europes' where men sought their fortunes.

To the west, Iran started somewhere beyond Zahedan; their Balochistan resembled ours—a vast, brown desert inhabited by turbaned people similar to those in Makran. Urban Iran, however, was distinctly Persian, full of pride in its cities like Shiraz, Isfahan, Tabriz, Yazd, and Tehran. Mashhad was an exception in our imaginations; it beckoned with sanctity and tradition due to its holy shrines, topped by luminous minarets connected to the Prophet's lineage. We often saw black-clad Shi'i Pakistanis heading toward the border on rainbow-colored buses for pilgrimages to Mashhad or even further into Iraq.

Conversely, Lahore was seen as the place for education, while Islamabad felt too posh and remote. Stories of Delhi and Bombay, nostalgically told by our grandparents' generation, evoked vague images of white and brown-skinned people hurrying on their separate paths. Tales of a distant land, interchangeably called Englistan, Wilayat, London, or simply Britannia, described a place that once ruled over us, building roads, schools, and cantonments, before its people returned to their cooler, greener fairyland. These British were said to have worn pith helmets and spoke a mix of English and Urdu called Hindustani, often in an authoritative tone, while native men spoke in hushed voices and exchanged winks, especially when talking about European women, the memsahibs. Barbers, musicians, cobblers, and other laborers gathered around elders and clerics would often talk about the pale skin, blue eyes, and fair hair of the Wilayati women, who wore floral dresses and carried parasols, as servants shooed away onlookers from the streets of Quetta, Tehran, Delhi, Bombay, and Karachi. These women's rare appearances, with their sunlit, milk-like complexion and wide-brimmed hats, inspired an almost celestial reverence akin to that which mullahs hinted at in their sermons. Some of the older generation whispered about their drinking parties and dances accompanied by music played on a gramophone, marked by the image of a dog listening to its master's voice.

The question of who these people were and what they were doing in our lands was a topic few understood well, though our parents' generation offered more informed explanations. Nonetheless, these stories lingered, their aura undiminished even as tales of newfound riches and luxury in places like Dubai, Kuwait, and Doha emerged. Curiously, these places, too, attracted white-skinned Wilayatis who found new opportunities after leaving our part of the world.

For my father's generation, particularly in the lower Indus Valley and its remote regions far from urban centers and the river, attitudes began to shift with increased education and mobility. The West was seen as a leader in education, technology, economy, and professionalism, and the realization grew that progress was possible without defensiveness or a sense of being 'lost in translation.' Lahore and Karachi became symbols of opportunity. My father and his peers sought to unlock these opportunities, seeing them as their due. Yet, there were those who wanted more, too soon, and felt stifled by the new colonials—first the Americans, then the military elite from Punjab—and retreated to the mountains, armed with guns and grenades to pursue utopian visions. The Soviets and their allies in Kabul offered support for establishing a classless society in a region that, in practice, allowed only two classes: sardars and peasants. My father's middle class was only just beginning to emerge.

Religious clerics were initially absent or confined to Zahedan and Quetta, but when the Soviets withdrew, religion and nationalism vied for dominance. This clash brought new waves of fear and violence. My father, refusing to be cowed by either the nationalists or the radicals, enthusiastically supported the education of my siblings Bahram, Anjum, and me. It wasn't an easy journey; he navigated a double jeopardy, but his wisdom, conciliatory nature, and resourcefulness as a senior civil servant saw us through. Yet, back in Turbat, we were never entirely out of danger, perceived as collaborators with the new rulers who obstructed the idealistic pursuit of a utopian world.

I was keenly aware of the divisions and tensions within our society, exacerbated by external interventions and geopolitical complexity. Living in England helped me view these issues more objectively. At times, I felt like a skeptic of the Westphalian state system, but realism made me acknowledge that there was no turning back. The path forward lay in building bridges across ethnicities, classes, denominations, and nations, especially those nearby. This belief in reconciliation meant that the unrest in Balochistan or the raucous chants of Brexiteers seemed at odds with societal needs. While I didn't become a Gandhian, I admired Gandhi's courage and tolerance. During reflective moments, I missed sharing meals with Lisa in Tavistock Square near my old alma mater. Gandhi and Bentham, so different yet so similar, shared the same purpose, as did Roy and Syed Ahmed Khan. Syed, who championed modern education for Indian Muslims despite resistance, wrote books while in London and even visited Bristol. I needed to learn more about his time in the West Country, but I had introduced Anne to his work during one of our tea sessions, speculating on whether he might have crossed paths with her great-grandfather in the late 19th century.

Syed's influence guided families like ours. Abu often spoke of him during my childhood in Turbat and later years. He was respected for not being an apologist and for recognizing the transformative potential of modern education, philosophy, and technology for traditional societies. Like Roy, he was an abolitionist ahead of his time, helping my father's generation overcome social taboos, even those against marginalized Sheedis like Aunty Zahra and others.

Susanne and Terence were naturally curious about me and protective of Anne. Our subsequent meetings, including a dinner

101

at a country pub, brought warmth and familiarity. Terence, extroverted due to his military career and current work in Dubai, contrasted with Susanne's polite, observant, and slightly reserved nature. She wasn't just a book conservator; she was a bookworm with a growing interest in West Asia, reading American writers like Selig Harrison and Robert Kaplan, though she had many questions about NATO's actions in Afghanistan and Iraq. Her Scandinavian disposition for peace contrasted with Terence's regimental pride, which carried a hint of imperial nostalgia, though he didn't flaunt it.

With Terence back on assignment, I had tea with Susanne when I visited Claverton to present a paper on the political economy of the northern Gulf to a group of development studies scholars. Susanne, usually composed, was effusive in her praise:

"Gul, that was an enlightening presentation. I think many of us learned a lot. You provided a comprehensive overview of the situation on the ground and showed how Western development models, coupled with militarism, have worsened conditions for millions."

"Thank you, Susanne. I hope I didn't come across as overly negative. I try to steer clear of extreme nationalism and socialism. Nor am I an apologist for capitalism or religious exclusivity."

"No, you backed up your argument with primary evidence from your fieldwork in that part of the world. You're not a typical World Bank consultant sitting in a revolving chair, using local surrogates to compile facts and figures—mostly figures—to complete reports that may end up on a shelf or, in some cases, change the entire game, if I may say so!" Susanne continued, "Gul, opportunities and one's own effort play a big role, as I discovered while researching Narayan's Malgudi. Perhaps it's a bit easier for us in the West due to the institutional support we receive, but in my experience, international students like you are some of the brightest minds, with the potential to change the world."

"That's a generous assessment, Susanne. Yes, they often push themselves to make the most of their exposure to higher studies in the West. But after graduating in fields like development studies or economics, many end up joining Bretton Woods institutions, only to propagate prescriptive policies that spout self-righteous mantras, where the market, interest, and profit justify any means, even if it leaves people hungry or worse."

"Well, we all look for greener pastures. I'm settled here, even though many people claim that Scandinavia has the best social security system in the world. Salford may be an anonymous hamlet, but I don't have complaints. Every place has its strengths and flaws, yet the global North-South divide remains one of the most acute."

"Do you stay in touch with family back home, if I can use that term, Susanne?"

"I come from a small family. Except for one sister and a maternal uncle, the rest are gone. Anne might have mentioned my Jewish uncle and his ties to South Asia. Unfortunately, my visits across the Channel have become infrequent over the years."

"Anne did mention your uncle and his impressive collection of books and art. He must be a fountain of knowledge."

"Like the Swedes, Danes have their share of bigots, but my family members are bibliophiles, which partly explains why I chose to become a librarian. On another note, Gul, how are things between you and Anne?"

"Things are going well, Susanne. I think the flexibility we've built into our relationship has given it resilience, especially as we both focus on finalizing our research and degrees before entering the job market. Anne's work with Attenborough's team, which she enjoys, could be key to landing a tenured position. I plan to teach and write; perpetual student life isn't sustainable for me."

"That sounds practical and reassuring. Anne told me she might need another six months to finish her doctoral research and is dedicating more time to writing and revisions since returning from her recent trip to the United States. I'm curious if she'll pursue a full-time academic career or a role at the BBC that would allow her to travel and write, even if it doesn't align perfectly with her research."

"I think she could do both. Her job should permit her to publish academic papers and monographs in her field while continuing her nature and habitat work and possibly teaching part-time. Just speculating, of course."

Back in Totterdown, I reflected on our conversation and was somewhat surprised that Susanne hadn't mentioned the possibility of Anne and me getting married—a presumption some parents would make after nearly three years of knowing each other. Perhaps Anne hadn't encouraged that line of thought, or maybe Susanne, like many modern skeptics, didn't see marriage as a necessary culmination of a relationship. Instead, she might have viewed it as contrary to genuine love and passion. That tea session left me with the impression of Susanne as an insightful, well-read, and forward-thinking individual.

A few months later, I had another chance to meet Susanne during a three-day South Asia conference in Bath. With Anne away on assignment in London, I chose to stay on campus at Claverton, allowing me to socialize with other participants. I had informed Susanne, and we arranged to meet for dinner on the second day at Bill's, a cozy spot behind the Abbey and the Roman Baths. The casual atmosphere and reasonable menu made it an easy choice for sharing Sicilian and Spanish tapas as appetizers—perfect icebreakers.

Susanne, visibly more relaxed, exuded elegance that day, drawing attention as she entered the bustling restaurant in a floral dress with a matching necklace. Her well-coiffed dark hair and tall, poised frame made her entrance feel almost regal. I had just taken a seat at a table by the wall adorned with rustic shelves holding pickle jars, wine bottles, and old-style pans—an attempt, perhaps, to create an air of authenticity or homey spontaneity.

"So nice to see you, Susanne. You look wonderful, as always," I said, extending my hand, uncertain if a handshake or a light hug was more appropriate.

"It's lovely to reconnect, Gul. I wrapped up work early, which allowed me to squeeze in a quick swim before coming here. You look as fresh as ever." She lightly embraced me, exuding warmth that was as disarming as her polished sophistication. Her dark red lipstick shimmered under the dim lights, adding a touch of formality that contrasted with her casual friendliness. As I returned her hug, I noticed that her tall frame almost reached my eyes—a nod to the classic Nordic height.

"I suppose your shift schedule is flexible enough to let you take time off when needed, instead of the usual nine-to-five grind."

"Yes, it helps, but evening shifts can be a drag, even if they let me sleep in or meet a friend for coffee the next day."

"I imagine Salford must have a few cafes, so you don't always need to come to Bath."

"Salford is more residential, with more pubs than cafes. The cafes are mostly Chinese and Indian takeaways. Bath, on the other hand, offers charming, cosmopolitan spots that I prefer."

"Salford does give you more garden space and easy access to nearby cities."

"And, frankly, it's dull. Sorry for the bluntness. Bath and Bristol overshadow it completely, and there's not much to do if you're single, especially as a woman. You can't go anywhere without being noticed, and eating alone in a pub doesn't offer as much privacy as one might think. The Globe is a better option, but even there, you run into neighbors who give you funny looks, as if they're pitying you."

"But Susanne, many of those people probably harbor their own desire for solitude, to break away from domestic monotony."

After a few sips of our Chilean wine and a toast to Anne, we continued where we had left off.

"Yes, Gul. Many people do long for domestic life—even some of the feminists I know at the university. They romanticize the idea of family and children, while others feel overburdened by their roles as parents, juggling their time and losing their own priorities. It's tough for fathers too, and even harder for single parents who, beyond the hard work, carry a sense of guilt for not maintaining a 'complete' family."

"With Anne grown and independent, you must have more time and privacy, especially when Terence is away, though that must come with its own challenges."

"I don't know whether she ever mentioned this to you, but Anne sometimes worries about me being on my own in a small town for long periods, though I never complain. She's a smart person, don't you think, Gul?"

"Yes, she's incredibly thoughtful and mature beyond her years. I suppose, aside from your upbringing, I'd like to think I had a bit of influence on her, even if she wouldn't admit it."

My quip made us both laugh, breaking any remaining formality with a warm undertone.

"I like your sense of humor. Anne will find that amusing too, and being a Daddy's girl, she'll credit her father for it. Just a guess. Terence is quite the charmer. You see, he swept me off my feet when I was just nineteen and came here to study. We ended up married, and Anne was born within a year. Time flew by so fast."

Susanne enjoyed her Greek salad and chargrilled chicken breast, while I savored my beef steak with roast potatoes and greens. Without being intrusive, she inquired about my family and my career plans. She seemed relieved when I spoke about Bahram and his wife, Shireen, who were happily balancing work and family life in Karachi.

"Your parents must be so proud, raising three successful children and sending you all to good schools and universities. I know families in Pakistan tend to be larger and more close-knit than here."

"Our parents were ahead of their time and placed great value on quality education. Yes, middle-class families in Pakistan are usually larger if you include grandparents, cousins, children, and even servants. In Balochistan, life can feel like a pre-industrial era—more like Victorian times—where dependence on household help is common."

"I'm skeptical about the 'post-industrial' label; it has cast us into what I'd call a 'post-normal' mode. But maybe that dissatisfaction has been the case throughout human history—it's that restlessness that has brought us to where we are today."

As we refilled our glasses, I asked Susanne about her family back in Odense.

"Odense is well-known for Hans Christian Andersen, but it's more than that. Like most of Denmark, it has a diverse economy, excellent universities, and a vibrant urban setting where more people ride bikes than drive cars. It's mostly flat and has fertile land, making agriculture strong. It's also known for having a high proportion of students, so it's far from a dull place to live or study. My mother was Jewish, and the rest of the family was mainly Lutheran, but on the secular side. My uncle David, whom Anne mentioned, has visited the subcontinent a few times and shared fascinating stories about the Jewish community in Cochin, which, as you might know, is dwindling. His stories sparked my interest in R.K. Narayan's work, helping me understand British India a little better."

"Yes, Anne did mention your uncle's impressive library. I have a theory that the Jewish community is one of the most urban and professionally oriented groups in history. With Israel, they now have a strong agricultural sector as well. I have some friends at the University of Southern Denmark who tell me about Odense and its cycling culture—it sounds a lot like Oxford or Cambridge."

"There were Jewish farmers in the Levant, Maghreb, and Spain centuries ago, but due to racism, insecurity, and migrations, they often ended up in urban ghettos. Israel has allowed Jews to reconnect and diversify their professions. That's why their agriculture has benefited from modern technology, though I'm not a fan of the policies of Sharon or Netanyahu. I'd love to see Israel become a true multi-faith society with equal citizenship for all. So here I am, half-Jewish, married into an 'imperial' family, living in the West Country and surrounded by books."

"Let's toast to that, Susanne. 'People of the Book,' as these Abrahamic religions claim in their exclusive way, although the Hindus, Zoroastrians, Buddhists, and now the Sikhs also have their holy books."

"To you, Gul. I'm so glad my daughter is close to someone as sensible and responsible as you, who values books."

"From books to books; to Susanne and Anne!"

Susanne chose crème brûlée while I opted for strawberry and hazelnut cheesecake, finishing the last of our Chilean wine. She seemed more effervescent than before, observing, "I dressed up tonight partly to celebrate Anne's friendship with you and partly because I don't get out much. This evening has been such a joy, like catching up with an old friend."

"Susanne, I'm honored to be here with someone so knowledgeable and elegant."

"So, where are you with your research? Forgive me for being so abrupt, Gul."

"Not abrupt at all, Susanne. I submitted my thesis two weeks ago, and it's been sent to two examiners—one here and one overseas, probably in the U.S. If all goes well, I'll have my viva soon, and then I'll be better positioned to secure a teaching role, though it all depends on the outcome."

"I'm confident you'll pass with flying colors. It may take a few more weeks, but you'll get there. Will your parents come to the UK for your graduation?"

"If all goes as planned, I hope to invite them. They deserve it. I'm not sure if Anjum, Bahram, or Shireen will make it, given their busy schedules, costly airfares, and visa restrictions."

"Anne is expecting her viva soon too; her reports have come in, and she seems optimistic. It would be wonderful if you both graduated on the same day—that would bring us all together."

"Anne has put in so much hard work, and I've seen her long hours, field research, and sessions with her supervisor—all while working nearly full-time. Sharing a graduation day would be the perfect way to celebrate."

I walked Susanne to her car behind Queen Square and politely declined her offer to drop me at the university guest house, as it would be out of her way and I planned to catch the bus back to Claverton.

"Let me be a little bold, Susanne. You were the most radiant presence in that corner of Bath tonight. Your company lifted my spirits. I'll tell Anne to make her jealous."

"It was lovely being with you, Gul. It's no wonder my daughter values you so much."

Assuming Susanne would share our evening with Anne, I still felt the need to tell Anne about our dinner myself. I could hear her giggle on the phone, though she wouldn't explain why and promised to tell me over the weekend after nearly three weeks of busy, separate schedules. Our reunion at my place picked up right where we left off on the phone.

"Oh, I'm sure you both had a great time. I have reasons to be concerned—especially when you're so charming and my mother has been reading Gillian Flynn's Gone Girl. It's all about the 'new woman' and her boundless potential."

"I've read reviews of that book. It lets men imagine all sorts of extreme scenarios in their relationships with women. But your mother is extraordinary—graceful and brilliant. People like her are rare."

"Gul, I'm glad you appreciate her, but she is a loner because of those very traits. With Dad overseas, that's partly why I returned to the West Country for my studies and work. I wanted to be nearby but still have my space, and it's worked out well for both of us. On a lighter note, I do worry you two might hit it off too well, and I'll have to step aside."

"Don't be dramatic, you schemer. Now I know how to make you jealous. Divide and conquer—it suits me."

"Don't get too confident, Stani Baloch. My blood comes from two imperial lines that stare each other down across the Channel. Now, what's your plan for this sunny day?"

"Former colonials have softened up, so I'm not intimidated. Let's cycle to Clifton, cross the bridge, and spoil ourselves at the Matthews' café. What do you think?"

"I'm all in. Let's go."

The unveiling of the Matthews took place in 1995 to commemorate the 500th anniversary of its predecessor's pioneering trans-Atlantic voyage. After the initial celebrations, the replica settled into its role as a commercial attraction, drawing crowds, especially on sunny weekends. Now functioning as a restaurant, it welcomed visitors, many of whom might not have even heard of the Italian explorer John Cabot (or Caboto), who served under the English crown. To its credit, our high tea was far from disappointing. The cucumber sandwiches, scones, strawberry jam, and cream were all fresh and delightful. Given our uphill ride to Clifton and the detour after crossing the Suspension Bridge, we devoured everything hungrily, ignoring calorie counts and the curious glances from those around us. Satiated and buzzing from a sugar rush, we began to explore our surroundings.

"Gul, look at those high-rises behind you," Anne said. "They resemble colorful square boxes stacked vertically—not too overwhelming to look at. Would you ever live in one of those?"

"They're definitely eye-catching with their rainbow hues. Quite a clever design by the architect. I wouldn't mind living in one if I had a permanent job and the right North European company," I teased. "Then, maybe I'd stop regretting for the Matthews."

"Enough with your regrets. You already have the company you desire—unless Glynn's fiction is influencing you too much. I have a couple of hours to spend with a tolerable Stani, if that's what you're thinking."

With Totterdown nearby, our bikes swiftly delivered us back to my place, where the sun shone brilliantly. As soon as we stepped into my room, we found ourselves in a close embrace. Anne whispered sweetly in my ear, the words barely discernible, as though she were exhausted from our long journey. "Time to celebrate our submissions, Gul."

"Submissions can mean many things," I said, smiling. "Never mind that—let's savor these precious moments."

We turned in bed, exploring one another with an intensity that left words unnecessary and unintelligible. The silence between us was more eloquent than speech. The only sounds were those of our bodies, and for once, I noticed pearl-like drops of sweat forming on Anne's skin. For a moment, I was aware we had forgotten to close the curtains, but I refused to move. Even the briefest pause felt unacceptable. Whatever fleeting hesitation I had was erased as Anne took control, and I surrendered willingly.

"That was a proper celebration, Dr. Sandeman," I murmured, my eyes half-closed.

"Climactic, indeed, Dr. Baloch. Hold me tight—I feel safe and cherished when you're here with me."

"Your love elevates me to new and pure heights, Anne."

"Even when you're not around, I sense your presence. It's as if you're always with me."

"It's amazing how our minds and bodies connect, defying distances, cultures, and logic. It feels like fate, even if one might be a happy atheist."

"This is probably the right time for me to share something deeply personal," Anne said, her tone shifting. "I'm not sure if it's the right moment, but I need to be honest, even if it risks everything."

"Anne, I'm all ears," I said, suddenly alert and curious.

"Gul, are you sure you want to hear this? It's about our future."

"Yes, please go on. I need to know."

"Well, you might have thought I was on birth control, but I'm not. I can't get pregnant. In my late teens, I developed cancerous cysts, and a hysterectomy was the only option. I recovered quickly and am healthy now, but I can't have children. I don't menstruate anymore. I should have told you sooner."

"Anne, don't be ridiculous. You are incredibly precious to me. I love you for who you are, not as a potential mother. That doesn't diminish the importance of motherhood, but my feelings for you go far beyond that."

"I knew you meant what you said, but I needed to be sure. If you ever decide to part ways, I'd understand, even though it would break me."

Holding her close, I looked into her teary eyes. "We're perfect for each other, and that has kept us strong. Our love is whole and doesn't need to change. Don't walk away thinking otherwise."

Tears streamed down her face as she rested her head on my chest, her fingers tangling in my hair. She raised herself and kissed me deeply, her eyes still shedding tears that I wiped away gently as I held her close.

"This is a huge decision, Gul. Think about it. You don't have to spend your life with a woman who can't have children, no matter how beautiful or educated she might be."

"Stop, Anne. Don't hurt me with this talk. I adore you now more than ever for your honesty and courage. I'm the lucky one here."

"I've always thought of you as a true gentleman, and you've just proved it. The surgery took away my ability to have children, but not my femininity or desire for intimacy, as our relationship proves time and again."

"You are a gem, Anne. You make my life brighter and more meaningful. Let me get us some drinks and snacks to celebrate this moment, my dear Colonial Ma'am."

Anne decided to stay the evening. As I ran my fingers through her soft, dark hair, I watched her eyes—slightly swollen from crying—give me a final glance, brimming with love and a sense of safety. She nestled her head on my chest like a child seeking comfort after a long day. I gazed at her, seeing in her a blend of innocence and grace that artists strive to capture in their most evocative works. As she slept peacefully in my arms, the faint sound of her breathing was soothing, as if she had finally released a burden she'd carried alone for too long. Despite the intimacy of our relationship, I had never noticed any scars nor seen any signs that hinted at her secret. This evening was transformative, bringing us even closer. Anne was my Balochistan—vast, deep, kind, and majestic. She was the embodiment of everything that was resilient and nurturing.

I lay still, reluctant to disturb her, savoring the way she fit against me. Though I felt the pangs of hunger since our snacks had been sparse, I refused to move. Time felt suspended, and I wished I could freeze that moment forever.

As the first light of dawn approached and the milkman made his rounds, Anne opened her eyes, a mischievous smile on her face. "You stayed awake all night, didn't you? Sorry for keeping you up. How long did I sleep?"

"I was counting my blessings as you lay here, and I didn't want the night to end. You're my devi."

"You have a way with words, Gul. Your poetry makes me want to wrap myself around you and forget the rest of the world."

And in that quiet morning light, time seemed to pause. Yet, an insistent urge for food finally pulled me from bed. I threw on my gown, made two loaded brown toasts with butter and marmalade, and boiled eggs. When I returned with steaming tea, I found Anne wearing my shirt and trousers, combing her hair in front of the mirror.

"In that outfit, you look like a Baloch youth, though you're missing a white turban and its proud twists," I said.

"I am your Balochistan—vast, deep, warm, resilient, and barren in parts. You'll never tire of exploring my many layers."

"That aridity has its own serene depth and responsiveness, no less entrancing and daring, Madam!"

"We sought our nirvana here yesterday with the sun peeping through those windows, and now it's back again. Shall we head to our Lahori joint in Easton? We desperately need some sustenance."

"Why not? I'm starving and craving that Punjabi fortification."

After that stormy and testing night, life settled into a steadier rhythm as preparations for my viva, finalization of the EU project, and the strenuous job hunt consumed me over the following months. The reports from the externals were positive, and my oral defense went smoothly, leaving me awaiting convocation while I submitted a paper to a research journal that sounded promising, bolstering my résumé. My supervisor's commendation of my research, shared informally with faculty members at Claverton, enhanced my job prospects, resulting in an invitation for a comprehensive interview at Bath. James Topsfield and his colleagues in the development studies department were already familiar with my seminar papers and international conference presentations. Eager to expand their teaching scope, they offered me a position starting in the next academic year. I had a fondness for Bath and appreciated the university's rising status in league tables, making it my first choice, though the renowned triangle further east remained alluring. Susanne, for her part, did everything to persuade me to join her university and stayed vigilant as July approached and I applied for visas for my parents and siblings to attend the early September convocation.

Anne's viva sailed through smoothly, with the board impressed by her research and articulate responses. Like me, she applied for jobs and received an offer from Exeter, a picturesque city west of Bristol that reminded her of Bath and was easily accessible by train. Her interview invitation came before mine, and we drove to the university together, admiring its hilltop campus surrounded by manicured lawns. After her interview, we strolled into town for an early meal, during which she received a call from the chair of the English department offering her the lecturer position. She accepted with a beaming smile, and we clinked glasses to celebrate. Throughout the meal, her knees brushed against mine and a playful smile tickled her lips. Susanne, sipping sparingly since she was the designated driver, watched with amusement. Before heading home, we toured the medieval cathedral, rivaling those in Wells and Salisbury, and stopped briefly at St. David's train station, Anne's future commuting hub, as she intended to continue living in Bristol while working part-time at the BBC.

After that tumultuous night in Totterdown, life found its momentum. We both earned our degrees, secured jobs, and prepared for our convocation. For me, finding an apartment in Bath was an added but essential task. I found a place in Bear Flat, close to the city center and Oldfield Park. Directly across from my new home stood a pub with a large bear sculpture on its roof, leading me to wonder if it inspired the neighborhood's name. I later learned from Joe that Bear Flat originated from "berewick," an Anglo-Saxon term meaning "barley settlement," hinting at its agricultural past. I planned to move in just before graduation, giving my parents space to stay if they could join me. The area had guesthouses nearby, and the Two-Tunnels Greenway was only a short walk away.

Regrettably, John, having retired from teaching at Newton Park, left in July, as did the other residents, closing a meaningful chapter in our lives. Moving from Totterdown to the more affluent Bath felt like a significant transition. Bristol had been kind to both of us, but Anne chose to stay another year due to its convenience and her commitments at the BBC. Susanne approved of my new flat, though I noticed a hint of worry on Anne's face. Nevertheless, she understood my reasons for moving. We received disappointing news from Anjum that my parents couldn't join us for my special day, though Bahram and Shireen were granted visas, which was some consolation. Anne drove me to Heathrow to pick them up and brought them to Bath, where I had arranged for them to stay at a guesthouse next door. They spent most of their time at my place, with Shireen redecorating and making frequent trips to the city center with Bahram. Bear Flat, perched on a hill across from the Avon and railway tracks, gave them a workout on their way back, which they enjoyed.

They met Susanne, Joe, and my friends in Bristol, visiting the Hawthorns and savoring a Lahori breakfast with Anne in Easton. Shireen joked with Anne about her "colonization" by a Turbati Baloch on her home turf, while Bahram and Susanne discussed literature over countless cups of English tea, which Bahram found too weak and compensated for with generous amounts. The cooler, rainy weather perhaps explained his increased tea consumption, though he enjoyed the occasional visit to the Bear and other pubs by the Abbey. Twice, Bahram and Shireen tried fish and chips at the Huntsman but preferred eating at home, as

Shireen enjoyed cooking and wanted to ensure I learned now that I was no longer a student. They praised Bath's architecture, found Bristol engaging, and were enchanted by Newton St. Loe and Newton Park. They were less impressed with the service at the Saracen's Head, with its Arab figure on the sign, but they loved the George Inn by the Kennet and Avon Canal in Bathampton. Bahram adored the village cricket ground, which he found as charming as the one in Gilgit, surrounded by the towering Karakorams and guarded by Rakaposhi.

Our convocation ended with tea at Brown's before gathering at Martini's in Bath for an Italian feast. The celebratory air was palpable, although we missed Terence and my parents. Anne, despite her best efforts, failed to convince Shireen to take a sip of Chianti, though Bahram needed no encouragement.

"I avoid drinking out of fear I might get hooked," Shireen said. "I don't mind if Bahram or others do, though."

"You can find alcohol in Karachi, but unless you buy imported brands—which are expensive—you can't guarantee the quality," I added.

"We don't drink to excess, just the occasional red wine or gin in the evening," Susanne said. "I understand the taboos and the challenges in Pakistan. Well done, Shireen, for steering clear."

"I'm not much for alcohol, but I do have the occasional shot with colleagues. Scotch and vodka are popular in South Asia, but wines are harder to come by, even though we grow great grapes in the trans-Indus region," Bahram noted.

"Terence tells us that alcohol is available in Dubai, but it's expensive and restricted to hotel bars," Susanne added, highlighting how newer economies balance restrictions and liberal access to alcohol.

Shireen and Bahram invited Susanne and Anne to visit Pakistan, noting Terence's proximity across the Gulf. I felt Anne was more inclined to visit, while Susanne, except for a visit to Dubai, preferred the comfort of the familiar. Still, she hosted an afternoon tea for us at her spacious home, surrounded by a lush garden and tall birch trees. With Anne in Exeter, we toured her room and Susanne's impressive book collection while enjoying her homemade pancakes, Danish pastries, and scones.

The following weekend, Susanne and Anne hosted us at the Globe Inn after a visit to Newton St. Loe, which Shireen and Bahram found magical. Throughout dinner, I noticed Susanne casting thoughtful glances at her daughter, then at me, as if recalling Anne's revelation about her hysterectomy. She seemed caught between witnessing the deepening relationship and worrying about her daughter's future.

Shireen and Bahram left with cherished memories after visits to Oxford and London, just as I began my first teaching term at Bath, guided by Joe's invaluable advice. Though I missed my family, I promised to return to Turbat for Easter.

EXETER

Mother appreciated my belated but brave step of informing Gul about my hysterectomy and was curious about his reaction. For her, the entire episode revived painful memories of when I underwent the surgery during my youth and the lasting impact it had on my life. Being an only child and then rendered unable to bear children was never a trivial matter for my parents. Seeing me professionally successful and finding genuine love while still grappling with feelings of inadequacy only deepened their silent anguish. Susanne, as was her nature, always maintained a strong and confident exterior in social settings to boost my morale and defiantly confronted the inexplicable circumstances that had put her and Terence in such a position. Following her tea with Gul at the university café, she felt reassured by his sincerity and urged me to confide in him directly. For her, honesty was non-negotiable, especially in challenging situations, and she encouraged me to be open with Gul while preparing for any outcome. I trusted his fortitude and straightforwardness but found myself hesitant to share this part of my past. Eventually, with my thesis completed and my decision to join academia strengthening my resolve, I chose that intimate night in Totterdown to reveal my truth. His understanding and unwavering support overwhelmed me, and in the months that followed, our bond grew even stronger. Life may be full of pain and sorrow, but it can also surprise us with moments of profound joy, transforming dukkha into sukha—relief born from grief, as a Buddhist parable might suggest.

Susanne, despite her encouragement, initially felt uncertain about how Gul would react to learning about my inability to conceive. She valued our relationship and understood how important it was to my well-being at this pivotal stage in my career. However, seeing the enduring intensity and depth of our relationship bolstered her optimism. She began to nudge me more openly to be honest with Gul. My hesitation did not stem from fear of losing him but from wanting to protect him from an emotional shock. In retrospect, after three years together, I realized that sharing my truth empowered me rather than burdening me with guilt. Gul, in turn, felt prepared to embrace the reality.

Ambivalence, after all, is an ever-present element in even the most intimate relationships.

Gul's creativity, expressive skill, and warm personality secured him the EU fellowship, easing his financial worries and allowing him to continue his research in the UK. His seminars at Bath and Bristol boosted his confidence and scholarly direction, helping him secure a teaching position. Meanwhile, the deteriorating situation back home, especially after the debacle in Afghanistan and Pakistan becoming a battleground for Shi'a and Sunni militants funded by Iran and Saudi Arabia, introduced a sobering dose of realism. This tempered his enthusiasm for returning home to teach and support younger students. He held hope that the cycles of extremism and ethnic nationalism, fueled by external influences, would eventually subside, allowing for normalcy to return. Gul held the elites of such societies accountable for their failings but was also critical of the often self-righteous and militaristic Western models of development. He believed that indigenous education and empowerment were the keys to progress. History was an essential part of Gul's outlook; it provided a counterbalance to the pessimism that often accompanied geopolitics and economics. Yet he was cautious about romanticizing the past or accepting the idea of linear progress. He often spoke of exploring the historical and contemporary connections between Oman and East Africa with Balochistan, especially regarding migration and the slave trade, an under-researched area that would blend historical sociology and linguistics.

My job at Exeter and the train commute back to Bristol gave me valuable time to interact with aspiring scholars, future bureaucrats, and budding writers. Their idealism and curiosity reminded me of my undergraduate days at Balliol. Graduate seminars were rigorous and participatory, fostering debate and critical thinking. Like Joe, I encouraged informality and open dialogue to build analytical skills, social confidence, and persuasive argumentation. My personal interest in expanding beyond the Anglo-Saxon core of English literature resonated with postgraduates who engaged with authors like Achebe, Soyinka, Farah, Narayan, Laye, Llosa, Okri, Salih, Armah, Adichie,

Mahfouz, Pamuk, Suleri, and Gurnah. This enriched the literary landscape and challenged traditional pedagogical norms.

In private moments, I began conceptualizing a work of fiction that would explore non-Western settings and characters, creating a genre distinct from those shaped by Kipling, Conrad, Forster, and Masters. This new work would go beyond the travel writings that captivated general readers. I owed much of this inspiration to Gul's influence, as well as conversations with Joe, Bill, Gavin, and other academics in vibrant Bristol. While I was familiar with many South Asian authors and noted an increase in female voices, I found that the Arab Middle East was still largely dominated by male writers. Turkey, with its strong literary tradition, led the region, closely followed by the Iranian diaspora. Then, Omani writer Jokha Alharthi began making waves with her fiction in Arabic. Like Pamuk and Shafak, she found skilled translators to introduce her work beyond Oman. Her narratives offered a refreshing perspective on a region often defined by geopolitical analysis, breaking the stereotype that its people were inherently violent or lethargic.

With Gul's move to Bath, Bristol began to feel somewhat redundant. I missed spending time with him, sharing tea and deeper conversations, whether intellectual or political, often intertwined with our cycle rides. My visits to the campus became infrequent due to time constraints from my commute and the influx of new students and faculty, though Joe still remained a familiar presence. One evening, Joe and Emma visited my flat, where Gul and I prepared a meal of South Asian and Chinese dishes. The gathering was informal and marked a celebratory mood, as it followed my graduation and job offer from Exeter. We had plenty of reasons to toast, and Gul and I could see pride in Emma's eyes as Joe shared his excitement about his upcoming trip to India with a group of enthusiasts. He had mapped out a journey through cities like Old Delhi, Lucknow, Banaras, Kolkata, and Chennai, with stops in Agra and Jaipur. Joe also mentioned recent departmental changes, including redundancies and the unexpected departure of Peter, the former department chair and long-time irritant. Joe, as an adjunct lecturer, had escaped the budget cuts, and we all raised our glasses to that.

"Here's to you, Joe! Best of luck with the book," Gul said, leading the toast.

"And to Peter selling milkshakes in Glastonbury!" I added, drawing laughter as we sat down for dinner. The table was set with mulligatawny soup, chapatis, and Russian salad.

"Gul prepared chicken karahi with added herbs and greens, mild on the chilies, while I sautéed some veggie noodles and chickpea pulao. Emma and Joe, bear with our gradual learning in the kitchen," I said.

"Yes, and the naans are from our favorite Lahori spot in Easton, and the chutney is authentically homemade," Gul chimed in.

"Anne and Gul, this is a feast! I see why Joe couldn't stop praising your last dinner party in Totterdown," Emma remarked.

"Well, not as accomplished as your cooking, but we try," I replied.

"I always admired John's research and how he challenged TV historians who gloss over the empire's flaws. I hear he's retired now—that must be a loss for Bath Spa," Joe said.

"Yes, John wanted to spend more time writing and being with his wife. They moved to Brighton to be closer to the sea and London. I still have his contact, though I'm not sure if he'll ever come back this way," Gul added. "John wasn't much into tech—he drafted his books and papers by hand for a secretary to type. He bought a mobile phone only recently, and we had to show him how to use it."

"Visiting John could be fun if we head to Brighton someday," I suggested.

"Yes, but not by bike on that old railway route that barely holds up beyond Midford," Gul said, grinning.

"Glad you know the Two-Tunnels Greenway. Emma and I enjoy walks there with our dogs but have to stay alert with all the cyclists and moms with buggies," Joe said with a smile.

"Joe, do you remember that time a horse rider came through the second tunnel? We could hear the hooves long before seeing her. She seemed so at ease," Emma said, reminiscing.

"I'm a bit further east, and I've occasionally seen a robed Buddhist waiting for the Newton Park bus. I should catch up with him one day," I said.

"That's Malinga, a Sri Lankan monk and faculty member at the other university. He lives near your place," Joe informed us.

"Bath is getting more diverse, but it's taking time. The international student population is definitely growing in Oldfield Park and Twerton," Gul noted.

"Anne and Gul, Malinga is quite popular, especially with women in town," Emma added, sparking curiosity.

"How so? Monks are supposed to be asexual and detached from worldly matters," I said, puzzled.

"Not like that," Emma laughed. "Mothers with young children often approach him for blessings. He's a holy figure, always robed, so they see him as a source of good fortune."

"I should meet him—with Susanne or Anne in tow, in case he's more reserved with men," Gul joked.

"Why assume that? He might be approachable to anyone. But it's worth trying, especially since he's practically your neighbor," I said. "Who knows, maybe he's a cricket fan too."

As the evening wound down, we finished with bread-and-butter pudding and green tea. Gul caught a ride back to Bath with Joe and Emma, and his departure left a pang of longing; in the past, such evenings would have ended with us tangled together in bed. But I knew another visit awaited that weekend in Bath.

With my books, clothes, and some walking shoes packed, I set off for Bath on Saturday morning after a hearty breakfast, almost ten days after hosting the dinner. The days had felt like years. Listening to Fleetwood Mac and passing light traffic, I drove by Salford without stopping, planning to meet Susanne later that evening. Gul was waiting by his front door when I arrived, and he embraced me before we even moved my bag inside.

"See that bear on the pub's roof, Anne? It's a reminder to give you a bear hug when you arrive," Gul said.

"With discretion, please. I'm too precious to be squashed. But first, I need a strong cup of tea before any more 'transgressions,'" I teased.

"Alright, come in and make yourself comfortable while I get the tea ready."

"I met a neighbor who teaches history at Newton Park. Ryan is from Ireland, has a doctorate from Chicago, and has published work on cycling and women's empowerment in 19th-century Ireland. It's fascinating how a bicycle could symbolize mobility and personal freedom for women," I said.

"Yes, it was a colony back then, and Catholicism imposed restrictions on women. But Victorian England wasn't much better—there was a hint of bluff in being a 'Ma'am Sahib,'" Gul replied, setting the tea tray down.

"I'd hold you tight, but I don't want to risk spilling tea on that shirt. The last thing I want is tea burns on that handsome chest. Ryan mentioned knowing Malinga, though we didn't go into detail. Maybe I'll invite him for a drink at the Bear sometime."

"I wouldn't mind a Guinness now and then. And speaking of aesthetics, I'm partial to its brown richness over translucent beverages. Scotland and Ireland share a long, intertwined history—rivalries and all, even in football."

"Well, parochialism can be both universal and local. I don't mind it, Anne, as long as it's for fun and not for friction."

"'Fun and Friction'—that could be an apt title for a piece in literature or cultural studies. Susanne is planning to join us later in the afternoon before we head to the city centre."

"With such a warm, dry day, why not take a walk around my neighborhood before your mum arrives?"

A few streets from Gul's place, we found ourselves on Greenway Lane, flanked by tucked-away residences and a school enveloped by tall oaks. The lane led us to Rosemount Lane, a steep descent that sent a thrill through us as we let our bodies find their own momentum down the slope.

"This must be nearly a 70% grade! Whether cycling or driving, this would be quite the adventure. I wonder how the residents feel about people being so daring on this hill."

"Bath's hills make it all the more spectacular. I've walked up Widcombe Road to the university—it's a long, uphill stretch that's great for muscle work. Coming down is, of course, much more relaxing. We can take the Prior Park Road and pass through Widcombe, which is a sleepy, charming neighborhood."

"Gul, I'm amazed at how well you know these quaint lanes and neighborhoods. They're so picturesque, especially on an autumn day like today. I can see why you like Widcombe—it's serene, watchful, perfectly nestled between the university and town. And this place isn't far from your monk neighbor or the Irish academic."

"Bath and its hamlets—like Widcombe, Lansdown, Bathampton, and Old Weston—epitomize English reserve and the tendency to retire into peaceful obscurity. I wonder why that is."

"It's not unlike a universal human desire to seek out scenic, tranquil nooks. Some attribute it to island life and the inclination toward solitude, while others see it as a self-indulgent retreat after centuries of global involvement."

"Imagine an impeccably dressed Englishman with a necktie and pith hat, climbing a tree with ropes to trim its branches while speaking in a Cockney accent."

"I can picture all sorts of scenes, including one with you in a yards-long turban and leathery shoes, wielding an ornate dagger as you chase down a cattle thief in Makran, only to find an Anglo-Saxon ma'am with a parasol taking her morning walk."

"What a story! Only a true writer could come up with such scenes. You should write it, Anne."

"I just might. By the way, we're nearing the point where the canal and the river meet."

"Let's stop at the White Hart. Are you up for a bite?"

The soup and salad, along with bread rolls, provided the perfect boost as we sat by the window, soaking up the sun after shedding our jackets.

"I can smell coffee brewing at the bar. I can't resist a strong Americano. Want one, Gul?"

"I'll have one if it comes with such delightful company."

"Typical man, casting his feelers at a naive country girl."

"A lucky man, indeed, and he knows it." Gul paused. "We need to pick up a cake and some buns from Sally Lunn's on our way back. Your mum will be here soon."

"Thoughtful and clever. Susanne will be thrilled; Sally Lunn's is her favorite tea spot in Bath."

"Everyone has a bit of a historian in them. Even in modern times, we hold onto traditions and the aura of the past. Americans and Australians may start with Columbus, Cortez, Raleigh, and Drake, but they still feel a pull toward antiquity."

"This Colombian coffee is doing its job. I wonder what Guinness would do for your Baloch warrior instincts."

"We can try it later, Anne. For now, let's get moving."

Susanne arrived just after we returned to Gul's flat, carrying groceries, a cake, scones, and olive ciabattas. Gul prepared tea with Darjeeling leaves and cardamom, heating milk for an authentic touch. Susanne savored the creamed scones and buns with strawberry jam, as did we. After tea, we readied ourselves for an evening at the Royal Theatre. A short drive brought us close to the Little Theatre, and we walked through lanes bustling with tourists and street performers.

I'd seen Carmen in Oxford with my parents years ago, and its music stayed with me. This rendition, with a new Spanish cast, a majestic horse, real Travelers, and vibrant performances, left a lasting impression. Set in Seville, the opera told the story of Don Jose, an Andalusian soldier, and Carmen, a captivating Traveler girl who led him to ruin and, ultimately, tragedy. Premiering in 1873, George Bizet's production initially received mixed reviews but grew to be a classic, though Bizet never saw its success—he died after the thirty-third performance at just thirty-six.

During the interval, we sipped Prosecco, thanks to Susanne, and discussed the flamenco dancers and passionate scenes. Susanne and Gul recognized colleagues from their university, a reminder of Bath's cozy size and frequent encounters that big cities couldn't match.

On our return, we began preparing our meal through a spontaneous job distribution. I was assigned to concoct the salad, Susanne to boil rice, while Gul took it upon himself to prepare kabobs. I picked fresh baby spinach leaves, mixing them with rocket, corn, avocado shards, black olives, cherry tomatoes, and red onions, all soaked in pesto sauce and garnished with freshly squeezed lemon juice. I covered the salad with thin slices of smoked salmon, though in a smaller measure, as I did not want to preempt Gul's kabobs of minced lamb, enmeshed in herbs, tomato paste, green chilies, and coriander leaves, with some ground cloves and salt added to the paste. He began putting the mixture on individual skewers. His concoction had a thin layer of beaten yolk to hold the ingredients together as they simmered on the grill. Susanne was not to be left behind and, in addition to boiling rice seasoned with a dash of salt and black pepper, she prepared a soup by blending basil, butternut squash, fresh beans, and celery. By the time we sat down to dine, the spread looked incredibly colorful. We clinked our glasses, toasting with an aromatic Andalusian red that Gul had acquired during his forays into wine stores on Milsom Street.

"Carmen is certainly a masterpiece," Susanne began, "and the credit goes to Bizet, but it is entirely up to the cast to maintain its high standards."

"I understand that Travellers still have a visible presence on the cultural scene in Andalusia and live in specific areas like Granada," I said, hoping Gul would comment. We all intentionally avoided using the 'G' word, though I remembered a street in Oxford called Gipsy Lane.

"The Indian origin of the Travellers is well-established, and their interaction with the few remaining Muslims, or Moriscos as they were latently called, ensured the survival of various multicultural traditions, such as the flamenco dance. A former Guardian journalist, Giles Tremlett, who was based in Spain, provides an exhaustive perspective on the Travellers' culture in Andalusia. I read his Ghosts of Spain after following some of his reports and found it fascinating how Spain's connection to the South still resonates. This theme is echoed in Gabriel García Márquez's One Hundred Years of Solitude, where Arab hawkers and Travellers are not just on the periphery but integral stakeholders of a hybrid culture."

Gul shed light on post-1492 Spain, where the Reconquista and the Inquisition wreaked havoc on its Jewish and Muslim populations, unleashing ethnic cleansing on an enormous scale that continued for nearly two centuries, often resulting in forced conversions or abrupt expulsions. Ironically, these tactics were later applied with an arcane expertise in South America and beyond, targeting indigenous peoples through the efforts of Conquistadors like Columbus, Cortés, and Pizarro. Bartolomé de las Casas, Columbus's one-time clerk and a converted priest, documented these events in his pioneering eyewitness account of the destruction of the Indies. Unfortunately, Las Casas's slim but powerful work did not appear in English translation until the late nineteenth century, by which time Spain—once the queen of the Western Hemisphere—had become a spent force.

"Anne and Gul, if I'm not mistaken, Don Quixote was the earliest Western novel that mocked the shallowness of chivalry," Susanne said, referring to Miguel de Cervantes, a Cordovan who had spent considerable time in North African captivity before writing his groundbreaking novel, which combined adventure, hierarchy, and satire.

"In my discussions with academics over the years, I've learned that many younger European Muslims travel to Spain, especially Andalusia, to connect with a lost past. They must internalize both a sense of belonging and loss. In places like India under British rule, and more recently in Bosnia, Andalusia has emerged as a poignant reminder of a diminished Muslim legacy. I'd love to undertake an extended visit to Spain at some point. My father back home has profoundly influenced me with his deep immersion in the Andalusian past." Gul said.

"Just as we Sandemans have our connection with Balochistan, you may find parallels with Cordova and the rest of Andalusia. In 2006, former Spanish Prime Minister José Aznar remarked that the Muslim presence in Spain was an extended colonial rule for which no Muslim ever apologized. Was he being logical or merely insidious, Gul?" I asked, curious to hear Gul's take on any parallel between early conquests and modern imperialism.

"Yes, Anne, it began as a conquest, but Muslims didn't leave, unlike the British and others in their colonies. Instead, they became an indigenous community within a pluralistic Spain. There was no 'home' country for them to return to, unlike recent European empires. The expulsions and forced conversions seven centuries later, like those of the Spanish Jews, were unjustified. That's where it becomes tragic. Once the Spanish and Portuguese crossed that Rubicon, it opened the floodgates for further conquests in the Western Hemisphere, Africa, and across the Indian Ocean," Gul concluded.

"Anne, you need to come back from Andalusia to this kitchen in Bear Flat to make us coffee, as there's dessert waiting in Gul's refrigerator," Susanne said with a playful smile. She had secretly prepared a surprise: a red velvet cake with ermine icing. "I made it this morning without artificial food coloring and anchored it on cream cheese frosting to avoid an overpowering vanilla taste. It's meant to celebrate your achievements in my two favorite cities."

While Susanne placed her layered, indulgent cake on the table, I busied myself preparing the coffee. Gul laid out the crockery, and in a brief private moment, I whispered to him about my intention to drive back to Salford to spend the night with Mum. Gul's comfortable apartment in Bath, with its tasteful furnishings and convenient location, added to my reflections. The logistics of working in Exeter, living in Bristol, and visiting both Salford and Bath had begun to wear on me.

While sitting in our conservatory back home over a late breakfast following Mother's gardening session, we tried to absorb the sun as we brooded over my commute. "The past few months have been quite favorable but endlessly fast-paced. From the viva to graduation, then the job in Exeter, and Gul going through similar stages and settling in Bath—it all happened too rapidly. A natural progression, I'd say."

"Yes, Anne, achievements of high caliber, no doubt. Seeing you so happy and thriving in your profession is well worth all those years of living in the West Country, often on my own in this otherwise comfortable home. Dad is quite proud of you, as am I, darling."

"Things have changed for the better, but there are new challenges as well, Mum. Instead of traveling between two towns, now I'm commuting between four. With you both here, living in Bristol feels slightly out of place, especially since I left the BBC to focus on teaching and writing. One option is to rent a place in Exeter and visit Salford every other weekend and perhaps catch up with Gul."

"Bristol is the hub for the West Country, as London is for the South-East. You could stay here, but the trains don't stop at Salford unless you keep driving. Exeter is a viable option, but you'd be anchoring yourself in Devon, away from Somerset."

I was refilling the teacups when Mum's phone rang. She didn't recognize the number, but her eyes narrowed quickly, her expression taking on deeper furrows.

"Thank you for your call, Doctor. It will take us time to absorb this shocking news. We know Terence is receiving proper medical care, but we'll need all the help we can get to bring him back to England as soon as possible." I knew instantly that Dad was hospitalized. I rushed to hold my mother as I saw her tear-filled eyes and her body slightly trembling. Yes, it was about Dad, who had been admitted to a hospital in Dubai after days of severe headaches and vomiting. Initially, he thought it was due to prolonged exposure to heat and excessive drinking over the previous weekend, combined with a stomach upset. But the tests revealed a tumor that had been growing for some time. The biopsy only heightened the apprehension, and Terence, who had kept the news from us, had requested repatriation. That call confirmed the urgency.

Life took a steep, dire turn with Dad's arrival in Bath, transferred by air ambulance to the intensive care unit at the Royal United Hospital, where prompt tests confirmed the diagnosis made in Dubai. At first, I hardly recognized him, and Mum sat in a chair wrapped in grief, trying to hide her tears. Gul was at the hospital when they brought in the stretcher. He held my hand firmly while supporting Mother with an arm around her waist. We sat by the bed in a room that was already buzzing with doctors, nurses, and medical equipment. It felt as if Dad's body, having weathered the storm for so long, had finally yielded to fate. His shrunken face and half-closed eyes bore witness to a losing battle against the relentless tumor.

Battling the daily onslaught of despair, we watched Dad's condition steadily decline. A week later, we were gently informed of the prognosis: a short span of time remained, during which he would be kept sedated for comfort. Mum and I held his hands, massaging them gently and touching his pale forehead, speaking words of encouragement we knew he might never hear. Our valiant Scot's time was almost up. My aunt and Mum's elderly uncle flew in from Odense, and our home in Salford became quieter, despite visits from worried neighbors. And then, Terence was no more. We quietly filed out of the room as advised, while they took his body to the mortuary. Anger, grief, and shock surged within us, but Mum and I tried to maintain composure, even as we were broken inside.

Life changed dramatically after Dad's funeral. Mum agreed to stay with me in Exeter, where I rented an apartment near the campus. Movers helped shift our belongings from Salford and Bristol, while Gul visited whenever he could. Bristol and Salford seemed to vanish from my life, and I became an Exeter resident. Susanne took a long leave from her job to divide her time between Exeter and Odense, while Gul prepared for a trip to Turbat during the spring break. These significant changes enforced a pause in my once-constant travels. Teaching at the university became my focus, punctuated by regular walks with Mum, who gradually busied herself with reading and showed no eagerness to return to Salford. Although she didn't say it outright, she was more protective of me. A few weeks later, she left for Odense to be with family, while I reworked my thesis for formal submission to Columbia University Press, which had agreed to include it in their literary series on modern American writers.

Gul's calls from Karachi, Turbat, and Lahore were a lifeline during my lowest moments. True to his nature, he often talked about cricket, politics in his country, the latest harvest of the renowned Makran dates, and the annual gathering of Zikri devotees near Turbat. He spoke about Gwadar and the Chinese interest in revitalizing the old Baloch port, noting the mixed reactions from the Americans and Indians, while the UAE and Oman remained noncommittal. His long conversations and messages transported me to that part of the Indian Ocean, sparking a renewed sense of purpose in my writing and inspiring the synopsis for my proposed novel set in that region. I began to seriously consider visiting the places Gul described so vividly and found a renewed drive in my literary work.

GYMKHANA

With Terence's passing, life changed significantly for Susanne and Anne, as it does for any family dealing with the sudden loss of a loved one. Healing takes time and involves numerous everyday activities. For the first few months, Exeter and Odense occupied Susanne until she returned to her job at the library. However, Salford felt quieter and lonelier for the Danish expatriate. Meanwhile, Anne gained more research students, and the planning of her proposed volume served as a timely distraction. By the time I left for Turbat, Exeter had become Anne's home, and she often welcomed Susanne for weekend visits. While not quite Bath, Exeter was certainly more pleasant than Salford. Susanne, without saying it outright, considered moving to Devon and seeking a position at the university. She did not intend to live with her daughter but wanted to settle nearby. After my departure, she brought up the idea with Anne, who was immediately supportive, prompting earnest efforts for Susanne's relocation. I was still in Turbat when Anne informed me of this development, which I found plausible, though Susanne's departure would mean a loss for the university and an unsettling void for me.

The long-awaited visit to Turbat, with a brief stopover in Karachi, proved to be heartwarming, as expected. My parents, Aunt Zahra, Adil, and Abu's workforce on the farm were overjoyed, and Anjum's return from Lahore added to the celebrations. My parents were aware of Anne and Susanne, albeit without all the details. They were pleased and, slightly surprised, that a bachelor had returned with gray sideburns and an ever-present smile tinged with noticeable reserve. Within a few days, Shireen, Bahram, and Zeenat joined us, enhancing Ammi's joy and keeping her occupied. During our table conversations, she subtly hinted at missing the presence of young children in the house, which was otherwise filled with adults.

Zeenat, who lived with Bahram and Shireen, was nearing graduation. She had matured into a confident young woman with a sharp, alert mind that had already shown promise a decade earlier. Now, she was more reserved, speaking little to me but maintaining her lively interaction with Anjum and Ammi. Aunt Zahra, now with more gray hair, seemed ageless. Her presence affirmed her status as the family matriarch, with my parents often deferring to her judgment. She still maintained her ancestral home, which had been updated with modern amenities, but she was an integral part of our household.

Upon my return home, amidst all the familiar memories and connections, I noticed two significant changes. First, there were two armed bodyguards, and no family member ventured out without an escort, limiting the once-spontaneous trips to the bazaar, visits to farms, or travels to Panjgur, Quetta, and Gwadar, where Abu held agricultural and residential properties. Second, books by Edward Said, Noam Chomsky, Ijaz Ahmad, and Olivette Otele adorned a side table, suggesting that my room had been occupied by an avid reader.

Balochistan was, as I knew even from England, in turmoil due to the generals' belligerent mismanagement, which had exacerbated long-standing resentments among the province's fragile middle class. At the same time, fiery clerics, supported by jihadist allies across the border, pursued their own agendas, leaving the ordinary Baloch and Pashtuns caught in a perilous situation. The influx of foreign arms and tacit support for subversive activities, particularly against government workers, had created an atmosphere of volatility, further heightened by the grim addition of suicide bombings, necessitating armed guards for families like ours. This situation had also prompted Abu to invest in properties in Gwadar, although that port city, too, occasionally suffered from bombings and protests by its residents, who resented the influx of outsiders buying prime properties and taking desirable jobs. At the same time, a steady stream of Baloch and other Pakistanis sought traffickers' assistance to emigrate.

Abu's assessments were rooted in political economy and regional geopolitics, including the Chinese factor. However, my childhood friends Mukhtar, Zahid, and Raheem relied on stark conspiracy theories, frequently voicing grim, speculative statements. I tried to reconnect and relive the bawdy jokes, playful taunts, and late-night gossip that had defined our youth in Turbat, but my friends—now burdened with family responsibilities—

seemed preoccupied. It was as though Turbat, and indeed all of Balochistan, had lost its innocence during my time away.

My parents were discreet about broaching my relationship with Anne. They knew of our intimacy through me and from Bahram and Shireen, who had discussed our time together during their visit. A few days after my arrival, while having breakfast on the veranda, Ammi gently asked about my future plans:

"Gul, you've achieved so much by Allah's grace, but have you thought about settling down? It would be wonderful to see grandchildren playing here."

"Ammi, that's a valid question, and I'm grateful for the consistent support from you and my family throughout my career. But I need a bit of understanding. I'm involved with a former classmate who is now a colleague. Shireen and Bahram met Anne and her mother, but sadly, they lost the head of their family a few months ago to cancer. They are still mourning that loss."

"Do you plan to marry Anne once she's somewhat recovered from her grief? And would she be willing to adopt some of our cultural customs, even the more traditional ones?" Dad was direct, as usual.

"I haven't discussed this with her, nor has she brought it up. In the West, women, particularly those with good education and careers, often approach such subjects themselves with those closest to them. Our relationship is strong but has yet to reach any long-term commitments." I knew I was being candid, especially with the use of "yet," which made all five of my listeners squint slightly. I wasn't ready to discuss Anne's past medical surgery and its impact on her ability to have children—it was too soon and could cause unnecessary distress or turn the conversation into a nonstarter. Discussing this without Anne's consent would have ominous consequences on all sides.

"You know there are educated, modern Baloch and non-Baloch girls around whose parents could be approached, though the final decision would be yours and the bride's. We fully respect modern choices. From what we've heard from you, Shireen, and Bahram, we would certainly welcome Anne into our family."

Ammi's eagerness respected personal choice, and I felt immensely fortunate to belong to a family that never imposed unilateral decisions in the name of honor but respected individual preferences and dissent on significant matters.

Abu and Ammi left for a wedding in the neighborhood, leaving the four of us at the breakfast table. Aunt Zahra ensured a fresh supply of karak tea, two more parathas, and ample local honey.

"Anjum, how are you finding teaching at the all-girls college in Turbat after four formative years in Lahore?" I asked my sister as she carefully divided the parathas into equal pieces for each of us.

"It's a challenge, Gul, but it gives me more time at home and a chance to catch up on reading and writing. I wish our teachers were more motivated and ambitious, though the girls are. However, many of them get married before finishing their degrees or finding jobs. Our social environment doesn't foster strong work ethics, unfortunately. What do you think, Shireen?"

"I agree. In Karachi, things are slightly different, and even in Campbellpur, the situation is better compared to Turbat. Marriage is a priority everywhere, and girls internalize it to the point of sacrificing everything else for it. Even those from educated and prosperous families often prioritize marriage over their studies or careers due to peer pressure and personal preferences." Shireen spoke from her firsthand experience as a student and now a married doctor who managed to maintain her practice. Bahram, who had been waiting to contribute, added:

"It's a widespread problem. A recent study confirmed that 85% of female doctors leave the workforce after marriage, spending their days managing their homes and overseeing domestic help. What a waste! Most of them, if not all, probably idealized public service and professionalism during their student days."

"The percentage could be even higher, according to some of my colleagues," Shireen added with a tone of authenticity.

"Children, home, and in-laws are important, but what's the point of spending years in medical school and costing taxpayers so much if it leads to nothing? It's unfair." Anjum, like me, was well past the usual age for marriage in our society and spoke from her own observations.

"In our society, where premarital relationships are frowned upon, I understand the urgency to marry, unlike in the West, where physical relationships aren't solely for reproductive reasons. But unhappy marriages are common in traditional societies like ours." Bahram didn't hold back. "Gul, you can afford to stay a bachelor and even change partners as you go."

"That's not the case of being a bed-hopper. Maybe I'm not ready for more responsibilities yet, or there are other reasons behind it." I left them intrigued, but Anjum's announcement diverted the conversation just in time:

"I have wonderful news to share. The Islamabad office of the public service commission just texted to let me know that I've topped the civil service examination this year and have been selected for district management. Here you go, everyone!"

Extemporaneously, we all rose, holding our cups to celebrate Anjum's exhilarating news and began dancing around her, which brought Adil and Aunt Zahra out of the kitchen to check on our sudden burst of joy. They soon joined in, hugging everyone blissfully. When Abu and Ammi returned, they were elated and instructed the household staff to prepare a large meal for the less fortunate in our neighborhood, including the Sheedi mohallah.

Anjum had to leave for Lahore early next week to join her academy on the Mall, giving me an opportunity to accompany her. In the meantime, I indulged in the joyous atmosphere of Turbat. The next day, we all piled into our cars for a picnic at the farm. The group included Zahra, Zeenat, Adil, my childhood friends, and the immediate family. Anjum was already playing the no-nonsense civil servant, issuing instructions on the preparation of sajji, tikkas, salad, and naans, made by local professionals. The sajji consisted of seasoned mutton legs on skewers, slowly rotating over an open wood fire, while the naans were oblong and furrowed—a style brought into our cuisine with the Afghan refugees after 1979. I had tasted similar naans in London's Drummond Street and in Bristol, where they had to compete with their circular Peshawari counterparts. Ammi never encouraged fizzy drinks at home, so we enjoyed lemonade and lassi for most of the day.

Zeenat stood out in a flowery tunic and dark shalwar, with a Sindhi ajrak draped over her elegant shoulders. Tasked with making a salad from the farm's freshly harvested vegetables, Zeenat's colorful creation won praise even from the sajji purists, who usually bypassed starters and vegetables in favor of filling their plates with tender mutton and homemade chutney. I marveled at how much Zeenat had changed in recent years—from a bookworm into a poised young woman with a captivating charm. Her thick, dark, curly hair glistened in the sunlight as she moved gracefully, offering salad and naans to everyone. Shireen and Bahram watched her with pride, knowing how well she had done while staying with them. Zeenat had excelled academically, participated in sports and extracurricular activities, and created a warm home environment for my brother and his wife, whose children treated her like aunt.

"Shireen mentioned your impressive academic achievements, including your recent master's in history, Zeenat. Everyone in the family is proud of you. What are your plans now?" I asked.

"Thank you, Gul. Anjum and Shireen have encouraged me to try for the civil service examination while studying law at the same time. I hope to contribute to society in some way. It might sound ambitious, but working with the Sheedi youth in Lyari also keeps me occupied," she replied.

"That's wonderful, Zeenat. You're talented in so many areas—athletics, poetry, mentoring the younger generation. I wish I could do as much. I've become lazy, cycling a bit around Bath where I live and teach. Have you published your poetry and writings anywhere?"

"Yes, under the pen name 'Safeena.' Some of my poems, book reviews, and essays have appeared in newspapers, including Dawn, which allows me to keep up with some of your work, Gul," she said with a smile.

Abu and Ammi exchanged appreciative glances as I spoke with Zeenat, while my siblings and Shireen valued my interest in her endeavors. I knew I would see Zeenat again in Karachi after my visit to Lahore, but her image stayed with me—her self-confidence, warm personality, and graceful composure, especially considering her background, were nothing short of remarkable. Born without privilege and from an often-overlooked community, Zeenat's self-development and refinement were inspiring, reinforcing my belief in human potential overcoming adversity.

During our flight from Quetta to Lahore, Anjum asked, "I saw you talking to Zeenat the other day. How do you see someone like her, from an underprivileged background, achieving her goals given the colorism and class issues that pervade our society like a virus?"

"She already has several accomplishments under her belt, which will help her face future challenges. It's true that Sheedis lack role models, and societal odds are stacked against them, but Zeenat is formidable. With our support, she can overcome these obstacles."

"Leaving aside her background, she's undeniably beautiful. Shireen mentioned she's quite admired at the university, though she doesn't seem to have any serious relationships, unlike others," Anjum teased.

"Alright, Madam Bureaucrat, I get the joke. Just make sure your newfound authority doesn't scare away your suitors. I wouldn't mind a non-Baloch brother-in-law, as long as he's intelligent and caring."

"Where do you stand with Anne? I know she's beautiful and intelligent, and she seems responsible."

"We've been close for years. She might even visit us in Turbat, which would require special protection, thanks to your bureaucracy. But, as I told Ammi, we're still non-committal."

"Abu and Ammi wouldn't mind a British daughter-in-law, especially if it means you're happy and they get grandchildren to dote on."

"Can I share something I haven't told anyone else? I could use your advice."

"Of course, Gul. You can trust me."

"Anne told me some time ago that she had a hysterectomy in her late teens due to a severe condition. She can't have children. This hasn't affected our relationship, but it has prevented us from considering marriage seriously. I don't want to leave her just because she can't have children. But I'm not sure how to tell Ammi and Abu, or whether they'd still welcome her as part of the family."

"I'm so sorry to hear that, Gul. I can imagine how difficult that must have been for Anne. On the one hand, she loves you, but she might not want to hold you back from having a family. You both need to decide whether you can be content without children or if you should part ways, which might leave lingering guilt. There are many childless couples in the world, but nothing is guaranteed."

"Thoughtful as always, Anjum. But how do I tell Ammi?"

"Be honest with yourself and Anne, and take it from there."

"Easier said than done. I might need your support as a neutral party."

"Are you planning to see Naveena in Lahore?"

"Not sure. What's she up to these days?"

"There's nothing wrong with meeting her for coffee, unless she's married to someone insecure. Our relationships evolve, so you might see her as a good friend now."

"She was always a good friend, and we were both broad-minded."

"My academy is on the Mall, just before the Gymkhana. It could be a good spot to meet. Some of your old classmates are in Lahore; they might have updates on Naveena."

My little sister was the brightest of us all, mature beyond her years, and I felt an immense sense of happiness that she had achieved what she deserved. While enjoying Russian salad and pasta at Gymkhana's Caffe Nine, I noticed Jamil walk in with a woman. He recognized me immediately.

"Gul! Back in Lahore? What a wonderful surprise! Zarina, this is Gulbaz Khan from Balochistan, a fellow Ravian and session mate. The bookworm who left for England years ago. Still single, this free bird! And Zarina, my better half—more into books than this old chatterbox here."

"It's great to see you, old friend. I just arrived from Turbat via Quetta. It's lovely to meet you, Bhabhi Zarina. How did you end up with this busybody?"

"We met through mutual friends who were part of Lahore's social scene about a decade ago. Now, they're all balding and busy with kids while we spouses are turning gray and heavy from eating biryani and Lahori breakfasts. I've heard about you from Jamil and Naveena—all good things, by the way," Zarina said, smiling.

"Join me at the table—no biryani this time. Their pasta is just as good as it was when I used to come here with Abu and Ammi."

"Yes, you brought us here a couple of times to show off. Naveena wasn't too impressed. No surprise she married a military man—high up the ladder with power, land, and privileges. Unlike us civilians, still slogging away in the Old Anarkali secretariat infested with jinns and rotting files," Jamil said, his tone dripping with satire.

"Don't be so self-deprecating, Jamil. You bureaucrats have your own way of feigning humility while being just as adept at wielding power. Right, Bhabhi Zarina?"

"Absolutely, Gul Bhai. These so-called humble civil servants aren't far behind those hopping between cantonments and housing colonies," Zarina agreed.

"I'm here for another week while Anjum is at her academy. I might visit some archives, GC, and catch up with other old friends."

"Zarina, you might not know, but Anjum topped the merit list in this year's civil service exam. What a brilliant family from far-off Turbat! It's all thanks to our Sassi, the traveler girl who defied odds, walking hundreds of miles through the heat and dust to reach her Punnu, who, like Gul, was from Turbat but abandoned her in the deserts of Sindh before she caught up to him."

"Typical city-dweller's tirade against the Baloch. Never forget Ibn Khaldun, the father of sociology, who credited nomadic and tribal people like us with the rise of civilizations while city folk like you contribute to their decline. Any news of the other metropolitan, Naveena?" I asked.

"She's somewhere in Lahore, married with children," Jamil replied.

"I shouldn't bother her, then. I had thought of meeting her for coffee in Gulberg but don't want to cause any concern. Maybe Punnu was just as mindful of Sassi's reputation when he quietly left for Makran."

We shared a few more sessions in Lahore, where Anjum and Zarina grew more comfortable in the candid discussions that characterized my relationship with Jamil. I also found time to dive into archival research, particularly on the East India Company's early activities at Ranjit Singh's court. Alexander Burnes, hailed by some Victorian writers as an incarnation of Alexander the Great, embodied the audacious spirit during his Indus voyage to Punjab and beyond. However, his overconfidence caught up with him when he met a brutal end during Akbar Khan's campaign following the Company's initial victory in Afghanistan. Paul Masson, a self-taught archaeologist who unearthed Alexandrian coins at Bagram, fled his Company tormentors and found refuge in my homeland. He had allies in Bombay who supported him and secured his sustenance.

Reading about Masson and other Britons "serving on the Frontier," including Elphinstone, Pottinger, Connolly, Stoddart, the Lawrences, Edwardes, Abbott, Jacob, Nicholson, and others, I visualized the upper Indus turning into a cauldron of warfare, intrigues, and international power plays nearly two centuries ago—a legacy that continues to this day. Anne, who was fascinated by my findings in Lahore, expressed interest in how Balochistan became a supply route and recruitment ground for attacks on Afghanistan. Ranjit Singh's refusal to let the Company pass through Punjab shifted the route, culminating in the conquest of Sindh by James Napier in 1843 and opening pathways through my homeland into Afghanistan and Iran. The next generation of colonial figures, including Richard Burton, John Jacob, and Robert Sandeman, left an indelible mark on the lower Indus region.

The murals at Lahore Fort, the expanding historiography on the Great Game, and biographies of these figures nearly transformed me into a historian. My long-standing interest in Baloch culture and diaspora, rooted in a subsistence economy, enriched my research. The British land settlements around Quetta, Chaman, and Fort Sandeman introduced new administrative structures, with railways connecting British Balochistan to India, Persia, and Afghanistan. More than naval power, the Company— and later the Crown—succeeded through political patronage backed by military strength, peaking under Lord Curzon. This policy led to wars with the Pashtuns and complex loyalties, with the Baloch and Punjabis often siding with the Raj for their own benefits.

Time flew by as I sifted through aging files and engaged in heated debates with academics in Lahore. I mingled with old friends and enjoyed outings with Anjum, who even arranged for me to give a lecture at her academy. I invited many of my long-lost friends, though Naveena didn't come, despite me slipping her an invitation through Zarina. Anne, some colleagues from Bath, Zeenat, Shireen, and Susanne from Odense joined online, witnessing the diverse, youthful face of a country known more for its challenges than its achievements. The discussions touched on unrest in Balochistan, politicized religion, Chinese involvement in Gwadar and Chaghi, militarized ethnicity, and women's empowerment—all of which piqued my curiosity and broadened the scope for future research.

As I left the venue, one question lingered: How do capable, well-intentioned individuals, brimming with qualifications and youthful idealism, succumb so easily to systemic dysfunction after joining the civil service? If the country remains trapped by corruption, inefficiency, power abuse, and religious extremism, there must be a deep flaw in its "steel frame." Despite my unease, the communal spirit and camaraderie of these gatherings nourished my optimism, though I often wondered how Anne or Zeenat would react in such settings.

Before long, it was time to depart for Karachi and beyond.

Shireen and Bahram provided me with peace and privacy during the week I stayed with them before returning to England. It was during this time that I began drafting a paper on karez, the underground water channels in Balochistan that serve as lifelines for the Baloch and Pashtun people across three states. The intricate work of digging and maintaining these channels, ensuring they remain unblocked and protected against evaporation during the long, dry summer months, has been a longstanding communal effort. This work involves job distribution, maintenance, land allocation, and regulated water usage. My inspiration partly came from a paper on water resources in the arid Baloch terrain that I had read in Bath. It was strong in statistical data but surprising in its lack of firsthand experience—the author had never visited the region or spoken the local languages. Instead, a research assistant in Quetta had supplied the data to the London-based author. Given the global focus on climate change, the paper naturally attracted significant attention in academic circles.

In addition to gathering evidence on southeastern Balochistan from colonial gazetteers, revenue reports, land registries, and ethnographic accounts, I conducted interviews with several Baloch notables and writers in Karachi and Jacobabad. Abu also sent me old revenue records containing detailed information and hand-drawn maps of karez, meticulously drafted by patwaris who knew these details by heart. These records dated back to the sixteenth century under Sher Shah, the Afghan king of India. Later, the Mughals, the British, and successive Pakistani regimes updated them, adding information on landholding families, harvests, and revenue assessments.

In Karachi, I focused on my paper, which examined the history and political economy of this unique irrigation system. It emphasized traditional and successful conservation methods. Zeenat, ever supportive, kept a steady supply of tea coming and engaged me in conversations about Karachi's literary scene. She accompanied me on visits to Lyari, a predominantly Baloch area with a significant Sheedi population, street artists, lower-middle-class writers, and a notable number of Zikris—a Baloch community often misunderstood for their spiritual beliefs.

Our first visit to Lyari together turned into three as my interest grew in this diaspora community, now a hub of urban and regional politics with connections across the Gulf. We enjoyed street food at chai khanas, and I bought Zeenat traditional Baloch attire and jewelry at her nod, which she proudly showed off to Shireen. These shared excursions, alongside my academic work, deepened our bond. We often shared jokes while debating political views on Baloch leaders and Imran Khan. Zeenat, while admiring Khan's cricket career and charity work, was critical of his erratic politics and stayed away from cultist loyalty. We both agreed that the military should return to the barracks. Despite the self-serving actions of ethnic politicians in Karachi, Zeenat had no patience for so-called strongmen who were heavy on rhetoric and light on results. She was a democrat through and through, and I was captivated listening to her.

"How do you find time to read and think about all these diverse topics, Zeenat? It's impressive, especially given how active you are academically and otherwise," I asked, genuinely curious.

"Gul, it's because of your family's love for books and the encouragement I've received from your brother and sister-in-law here in Karachi. I also wanted to prove to myself that life doesn't have to be a monotonous routine, turning one into a robot. Exercise and intellectual discussions help keep me going."

She spoke with such passion that I found myself looking deeper into her beautiful almond eyes, framed by long, dark lashes. Her expressive face was illuminated in the morning sun, and her full lips moved rhythmically as she spoke with conviction. Occasionally, a breeze would push her loose headscarf back, revealing thick, dark curls cascading to her shoulders, which defied the floral silk cloth trying to contain them. With elegant, slender fingers, she toyed with a fork, picking at the carrot cake the waiter had brought with our tea. We both devoured it eagerly after wandering through the labyrinthine streets of the world's largest Baloch settlement. Walking beside her, I couldn't help noticing how her profile drew admiring glances, making me more self-conscious. Yet, despite her striking presence, she blended seamlessly into her surroundings, evoking memories of strolls with Anne back in Bristol.

"Do you see yourself as a civil servant, like Anjum, in the near future, or do you plan to pursue another profession, Zeenat?" I asked.

"I wouldn't mind trying my hand at the civil service exams to empower young girls in Lyari and Turbat. But honestly, I'd love to travel and write books like you. It's an honest confession, and even though you're only five or six years older than me, you're miles ahead in terms of scholarly work."

"Don't be too impressed by my apparent success. I'm still just a beginner on that journey. But what if Aunt Zahra gets you married off?"

"There are always hazards, and I would never defy my hardworking mother. But I'm determined to explore myself, see the world, and accomplish something meaningful before settling into what could become a rigid and monotonous life. Sorry if I sound non-traditional."

"Not at all, Zeenat. I admire your courage and passion to explore your potential without turning into a rebel. I'm sure Anjum and Shireen will support you wholeheartedly." Unconsciously, I held her wrist but quickly let go, realizing it might be seen as a transgression. She didn't seem to mind, as her expression took on an inviting glow. I wanted to continue the conversation, but we needed to head to Aga Khan University for my lecture that afternoon.

"Can I attend your lecture, if you don't mind, Gul?" she asked.

"Only if you're free and willing to risk being bored by academic rambling! I'm sure my hosts would be glad to have you, though I might discreetly request they keep you away from the refreshments—I wouldn't want you to see me devouring homemade Ismaili sweets."

She laughed heartily, revealing her shining teeth and the tip of her tongue caught playfully in a smile. "Let's get a rickshaw; I love those noisy two-seaters driven by the handsome Afridi Pashtuns from the Khyber." I hailed one, and we made our way to Liberty Books, where I wanted to pick up some Urdu volumes and check out new acquisitions in the humanities.

I bought a few fiction titles by Pakistani women writers for Anne, which were hard to find in Exeter, as she was planning to introduce a course on South Asian literature featuring classic Urdu poets like Mir, Ghalib, Iqbal, Shakir, and Saahir. I also picked up Destiny Disrupted by Tamim Ansary and Corelli's Mandolin by Louis de Bernières to gift Zeenat.

"I already browse your collection at home and appreciate this so much. I'd heard of these authors but never had the chance to read them," she said, her eyes lighting up.

"These other volumes are for Anne Sandeman, who teaches literature at Exeter and, like me, studied at Bristol," I added as we strolled out of the store on our way to the university.

"Her last name sounds familiar—Sandeman, as in Fort Sandeman. Is she related?" Zeenat asked.

"Correct. She's the great-great-granddaughter of Robert Sandeman, who spent his career in Balochistan during the 19th century and played a key role in establishing what became British Balochistan. He passed away in Las Bela, not far from Karachi. Sadly, Anne's father died of cancer not long after taking an advisory job in Dubai, and he never got the chance to visit Balochistan as he'd hoped."

"That's so tragic. It must have been a tremendous loss for Anne."

"Yes, she was devastated. Terence had only recently moved to Dubai when he fell seriously ill and was flown back in critical condition. Her mother, Susanne, who worked as a librarian at my university, moved to Exeter after his death."

"Do you think Anne might still be interested in visiting Balochistan? Some areas, especially ours, are quite restive at the moment, and the weather is harsh—we're the largest gravel desert in the world, after all."

"Deserts have their oases, and inspiring individuals like you, Zeenat."

"And like you, Gul. I'm sure our Punnu wasn't as bad as those Punjabis and Sindhis make him out to be while glorifying their Sassi. But as a woman, I should probably side with her over a fellow Baloch man. Yet, some exceptions do exist." She gave me a playful nudge on the elbow.

Zeenat was certainly not an ordinary person; she spoke her mind freely and with conviction. She embodied the best of both Africa and Balochistan, though I kept that thought to myself. It lingered with me for days until I boarded my flight to Istanbul, where I would change planes for Heathrow.

After returning from my travels, I focused on completing my research paper on karez, which, after revisions and addressing feedback from anonymous referees, was published in a leading North American journal. This achievement was followed by a seminar at UCL, where Anne accompanied me to London. We stayed at a hotel in Bloomsbury and enjoyed a brief picnic at Tavistock Square by Gandhi's statue. Our visit to the British Library coincided with a literature festival co-sponsored by the Jaipur committee, which gave us a chance to explore recent works in our fields. I was slightly rushed during the lunch break as I prepared for my seminar that afternoon. Anne noted that my presentation, rich with historical and technical details, resonated well with the audience, as evidenced by the engaging discussion during the Q&A. My former tutor was present and, after sharing his appreciative remarks, invited us both to lunch at the college the following day.

Later that evening, I took Anne to the Jeremy Bentham pub— after visiting Gandhi, it only felt right to pay homage to my old Utilitarian friend. Anne enjoyed the lively atmosphere of Bloomsbury and chose her dishes at Diwana in Drummond Street, though I quietly missed heartier fare like kabobs but made do with vegetables and daal. I must admit, their bhajis—our pakoras— were quite uplifting with their perfect blend of herbs.

Slightly tipsy, I updated Anne on the happenings back in Turbat: Anjum had been posted as the head of civil administration in Attock, and Zeenat, after her exams and interviews, had joined the academy for the country's foreign service. With her initial training in Lahore nearly complete, Zeenat was set to move to Islamabad for specialized induction and hands-on experience at the ministry. A promising diplomatic career awaited her, offering opportunities for foreign postings and interactions with diverse people—a remarkable achievement for someone from the backwaters of our province and a marginal community. Aunt Zahra, Nuzhat, and the entire family were ecstatic, as were her brothers in Oman and Peshawar. The Sheedis of Turbat were setting new benchmarks, even for the more self-assured Gichk is and Gashkoris.

Anne's desire to visit Balochistan had only grown stronger, especially since Terence's passing had left this dream unfulfilled. Since then, Anne and Susanne had made Exeter their home, though Susanne still visited Odense periodically to reconnect with family. With two scholarly monographs completed, Anne was seriously considering writing a historical fiction. Besides her connection with Balochistan and her friendship with me, Celestial Bodies had inspired her desire to visit Muscat and meet Jokha Alharthi.

"Gul, I want to visit Oman and Pakistan, and I'd love to see Iran, particularly Zahedan and Bam. I've heard so much about Isfahan and Shiraz; I could spend a month there. And, of course, I'd like to meet Anjum and possibly your parents, if that's not an inconvenience."

"No problem, Anne, but there are two caveats: we'll need to get time off from work, and we'll need to consider the weather. Balochistan turns into an oven during the summer, making travel difficult. My family would be thrilled to host you, but in Turbat and nearby areas, we might be perceived as a married couple, as pre-marital cohabitation is frowned upon in our culture."

"I'm unsure how to handle the second issue. What would you suggest, Gul?"

"I don't have a clear answer. I don't want to put you in an uncomfortable position just for the sake of convenience."

"Gul, to be honest, I wasn't in favor of marriage even before you shared your personal details with me. But I hate to think that I'm keeping you in a situation that benefits me without any commitment on my part."

"I appreciate your honesty, Anne. You're right—my parents and even Susanne might want us to marry for their own reasons, and those reasons are genuine. I don't want to trivialize their expectations, especially as we're not getting any younger."

"Since we've always been open about our relationship, which is what has kept it strong over the years, I should tell you that my mother wishes for me to marry and have children. I shared your medical history with Anjum, and she advised me to discuss it with you before talking to my mother. It's easier said than done."

"So, what's your plan? I understand your dilemma—being caught between parental love and personal freedom. My situation is clearer but no less ironic. I hate being seen as 'barren,' even though I love children."

"Staying honest is the best way forward, even if it's difficult. My being away from Turbat has helped me avoid the conversation, but we'll need to face this after our visit."

"How will you describe our relationship to your family?"

"Former classmates, now colleagues, friends, maybe fiancés—people who happen to sleep together but keep it private. Partners in obfuscation, if you will."

"That's quite the explanation! Let's head back to the hotel before I change my mind about the trip."

"No, we'll go together, even if it means practicing 'blatant hypocrisy' in Turbat."

"You're a ruthless desert dweller, Gul. But I'll come as myself, not as anyone's appendage. Remember, I have Sandeman blood, Viking spirit, and a touch of Jewish resilience from Susanne."

FORT SANDEMAN

"They're called Zikris because they chant hymns to Allah, the Prophet, and Syed Muhammad Jaunpuri, who claimed to be the promised mehdi, or redeemer, as Muslims call the figure who will appear before the Day of Judgement. Others might refer to this figure as the Messiah. Jaunpuri, a millenarian, lived in India during the fifteenth century, and his followers became known as Mahdawis. The Zikris are a splinter group, distantly related to the original sect. They gather annually during Ramadan and, along with specific communal rituals, engage in barter trade, arriving with their families and beasts of burden laden with harvests, crafts, and sweets for sale. It's reminiscent of traditional fairs in premodern tribal and rural societies," I explained to Anne as we made our way to Koh-i-Murad, a few miles outside Turbat.

"They're called Zikris because they practice zikr, or chant, which is a Sufi tradition," Anne noted. She was familiar with some Sufi tariqas that praise Allah vocally, with or without music, often accompanied by eulogies for the Prophet.

"To our ethnic nationalists, the Zikris are seen as the authentic Baloch, supposedly untouched by mixed marriages or urbanization. With their semi-nomadic lifestyles, they are perceived as a community in transition, lodged between their tribal origins and a rural present. Many now live in Lyari as laborers. Their dances, music, and tributes to Muhammad Jaunpuri—their saint—are frowned upon by puritans and have led to exaggerated rumors that place them outside mainstream Islam, which is untrue. Contrary to these misconceptions, their hilltop is not a separate Kaaba for pilgrimage; it's simply a sacred place for their annual gathering. To me, they're like Baloch Bedouins."

"I'm eager to see this sanctuary, Gul. It's likely that their poverty and dispersal over such a vast area haven't helped their cause. It's reassuring, in a way, that some nationalists claim them, which may offer some semblance of protection."

"True, Anne, but those nationalist claims can also put them at risk by overstating their influence."

Koh-i-Murad blended seamlessly with its surroundings, appearing as a typical desert plateau with gravel, mounds, and cacti, but it lacked trees and arable land. We spotted a mosque-like structure—the only constructed area—with a few berry trees, places for ablutions, and a mihrab facing Mecca. Copies of the Quran sat on a shelf, and earthen oil lamps meant for providing light in the absence of electricity. A solitary hand pump stood next to an open water trough, holding a small amount of water spared from evaporation. Inside the mosque and its square compound, about a dozen handmade mats spoke to the stark austerity of the site.

Climbing a hillock behind the mosque, we reached an open space resembling a large football field, where the Zikris would gather to perform their mystical rituals, cook, and engage in communal activities. Following our driver and guard, we removed our shoes; though Anne wasn't required to do so, she respectfully took off her Balochi moccasins. The ground, bare and rough with gravel and thorns, tested our feet, but we pressed on, taking in the strange, serene atmosphere. Aside from the lone caretaker, the place was empty, and the quiet was eerie, heightened by the setting sun casting its reddish glow across the horizon. The sun, though no longer burning, still resembled a giant fireball in the clear, expansive sky.

On our way back, we spotted a thin jackal and a couple of agile, fleeing buzzards, along with doves hastily feeding before nightfall. As we navigated a turn on the unpaved trail, a full moon rose from behind the hills, cool and silver against the deepening blue of the twilight.

I could see Anne gradually becoming absorbed by the rugged, mysterious expanse of Balochistan. Though often perceived as a desert, the region displayed an exceptional variety of geographical features. Our jeep ride on the newly paved road to Gwadar offered glimpses of a stark landscape punctuated by oases and small hamlets, while camel caravans moved parallel to the road, reminiscent of the tales of Sassi and Punnu or the saint who once sought refuge here from fanatics in Delhi and was protected by local nomads.

Gwadar and nearby Pasni had long sent Baloch traders and warriors across the Gulf to Muscat and beyond in search of opportunity. Some never returned, lost to the sea, while others came back with slaves and tales of the Arabs and Africans, whom they called Abyssinians. Despite being seen as nomads with little history or reach beyond their villages, these traders used camels and later dhows to venture into Persia and as far as Muscat and Salalah. These places, with their familiar landscapes and customs, mirrored the terrain they had left behind, even as their journeys were guided by fishermen and sailors heading to Basra and beyond.

"Geopolitics has led to an exaggeration of Gwadar and our coastal towns, contrasting with pundits who trivialize what you see here—where rough brown earth meets mellow blue sea, seemingly aimlessly. The Greeks halted here, their forces depleted after marching for hundreds of miles under a relentless sun. Spies like Masson and Burton disguised themselves in large white turbans, speaking Hindustani and Persian as they slipped into Persia and beyond. Cities like Kandahar, Kabul, Herat, and Balkh served as conduits for covert observations of Bokhara and Khiva, away from prying Russian eyes."

"That's quite some history, Gul, still largely unwritten. I can picture Paul Masson, like Jaunpuri, holed up in a Baloch village, jotting down his accounts of Harappa, Bagram, Kabul, Kandahar, and Peshawar while staying clear of the Company Bahadur he deserted, yet maintaining contacts with his former patrons," Anne said, her grasp of those early escapades as impressive as ever. "To reach India from British ports by circumventing Africa and the Sultanate of Muscat must have been an incredible feat for early colonials, explorers, or 'do-gooders,' as you call them, Gul." She was in a playful mood, still captivated by the determination of those voyagers who ventured out long before the steam engine or the Suez Canal, protected by the Royal Navy from marauding pirates.

"I'm sure those individuals—including the one next to me now—were motivated by all sorts of aims and ideals. Unlike many others, the British, blessed with knowledge capital and a sense of mission, destiny, and invincibility, undertook those extraordinary journeys," I said. "From wet Bristol, grey London, and overcast Glasgow, deciding to embark on a lifetime journey to distant and challenging lands must have been the boldest choice any of those islanders ever made."

"Those green and grey lands seem so far away from here—your khaki Turbat—though no less captivating. Perhaps the distance, heat, solitude, diseases, new languages, and landscapes dared Grandpa Robert and his kind to discover themselves. They were the Zikris of their time, only better equipped and more confident," Anne said.

By then, we had reached the outskirts of Gwadar, where well-paved roads, roundabouts, planted trees, and towering billboards marked the approach to the newer parts of the city. These developments overshadowed the fishermen's huts and the old town that seemed lost in time. We checked into a new hotel overlooking the Gulf on one side and the orange-hued mountains on the other. As evening approached, we walked barefoot on the warm sand. Anne, still modestly dressed with her head and arms covered, joined me as the sun began to set behind the hills, painting the horizon crimson. I yearned to plunge into the sea, away from prying eyes and the looming cranes and moored boats.

Anne's skin, now a coppery tan replacing her initial salmon-pink complexion, intrigued me as much as the moment. No place could be more enticing than this expanse where desert and sea embraced, miles from any human presence.

"Gul, this is magical. It feels untouched by modernity and human noise, though I know your Chinese friends are somewhere in their guarded enclaves," Anne said. "This place will be the setting for my next book. What's on your mind, Gul?"

"Just warding off some mischievous thoughts but trying not to be reckless."

"I appreciate your honesty, but I won't be writhing in the sand where the waves are breaking. The muslin clothes your mother gave me are comfortable, but I do want to dip in the sea. Here I go," Anne said, stepping into the water.

I followed, swimming a few yards beside her.

"Isn't it funny swimming fully clothed, Anne?"

"Gul, I noticed you tossed off your shorts before jumping in. My shalwar-kameez isn't stopping me from enjoying this warm, gentle water. Soon, it'll be night, and your Baloch moon will rise over the Arabian Sea. Until then, enjoy the moment, you rogue."

Before I knew it, I found myself holding Anne's muslin garments, which she had shed. I discreetly swam back to the shore, spreading her clothes over my own to dry. Though we were far from the hotel and port, and the dusk offered us complete invisibility, I still felt cautious. Yet, the isolation allowed us a moment of freedom.

"Gul, you can't see the different shades of my tanned skin; the darkness has its perks," Anne teased.

"But I can feel it, and it's as warm and welcoming as when a certain Englishwoman met a Baloch man years ago," I replied, pulling her close as our lips met, our bodies moving in a rhythm only we understood. The sand crested over us, and the waves caressed our feet.

"I feel so alive in moments like this, Gul. I wish I could give you a family, a train of children. Sometimes I feel inadequate, but my love for you is more than just physical. I adore your family and wish I could give back all the affection they show me."

"Anne, you're so much more than maternal potential. Our relationship is beyond that. Your wisdom, warmth, and humanity are deeper than the sea. And by the way, we should call it the Baloch Sea—our land is the largest bordering it, and Oman on the other side is part Baloch, even if only in spirit."

"Is it the pilgrimage to Koh-i-Murad that has made you more esoteric, or is it the hour, the place, and me?" Anne asked, a mischievous glint in her eyes.

"All three. Once we're back in Bath, I'd like us to visit Stonehenge. Maybe we could join the Druids for the Solstice; they remind me of our Zikris."

"Why not visit Salisbury and then Glastonbury? We might even find some Sufis there. For the music festival, we'd need to tap into Susanne's connections—she's quite resourceful with that sort of thing."

"Susanne's charm is disarming. We can count on her. But before that, we still have a couple more days in Gwadar, and I'd like to visit Jiwani, the closest point to Iran, before we fly to Quetta

Following another dip in the sea, we squeezed into our wet, sand-covered clothes and walked back barefoot to the hotel.

"You know, Anne, during the First Anglo-Afghan War, a religious leader of a Muslim denomination stopped here on his way to Bombay. He found India safer than his native Persia, and the British endorsed him as the spiritual leader of the Ismailis, even granting him the title of Aga Khan." After refreshing myself with some food, I had enough energy to share local history while the dining hall buzzed with a mix of Pakistanis, Chinese, and Arabs.

"The Aga Khan—now I understand that the title originated in India," Anne said. "These are your Shi'i Muslims who believe in a living imam, unlike some other sects."

"Exactly. Interestingly, an Ismaili entrepreneur owns this hotel, along with others in Quetta, Karachi, Islamabad, Gilgit, and Kabul. Sadruddin Hashwani is an Ismaili who, beyond his spiritual ties, sees great commercial potential in Gwadar."

Anne enjoyed the sun-drenched days by the sea, often stretching herself near the grand window of our room. The location was exclusive and private, affording her a sense of freedom. In the days we spent there, her skin developed a warm, even tan. This routine was briefly interrupted when we took a short trip to Jiwani, a border town known for its untouched beaches and a rare mangrove forest that stretched into neighboring Iran. Just thirty-five miles from Gwadar, Jiwani bustled with traders, anglers, and shopkeepers—a blend of African, Arab, Baloch, and Persian ethnicities.

We spoke briefly with border sentries, enjoyed kabobs and naans at a roadside café that served us complimentary Iranian salad and sweets, and took a short dhow ride on the Gulf of Oman. The sailor pointed out the Victoria Hut, said to have been built to welcome the newly crowned Empress of India. The Queen never ventured beyond Switzerland, but Curzon once made it to Pasni, another port town, which for a time was even called Curzonabad.

History, geopolitics, and trade intersected palpably here. While troops, traders, pilgrims, and traffickers pursued their interests, Western powers kept vigilant eyes on Iran, China, and Pakistan. Chahbahar, an Iranian port just fifty miles from the border, underscored the region's significance. But our priorities were different: we wanted to witness the breathtaking sunset at the westernmost corner of the country, where the air was clean, the sand was soft, the hilltops stood dignified, and the waves moved poetically. We lingered on a cliff, watching as the horizon shifted from gold to a soft rose, finally absorbing the sun. The place where the day's ruler rested seemed like the spot where earth and sky merged seamlessly. We stayed there long after the sunset, gazing at the sea that now mirrored the darkening sky, scattered with stars. The experience left us speechless until we returned to Hashwani's modern hotel.

A short flight took us to Quetta, a city shaped by human and geological upheavals. The devastating earthquake of 1935 almost obliterated it, and the events of 1947, along with the Afghan wars and the Iranian revolution, dramatically changed its demographics and urban landscape. Today, Quetta is a melting pot of refugees and ethnicities, a crossroads of Asia. Anne was surprised to see schools, roads, and hospitals still named after Robert Sandeman. The sight of Hazara Pakistanis in the streets also intrigued her; their ancestors had moved to Quetta in the 19th century to escape discrimination in Afghanistan and seek better economic opportunities. Quetta, predominantly Pashtun with a significant

Baloch population, has become a city of challenges, standing in contrast to its earlier identity as a hill station like Shimla, Murree, or Shillong, but with fewer trees.

"Are you ready for the 350-mile journey to Zhob, formerly known as Fort Sandeman, named after your great-grandfather? It's nestled right in the middle of Pashtun lands, under the Sulaiman Mountain," I asked as we navigated Quetta's labyrinthine streets.

"Absolutely, Gul. I'm fully recharged by the sun, the sea, the delicious food, and, I must say, decent company," Anne teased.

"With the new road, the trip shouldn't be too taxing. We could have taken the train to Chaman, near the Afghan border, but Zhob is just as close to the frontier. Abu, with his connections in the bureaucracy, has secured a reliable ride for us and arranged for our stay at the fort itself."

"I can imagine your dad being so well-regarded that even in retirement, his colleagues help out with logistics like this. I bet your mum has her own extensive social network, though Anjum would probably know more about that."

"Anjum is very much like Abu—firm yet friendly. I'm more laid-back when it comes to socializing, though there are exceptions," I said, playfully pinching Anne's arm with a wink.

Anne, through her prior readings, was well-acquainted with the history of our next destination. Zhob, which means "oozing water" in Pashto, lies beside the river of the same name and is watched over by its notable castle perched on a hill. The town has been known by various names, including Appozai, Fort Sandeman, and, since 1976, its current name. Robert Sandeman, son of a Scottish general, had served the East India Company during the siege of Lucknow in 1857 and was closely associated with prominent colonial officials like John Nicholson and the Lawrence brothers, who focused mainly on Punjab after acquiring it from the Sikhs in 1849. Sandeman began his service as a collector in 1866 in Dera Ghazi Khan, a border district in southwestern Punjab, which was predominantly inhabited by Baloch tribes such as the Mazaris, Khosas, and Lagharis. From his base near the Sulaiman Mountain, Sandeman negotiated with Baloch and Pashtun chieftains and maintained relative peace during the Second Anglo-Afghan War of 1878, even when the British faced a defeat at Maiwand.

Controlling territories that stretched to the Gomal Pass, Sandeman based himself in the castle built in 1890. He passed away two years later in Las Bela, after spending most of his active life in Balochistan. Known variously as governor, political agent, and lot sahib, he managed to keep his Pashtun allies in good humor during the Raj's aggressive forward policy towards Afghanistan and Persia, which later came to be known as the Great Game. With humor, bluff, and sheer audacity, the Raj maintained control, supported by improved communication networks like railways and telegraphs, an organized regimental system, and the weakened monarchies of Persia and Afghanistan. This ensured that British control over what became known as British Balochistan remained strong. Like the Khan of Kalat, the nominal head of the Baloch confederacy, the Emir of Kabul and the Qajar king of Persia were essentially vassals, similar to the 564 other rajas and nawabs across the subcontinent, until the seismic changes of 1947 redrew internal boundaries, leaving the external ones intact.

Quetta's bazaars offered Anne a vivid glimpse of the city's ethnic mosaic, with Pashtuns more prominent due to the influx of Afghans from across the Durand Line. Baloch, Hazara, and Punjabi communities clustered in their respective localities, while schools, universities, hospitals, mosques, hotels, markets, transportation hubs, and government offices brought them together. Despite their traditional backgrounds, many clung to their customs, languages, and clan identities, although the younger generation was gradually moving towards more fluid identities as they navigated increasing mobility. In my own family back in Turbat—hundreds of miles south in the heart of Balochistan—social boundaries were similarly shifting, creating opportunities and anxieties. It was no surprise that some resorted to ethnic identity as a banner of defiance, sometimes escalating into violence.

"Gul, I can see the difference between the Pashtuns and Baloch in how they wear their turbans and speak their languages.

Some of them seem bilingual and have a decent command of Urdu, which, along with shared geography, seems to connect them," Anne said.

"These are trans-Indus communities—the world's oldest surviving tribal formations—that have long fascinated anthropologists, novelists, and countless geo-strategists. Some writers argue that the Pashtuns have Jewish roots, while we Baloch are thought to be related to the Kurds. Why can't they simply be indigenous, without needing to originate from somewhere else?"

"Good questions, Gul. But you can't stop people from romanticizing. In the nineteenth century, Indians and the English were both claimed to be Aryans—an idea as far-fetched as the belief that Sanskrit is the ultimate source of Indo-European languages. Yet, those Oxbridge Indologists still attract a following."

When we reached Zhob, our conversation turned more specifically to Robert Sandeman.

"Anne, I wonder how Robert Sandeman spent his evenings, so far from any major city, worrying about 'things falling apart.'"

"Probably channeling that old American 'pioneering spirit,' I suppose," Anne said with a grin.

"He lived here, holding discussions with Pashtun and Baloch notables, drafting reports for Calcutta and Lahore while turbaned orderlies moved the big pankha and kept the flies at bay. In between, he'd sip his gin and tonic, taking breaks to play the piano."

"You want to relive Grandpa's life, don't you, Gul? I wonder how the Indian servants managed to carry him in a palki, given he was quite tall and stout!"

"Part of him lives through you, Anne. And now we're in the very room where he spent countless hours. The same room was later occupied by British and Pakistani officials. Reliving history is surreal; those distant olive trees may be younger, but the palms were likely here before your grandfather. Back in Kech, we claim our dates are the best in the world."

"Those dates certainly make Turbatis special, Professor Gul," Anne said, teasingly.

"When I was a child, our family believed that Harnai's blankets were the best in the world. The wool here had a unique quality due to the climate, terrain, and water from the Zhob River. You'd see Pashtuns carrying blankets on their shoulders in the bleak winters around the Sulaiman Mountain. Meanwhile, we Baloch favored cotton shawls, much like the Indus Valley farmers did. Even the Gandhara Buddha and Mahatma Gandhi wore simple wraps."

"Speaking of Gandhi, I remember from your UCL days that he supposedly experimented with sexual abstinence while sleeping next to young women."

"Yes, I heard that during a lecture by a Harvard psychoanalyst, though not in so many words. Who knows what he was trying to prove, if it's true. But should we defy the Mahatma's example in this king-sized bed, now that the air is cooler and the mutton karahi and naans have stirred up certain desires?" I asked, half-jokingly.

"I'd be lying if I said I hadn't thought the same, especially with all the organic food, unfiltered sunlight, brisk walks, and sea dips—all thanks to a Baloch academic who's equally at home in England's West Country and his native soil." Anne said, stepping into my embrace, her lips meeting mine as the Zhob River meets the Gomal. Our bodies, warmed by the evening air, moved in sync. Between pauses and whispered words, Anne asked, "How did Grandpa Sandeman entertain himself during long winter nights alone?"

"How could he be alone with all the power at his disposal, that Gora sahib? He played the piano religiously and knew this region like the back of his hand. I'm sure he must have had discreet liaisons, which other men likely accepted, given the awareness of his human needs," I said.

"A typical man defending his fellow species—that's what you are, my Baloch friend!" Anne teased, pressing herself against me on the sprawling bed. I responded, holding her tight:

"Reminds me of what Bob Dylan would say:

'How many roads must a man walk down

Before you call him a man?

How many seas must a white dove sail

Before she sleeps in the sand?

Yes, and how many times must the cannonballs fly

Before they're forever banned?

The answer, my friend, is blowin' in the wind,

The answer is blowin' in the wind.'

Anne continued with the next stanza:

'Yes, and how many years must a mountain exist

Before it is washed to the sea?

And how many years can some people exist

Before they're allowed to be free?

Yes, and how many times can a man turn his head

And pretend that he just doesn't see?

The answer, my friend, is blowin' in the wind,

The answer is blowin' in the wind.'

Together, we hummed the last stanza:

'Yes, and how many times must a man look up

Before he can see the sky?

And how many ears must one man have

Before he can hear people cry?

Yes, and how many deaths will it take 'til he knows

That too many people have died?

The answer, my friend, is blowin' in the wind,

The answer is blowin' in the wind.'

We found ourselves sitting on the edge of the bed, our earlier playful mood replaced by a quiet, reflective pause.

"I wonder how Robert Sandeman managed to get his piano all the way to this town," I mused. "Maybe it was shipped from Dundee to Karachi, then transported by train to Quetta and Harnai, and finally hauled 170 miles on a camel cart. The nearest train station in Punjab is 122 miles from Zhob. It's anyone's guess. Unfortunately, they removed it when some overzealous civil servant started renovating this castle, especially the residential quarters. They should preserve its originality, including that piano. And we probably shouldn't be frolicking here, even if one of us is his descendant."

"Gul, it reminds me of Chopin's piano that George Sand managed to transport from Paris to Majorca, though that was a shorter journey," Anne said.

"There are two statues outside this castle. The Gora figure doesn't resemble your grandfather.

"Anne, Major Barnes was once the collector here. Amid rising imperial revenues and directives involving the Khan of Kalat and the Emir of Afghanistan, the Kakar Pashtuns frequently resisted British control. They defied Sandeman more than once, as he often dealt with chieftains through threats and financial incentives. The ordinary Baloch and Pashtun peasants bore the brunt of this system of patronage. Sher Khan Jogezai even shot Major Barnes, and those two statues represent contrasting historical interpretations."

"So, the romanticized 'Sandemanian system' of pacifying the Baloch and Pashtun tribes—unlike the rest of the Frontier—is just a Victorian myth?" Anne asked.

"I'm afraid so. While patronage was framed with imperial and Christian altruism, it was primarily a means to maintain tribal hierarchies for peace and loyalty to the Raj. Figures like Sandeman, Herbert Edwardes, John Jacob, and John Lawrence perpetuated this approach. Sorry if I sound too critical or anti-colonial, but that's the nature of historical inquiry. Even Gandhi, the apostle of non-violence, is being sidelined in his own country by populist politics. And few today care about his celibacy, which we seem to be emulating here, Devon Professor," I added with a smile.

"I completely agree, including your selective Gandhian celibacy. There's no need to defend the Raj's shifting policies that alternated between romanticizing and vilifying the colonized, especially indigenous and tribal communities," Anne said.

We sat together, holding hands as the atmosphere turned pensive, our playful energy giving way to platonic comfort. We eventually fell asleep, wrapped in each other's arms, like the Zhob joining the Gomal downstream.

Early the next morning, the cooing of doves and chirping mynas woke us, though Anne mentioned that she'd already heard the call to prayer from a nearby mosque. Fully dressed, we enjoyed our breakfast of sizzling parathas and omelets seasoned with fresh, local herbs, washed down with milky tea. From the veranda, we took in the view of the sprawling town below and the green, oasis-like valley nestled within the arid, rugged landscape of Koh-i-Sulaiman.

"Anne, Koh-i-Sulaiman means 'Solomon's Mountain.' It's part of the reason people link the Pashtuns to the Lost Tribes of Israel."

"That might hold some truth, considering the exoduses from Palestine. Like others, Jews of the past likely moved eastward to avoid the Mediterranean, where their oppressors ruled," Anne reflected.

"Unfortunately, exoduses from the Holy Land haven't stopped; they've only increased in recent years."

"It's tragic. But now, I have some good news to share," Anne said, looking into my eyes. "I've been offered a professorship at the University of Southern Denmark, complete with benefits like sabbaticals, a housing allowance, and relocation expenses. I got the email while you were talking to the collector in the front room."

"That's fantastic news, Anne! It's a well-deserved acknowledgment of your expertise and your Danish roots. Congratulations! I wish I could get some champagne, but I won't risk any local brews, even though our bodies are now acclimatized to Balochistan's ruggedness."

"Thank you, Gul. I haven't made a decision yet. Leaving the West Country isn't easy, and neither is the thought of being apart from you—from what we share."

"Odense is Susanne's home, and Denmark ranks at the top of global quality-of-life indices. They probably don't have a spot for a Baloch like me, but if they did, I'd consider moving to Scandinavia. Then again, maybe I'm more at home in good old England."

"It's a big decision, not one I can make on a whim. I need to talk to Susanne and my colleagues in Exeter. They've been struggling with under-recruitment in the humanities, including creative writing, which isn't unique outside of Oxbridge and the Russell Group."

"Hans Christian Andersen would be delighted to have Susanne's descendant back in Denmark. But you won't leave until after my UCL interview and our visit to Gandhi's statue. For now, we should head to Quetta to catch our flight to Lahore tomorrow morning."

Anjum had reserved us a pleasant room at the Gymkhana, along with a packed itinerary of lectures, meetings, and dining experiences. Anne's initiation into the Mughal and colonial Lahore began with the Gymkhana itself, where the décor, golf courses, turbaned waiters, old hall with its piano, columned patio, and even some of the menu items evoked the bygone Raj. A stroll around the manicured lawns and the golf course reminded us that despite its harrowing pollution, Lahore still cherished its green patches. Tall trees hosted flocks of noisy crows, chirpy mynas, fierce kites, and curious falcons, all keeping a close eye on the ever-busy city. After a workout and an extensive swim, we settled into Caffe 9 to savor their mulligatawny soup, followed by spaghetti and meatballs. Anjum joined us for coffee after finishing a workshop at the civil service academy, which would be our destination the following morning before our visit to Aitchison College. Zeenat, who was completing her foundational training at the academy before moving on to her foreign service institution, came along with Anjum.

I was thrilled to see Zeenat: confident, poised, and strikingly beautiful, seamlessly combining her African and Baloch heritage. No longer a teenager, she was now a polished professional with an agile mind in a meticulously maintained body.

"This is Zeenat—a member of our extended family from Turbat. Zeenat, this is Anne, who teaches English at Exeter and has a close connection to Balochistan through her great-grandfather, Robert Sandeman," I said. My introduction was formal, but inside, I felt like the luckiest man alive, surrounded by three brilliant and captivating women.

"Anne, I've been looking forward to meeting you. I've heard so much about you from Anjum and was disappointed to miss you in Turbat because of my training here in Lahore," Zeenat said, holding Anne's hand. Anjum ordered cappuccinos and carrot cake as we settled in.

"That's very kind of you, Zeenat I thoroughly enjoyed my time in Balochistan. What a warm and hospitable place! My great-grandfather spent most of his life on that side of the Indus, and thanks to Gul, I've reconnected with my roots, even if they were imperial," Anne replied.

"My Baloch ancestors, like the Omanis across the Gulf, engaged in various enterprises and still recall their golden age under Mir Naseer Khan Kurd before Nadir Shah from Persia and Ahmad Shah from Afghanistan disrupted it," Zeenat said.

"Yes, our Baloch ancestors moved into Punjab and Sindh, and some of the largest landowners there are still Baloch. We, too, have imperial legacies, though our nationalists prefer to highlight victimization," I added.

"True, Gul. But my African heritage likely includes a history of subjugating weaker clans, only for Omanis and Baloch to gain the upper hand and sell them into slavery," Zeenat noted.

"We all have fluid identities, Zeenat. Look at me: my father's side is Scottish, my mother is a Dane of Jewish descent, and here I am reconnecting with my roots in Balochistan, surrounded by wonderful people—even if one or two are just bearable," Anne teased, nudging me and winking at Anjum and Zeenat.

"Mixed histories and fluid futures. That's what life is about, now more than ever," Anjum concluded.

As the three women shared stories about their university days, favorite authors, and musicians, I kept glancing at Zeenat. Her glossy, dark hair framed her warm, expressive face perfectly, and her brown eyes seemed as deep as the glacial lakes in the Karakorams. All eyes were on her as she entered, her regal, statuesque figure moving with grace and poise. Anne was enchanted, as I could tell, while Anjum's own intelligence and strength were equally compelling. Yet, with Anjum being my sister, my interest in Zeenat was naturally of a different nature, though not without complexity.

The next morning at the academy, trainee civil servants were intrigued by the presence of Robert Sandeman's descendant, engaging Anne with thoughtful questions that never strayed into criticism. Many, especially those from Balochistan, were curious about my research and teaching, but Anne remained the center of attention—a fact that Anjum and I admired. Zeenat asked me about my research on Balochistan's underground water systems in light of climate change and the spread of tube wells across the Indus. During a colonial-style tea session, served in fine china with Montgomery biscuits and pastries, Zeenat introduced us to her batch, allowing Anne to appreciate the group's diversity. Some of the women even shared their regret at not choosing academia, expressing envy at Anne's career as an academic and author who traveled freely, gathering inspiration for her upcoming fiction.

Our next visit was just across the academy on the tree-lined Mall Road. Anjum had arranged a ride and joined us on our trip to Aitchison College. This sprawling institution, once intended for the heirs of princely states, reminded Anne of Oxford's Keble College with its red-brick buildings, expansive cricket grounds, and extensive sports facilities, including horse stables and tracks. Here, students in starched turbans and college blues asked Anne insightful questions about her family, education, and recent visit to Balochistan—topics she had become adept at discussing.

The following two days were spent at Kinnaird and Government College, both established during the British Raj and known for producing some of the country's top scholars. The events were interactive and left us impressed by the students' caliber. In those two days, we chose to stay away from Lahore's upscale areas, dining instead in the Old City and visiting the Fort, Mughal mosques, gardens, and royal tombs across the Ravi River. Anne was entranced by the multi-layered history of Lahore but, like many others, concerned by its polluted, noisy traffic. We dined at a rooftop restaurant housed in a historic building, which offered a stunning view of the Lahore Fort and Badshahi Mosque under a faintly glowing moon.

With endless cups of karak tea at the Punjab Club, Gymkhana, and lively night spots in Gulberg, Anne immersed herself in the love stories of Punjabi folklore. She pondered the romance between Emperor Jahangir and Anarkali, and the mystical tales of Muslim Sufis and Sikh Gurus, which predated the East India Company and Presbyterian missionaries. Lahore, like Delhi, had survived repeated cycles of devastation and rebirth, showcasing an indomitable spirit that captivated Anne. I held her hand and admired her resilience, knowing our journey would soon take us back to where it all began.

Anjum, though not fond of gym workouts, compensated with brisk walks in Lawrence Gardens, Gymkhana, and the Punjab Club grounds, often turning them into jogs. Anne and Zeenat preferred running, followed by swimming laps. Once, they persuaded me to join them for a jog from Charing Cross to Gymkhana, passing Victorian landmarks like the Governor's House, Lawrence Hall, academies, hotels, and Aitchison College. Motorcyclists slowed down to gawk at the four of us in full-length tracksuits, particularly at Anne and Zeenat, who could easily be mistaken for African American. One cheeky rider shouted in Urdu:

"Bhai Sahib! Kiyya ayyashi. Do maghrabi, khoobsurat aurtain aapkay saath aur hum aik desi ko taras rahain hain." (Oh brother, what luxury! Two beautiful Western women with you while I can't even find a local wife!)

Anne sensed the humor in his tone, even without Zeenat translating. We laughed it off, sharing a moment of spontaneous, harmless amusement.

ODENSE

Shortly after Anne's departure for Odense, Gul moved to London, joining UCL—his former alma mater—after being recruited due to his strong research profile and a significant grant to study the qanat system and its potential revival in Balochistan. This was particularly timely, as Pakistan had become one of the most vulnerable nations to global warming. The country contributed only a minuscule share to global emissions, yet its glaciers were melting at an alarming rate, and cities were frequently shrouded in smog that threatened the health of millions across the Indus plains. Anne, who had taught in Devon for a time, left Exeter when the University of Southern Denmark (SDU) offered her a professorial position—a proposal she received while visiting Balochistan. By the time she returned to Exeter, under-recruitment in the humanities had already begun triggering job cuts across the South-West. With Gul's impending relocation to London, Anne's move to Denmark became the most practical option, allowing her to remain connected while advancing her career.

Odense, with its riverside walks, provided me a serene base for volunteer work close to both the University Hospital and the town's business center. Anne's transition to SDU was smooth, aided by the collegial environment of her department. However, I sensed Gul's wariness, particularly due to the growing wave of European populism that often targeted Islam. Since 9/11, certain politicians and media outlets had perpetuated the idea of Muslims as a demographic threat to Europe. Under the guise of free speech, provocative cartoons of the Prophet Muhammad were widely circulated, provoking resentment among Muslims and others who found such acts an unnecessary provocation. Figures like Geert Wilders, Jorg Haider, and Jean-Marie Le Pen exacerbated tensions by framing refugees as threats to European values—values that were never clearly defined but implied an inherent superiority over those seeking refuge from war-torn regions. Amid this turmoil, Gul was hesitant to extend his stay in Denmark, which unsettled both Anne and me. Europe had become an increasingly hostile place for immigrants, especially after the turbulence in West Asia spurred a steady influx of asylum seekers. Gul believed that Europe's long-standing hostility towards Islam had returned with a vengeance, never truly disappearing but lying dormant until reawakened by events like 9/11 and the subsequent migrant crises. To him, Britain offered more tolerance compared to the Continent, though Euroscepticism and figures like Nick Griffin, Nigel Farage, Tommy Robinson, and the English Defence League continued to stoke anti-immigrant sentiments.

Gul joined me in Odense, where we stayed at Susanne's welcoming home with its expansive lawn, extensive study, and multiple bedrooms. Before leaving Exeter, I had stored my belongings, as my flat was quickly taken due to the high demand for housing near the university. The day after our arrival, I borrowed Mother's bike while Gul rented one from a local shop, and we set off for SDU. The campus, a long, modernist structure with attached wings, was situated outside the city center, ensuring a safe and pleasant ride through the suburbs. Although my colleagues weren't expecting me until the following week, we avoided the department and instead explored the library, classrooms, and cafes. Unlike Oxford, Bristol, and Exeter, SDU had a distinctively modern and capsule-like design, though the students, lively and vocal, made us feel at home. Gul, who had little affection for concrete structures with low ceilings, wisely refrained from making critical remarks, though I noticed a flicker of disillusionment as he surveyed the endless, covered corridors. It brought back memories of his university in Bath.

Later, we shared a meal at Susanne's with her uncle and a cousin, a doctor at the nearby hospital. Our conversation spanned European politics, the Middle East, and the rise of right-wing populism. Discussing the 2011 massacre by Anders Breivik in Norway and the 2006 Prophet cartoon controversy—along with its resurgence in Paris—everyone agreed that freedom of expression had crossed a line, becoming disproportionately provocative. David, Susanne's uncle, pointed out that caricatures were often abrasive and inherently racist, though he condemned the violent reactions against Danish embassies and Western businesses in Muslim-majority countries. Throughout the evening, Gul remained reticent, which I attributed to exhaustion and the looming reality of our separation on either side of the Channel.

The following night, with snow gently falling, we headed to a cozy Lebanese restaurant facing Hans Christian Andersen's childhood home. Passing through the business district, we saw miniature Santas peering through elaborate Christmas decorations, their twinkling lights adding warmth to the cold air. The restaurant, run by a Syrian chef who had once worked in Aleppo, offered a blend of African, Arab, Persian, and Central Asian flavors. The chef had chosen Odense for its quieter pace, far from the hustle and bustle of Hamburg and Copenhagen. The place buzzed with diners, the atmosphere refined and carefully orchestrated, a stark contrast to our favorite Lahori eatery in Easton and the lively Diwana on Drummond Street. Susanne had invited Nasser, an Iraqi historian teaching at the university, who spoke about the subtle nuances between Damascene and Baghdadi cuisines. A Kurd from Mosul and an immigrant from Saddam Hussein's era, Nasser taught courses on Kurdish history, Iran, and the Middle East. He and Gul found common ground, discussing topics ranging from agriculture to urbanization and rural politics. It was heartening to see Gul animated and engaged, and I exchanged a knowing glance with Susanne, grateful for her thoughtful invitation.

Trying to add an academic angle to the conversation, I asked, "Nasser and Gul, I see many similarities between your communities, from names to shared vocabulary and their presence across multiple states. Is that enough to suggest a common origin?" Given my time in Balochistan and basic knowledge of the Kurds, I felt confident broaching the topic.

"Depends on what one is looking for, Anne. We share tremendously in areas like language, creed, political economy, cuisine and the demographic configuration of our respective communities divided into several states as are the Baloch though I may not be in favor of changing borders as that would only further destabilize an already fragile region. Susanne briefed me on your visit to Turbat and much more, the next destination could be eastern Turkey and northern Iraq though a factionalized Iraq and unstable Syria aren't happy reminders of the situation on the ground."

"Yes, Nasser, our British-Danish writer here can think of her next fiction focusing on your part of the world and I may benefit from a similar sojourn at places like Kirkuk, Mosul and Sulaymaniyah," Gul was not being outlandish, as Susanne backed him up: "Sure, as a non-specialist, I can still figure out Balochistan and Kurdistan resembling each other in almost every aspect and themes like political economy, irrigation system, local politics and relations with the neighbors can justify several comparative studies."

"Anne, I understand you're busy writing a novel on that part of the world. Can you give me an overview?" Nasser owed this inkling to Susanne.

"My fiction inducts Baloch, Omani and Persian characters within a larger Victorian context of the British empire where the latter is an instrument as well as a beneficiary and is using abolitionism as a moral justification to control the Indian Ocean. The plot revolves around an Omani character from Zanzibar, who is seeking retrieval of some recently kidnapped East Africans, apparently taken to Balochistan and in the process meets his future Baloch spouse, with whose help he retrieves three Africans from Basra. In the process, this resolute person must ward off chieftains and colonials all seeking their pound of flesh. Eventually, he discovers his own Baloch roots from Turbat, much to the amazement of all. Gul has a fair idea of the plot and remains a major influence and facilitator for this fiction. I'm still looking for an appropriate title."

While sharing this information, sub-consciously I sought some input from Gul, who noted: "I'm sure, Anne's novel will help us understand complex exchanges across the Gulf and beyond and, in a way, may move her readers away from the usual geopolitical preoccupation. She has completed the necessary groundwork which may guarantee her an eminent publisher and extensive readership."

"Finding literary agents is an uphill task since publishers leave initial screening to them and despite fiction claiming a lion's share in publishing, there aren't enough agents around." Susanne shared her first-hand knowledge of the industry, clearly driven by profit and competition.

"Sure, Mum. But despite all these bottlenecks both the US and UK keep publishing thousands of volumes every year, almost monopolising the entire business. The system seems to be working though remains affixed to bigger concerns," I slid in my assessment.

"Kurds and I'm sure, Baloch as well, are traditional people for whom story telling remains a favorite pastime but mostly it is oral. We have our own short story writers and novelists, but due to lack of translation, they remain unknown in Europe. Even though we have a growing Kurdish diaspora in the West, yet our literary representation remains almost miniscule." Nasser spoke with a tinge of dismay.

"I see more writings by Turkish authors, followed by their Iranian and Arab counterparts, yet Kurdish absence from literary scene is unforgiveable. Kurds appear only in political narratives and nowhere else, which is a travesty." I spoke emphatically.

"I guess one can say the same about the Baloch, Amazighs, Hazaras, Natives, Aborigines and the rest with several odds stacked against their creative efforts," Gul was not off the mark. "Though the way forward would be through undertaking local initiatives such as self-publishing using inexpensive organs of social media."

I could see Gul vibrant and vocal at the dinner with alacrity and humor somewhat restored. I enjoyed meeting Nasser and, in a way, felt relief over Susanne's socialization—a rebuke to her early life in Salford and even in Exeter that smacked of some provincial imprints though she enjoyed her job and outings in Bath. I needed to assume a similar path in Denmark while being away from Gul and England. It would not feel that acute if he remained in Odense helping me settle down in a flat and at SDU, but we both knew what our future held for us given our professional imperatives. Gul's estrangement, as I understood, accrued from this foreboding and let us admit it, from a Scandinavian context which hit him more than its English counterpart. After his initial enthusiasm back in Zhob, he did not display any interest in exploring teaching opportunities in Denmark though he admired the countryside, quiet neighbrhoods and English holding the forte across Scandinavia. Apparently, he was encouraging my move to Denmark but inwardly, he faced a gaping chasm. I too had retrospective moments, but any reversal was impractical given the squeeze on the humanities across the sector back in England amidst prospects for playing a formative role at SDU. Unlike my older bike back in Exeter that I had donated to a postgraduate student, my newer two-wheeler fitted in well with the thousands of its counterparts plying in and around Odense. Most students and the faculty lived in the town itself keeping the bike tracks busy and atmospheric.

Anne told me about a new colleague at her school in Exeter who had joined the archaeology department and was assigned an office next to hers. This proximity enabled them to meet in the tea lounge, where small talk eventually led to a proper conversation over lunch. As soon as Anne mentioned her visit to Balochistan with a Pakistani colleague, Lisa became more curious, and that is where my name came up. However, both academics, being smart, refrained from divulging their respective relationships with me. Lisa was intrigued by Anne accompanying me all the way to Turbat and beyond, though Anne left out the intimate aspect of our relationship that began in Bristol and continued since. Lisa, for her part, briefly mentioned knowing me from our time together at UCL but did not bring up our visit to the Peak District. Anne was intrigued since we had never discussed Lisa, though, to be fair, she had told me about her escapades with Boris and Grant back in Oxford. Her past liaisons didn't bother me, nor did she show any curiosity about my previous physical encounters. During her final days at Exeter, Anne didn't get the chance to probe Lisa further about our connection, and Lisa, now married, likely wouldn't have concerned herself with past romances.

It was after our first cycle ride to SDU when Anne unobtrusively mentioned Lisa during a coffee session:

"In the rush of events, I forgot to mention that just a few weeks before I left my job at Exeter, I met Lisa, a new colleague in the school appointed to teach archaeology. She specializes in ancient

Anatolia and is a former UCL graduate who said she knew you. Her husband still lives and works in London."

"What a small world! I met Lisa when I was at UCL. She worked part-time in the library and was planning a visit to sites in Turkey. That was ages ago."

"She came to Exeter from Norwich, where she taught for a few years while commuting from London, where her banker spouse is based. She seemed curious about my visit to Balochistan."

"Anne, I should've mentioned Lisa to you but somehow stayed reticent or didn't consider it relevant. I confess I've been less than honest, especially since, in the early phase of our relationship, you'd mentioned Boris and Grant. My apologies for being tardy!"

"I don't hold it against you, Gul, especially now when we're about to part ways after being so close for so many years. Your past relationship with Lisa doesn't matter to me."

"Lisa and I had several outings in Bloomsbury and even hiked in the Peak District while staying at her aunt's house in Eyam. We became physically intimate then, and that's when I, a Baloch, bid farewell to my long-held virginity. But after that, we went our separate ways."

"Lisa seemed like a no-holds-barred person."

"Yes, she was. But I regret not being more forthcoming about this past relationship, or whatever you'd call it, Anne."

"Well, the past is another country. There's nothing we can do retrospectively, though some early hints would have sufficed, especially given how close we've been for such a long time."

I held Anne's hand but didn't know what to say, and we both fell silent.

In the following days in Odense, a tinge of estrangement and introspection began to manifest, though with Susanne around, our mutual warmth would quickly return.

"Gul, I wonder whether you know more about Nasser and how he lost some of his family members in that chemical gas tragedy that Saddam Hussein perpetrated in the Kurdish area. His wife and their child were visiting her parents in Halabja in March 1988 when napalm bombs decimated the community, leaving Nasser a refugee in West Germany. It was slightly easier back then to find asylum. After studying in Bonn and Heidelberg, he taught at Hamburg before moving on to Odense," Susanne mentioned with a hint of grief and helplessness, reminding me of the infamous Halabja massacre. It had been reported in leading English newspapers in Pakistan, where readers generally sympathized with the Iranians following Saddam Hussein's invasion of Iran, which led to an almost decade-long war that claimed countless lives on both sides. For most of us in Balochistan, as elsewhere in the country, Hussein was perceived as being aided by Arabs, Israelis, and Western powers, resulting in both warring nations suffering immensely while igniting Sunni-Shi'i violence in Afghanistan and Pakistan.

"Susanne, those terrible years never seem to end, with two Gulf wars, continuous volatility in the region, and the outflow of millions of refugees—not to mention the emergence of militant organizations like Al-Qaeda and Daesh. Even my own province keeps paying the price with countless insurgencies that demand human lives relentlessly. Nasser is a survivor, though his conversation doesn't reveal any trace of bitterness."

"I refuse to believe that some population groups, like those in West Asia or Sub-Saharan Africa, are inherently prone to violence, as people like Geert Wilders, Tommy Robinson, Ann Coulter, and Robert Spencer try to force us to accept," Anne said with a hint of anger. "It's the geopolitics and economic deprivation that turn people into refugees, as we're witnessing right before our eyes."

On Susanne's recommendation, I chose an Italian restaurant and invited Ann, her mother, Nasser, and Astrid Nielsen, the chair of languages and creative writing at SDU. Astrid had been a student at the University of Edinburgh and had Erasmus teaching experience at universities in France, Italy, and Germany, which gave her a broad perspective on contemporary European fiction.

176

With Anne joining her faculty, Astrid aimed to strengthen the North American component of the department. Nasser's department focused on politics and fell within social sciences, but it was located next to Astrid's, and they knew each other. Nasser had been finalizing his second book on the Kurds in Iraq, covering the American invasion and the rise of sectarian militancy, prompting me to ask him about its content:

"I'm always curious about the Yazidis and their place among the Kurds, a fascinating subject for anthropologists. The world only came to know about them after the recent rise of Daesh. Do you include them in your study?"

"Of course, Gul. They've suffered for a long time. Although we identify them as Kurds, they share many similarities with their Arab neighbors. The name 'Yazidi' is both a misnomer and somewhat insidious, as most orthodox Muslims, especially the Shi'i, consider them heretical due to the association with Yazid, the Umayyad caliph responsible for the massacre at Karbala. This event, where the Prophet's grandson and his relatives were killed, holds significant historical weight. The Yazidis, who incorporate some Sufi and Zoroastrian elements, emerged during the thirteenth century amidst the chaos of the Mongol invasions and the Crusades, which fragmented Muslim sultanates in West Asia. Over the centuries, they often resisted Ottoman expansion in Kurdish regions. Daesh, being a Sunni organization, has persecuted the Yazidis based on misattributed prophetic traditions. Their plight after the fall of Mosul and Sinjar to Daesh became widely known through social media, raising serious moral questions about human rights. Amid this catastrophe, nationalist Kurds are now reclaiming Yazidis as part of their heritage. Apologies for the lengthy monologue."

"No need to apologize, Nasser. The threat to pluralism from so-called majoritarianism is a harsh global reality. Awarding a Nobel Prize to a Kurdish, Iranian, or Pakistani woman doesn't erase the harsh truths we face. In my region, for example, the Zikris faced backlash until a few years ago. Although it wasn't as catastrophic as what the Yazidis faced, it still involved significant persecution," I added, prompting Anne's sharp critique of double standards.

"Yes, during the 1990s, when Yugoslavia was in turmoil, Bosnian women were brutalized by their former compatriots. Cities like Sarajevo, Mostar, and Srebrenica endured years of suffering while military and political leaders simply pontificated. The UN, NATO, the EU, and Muslim rulers were content with issuing ritualistic statements of condemnation and did little more. Women's empowerment was used as a pretext to invade Afghanistan, yet after years of engagement, Afghan women, especially those in rural areas, are worse off, with many of their men either abroad or dead. It wouldn't be surprising if the U.S. and its allies eventually handed Afghanistan back to the Taliban. War fatigue is already palpable in Western capitals. Apologies if my statement seems steeped in despair," Anne said.

"Not at all, Anne and Nasser. You both speak for millions," Astrid said firmly. "In the post-colonial world, there is a profound disconnect between people and political leaders. While we can voice our dissent, we have more impact on domestic issues than on geopolitical ones."

Susanne observed the younger academics expressing their frustrations, while she and Nasser seemed resigned to the reality of international politics. Nasser refilled our glasses with Chianti as Susanne passed around pasta, fish cakes, and slices of olive loaf, calming our spirited discussion. Astrid expressed interest in my research and mentioned her plan to spend the next summer in London to complete her volume on literary criticism:

"I'd prefer to stay in or near Bloomsbury for easy access to libraries and bookstores. It would be helpful to meet academics from Birkbeck, UCL, and possibly King's College."

"Besides YMCA accommodations, you might consider residence halls in the area. I stayed at the International Hall eighteen years ago and found it both convenient and cosmopolitan," I suggested cautiously, not wanting to assume she needed advice. "Anne knows academics in Bristol and Exeter if you wouldn't mind traveling to the West Country."

"Former colleagues and teachers at both universities would be willing to help, though it may take some time to coordinate. But we can discuss it soon, Astrid," Anne reassured her.

Our evening, which began on a serious note, turned convivial as we settled into a more relaxed mood. The Italian espresso and array of desserts revived our spirits for a while before it was time to leave. Astrid departed on her bike, while Anne and I chose to walk, and Susanne caught a ride with Nasser.

"I'm glad to see Susanne and Nasser connecting," Anne confirmed what I had just suspected but hadn't voiced.

"They needed each other, and they deserve to be happy, just like anyone else," I said, squeezing Anne's hand.

Two days later, Gul boarded the train to Copenhagen to catch his flight back to Heathrow. A pall of sorrow and melancholy had pervaded their moods since their arrival in Odense a few days earlier. The warmth and spontaneity they had shared during their time in England gradually eroded, replaced by a growing sense of unease and dismay. Initially, both Gul and Anne attributed this significant shift in mood to exhaustion and the excitement of change, especially for Anne, who had left her colleagues and home turf. Yet, the feeling persisted. Gul sensed an ominous foreboding, as if the physical distance was initiating a looming separation. For Anne, this new phase in her career came with its own demands, presenting personal costs that now seemed starkly apparent. They spoke of continuity and consistency, but as worldly-wise individuals, they both knew that the departing train symbolized more than a routine journey; it marked a transition into the unknown. In Odense, they spent several sleepless nights tossing and turning, pretending to be fast asleep. Usually strong-willed, they now found themselves at the mercy of circumstances of their own making. Gul felt like a lonely leaf swept away by flash floods, while for Anne, the future looked bleak. Moving away from the West Country seemed like a long-overdue acknowledgment of a relationship that had stagnated. Life had to go on, even if love did not.

Their messages and daily conversations, slowly but steadily, began to lose coherence, underlaid with formalities and complaints about busy schedules and professional obligations. They missed each other intensely during the first few weeks, even to the point of feeling self-reproach for not staying together in

England. However, realism crept in, and pragmatism took hold. Anne started to enjoy the company of her new colleagues, including some Finnish and Dutch expatriates. Her students appreciated her teaching skills, Oxonian accent, and congenial accessibility, and soon, professional camaraderie replaced initial self-doubt. Occasionally, she met Susanne and Nasser for meals or coffee. Susanne had regained her old vibrancy and frequently visited the library to continue her research on Narayan. Nasser, too, showed renewed urgency in completing his book, and the two were often seen discussing their respective works in SDU's cafés or their favorite restaurants in Odense. On some weekends, they traveled to Copenhagen and Stockholm for theater performances, while Susanne's weekly visits to her Uncle David continued, his library being an added attraction for the aspiring author.

Anne's coffee breaks with Willem van de Graz in the staff lounge began to stretch longer. Willem, who was working on research related to Emile Zola and Albert Camus, was interested in Anne's literary ambitions and publications on American authors. He was curious about the influence of her travels on her fiction, which blended history, romance, adventure, and cross-cultural experiences within the context of the Raj. Anne's recently published novel Blue Waves, Brown Horizons had been named one of the best Christmas reads by The Guardian, while The Telegraph compared her work to that of John Masters and Ruth Jhabvala.

Willem, when not teaching or working on his next paper, dabbled in poetry. Even when translated into English or Danish, his verses retained their rhythmic quality, aligning with his laid-back, romantic disposition. While Anne was a skilled storyteller with her own flair, Willem was a talented wordsmith whose poetry showcased an exceptional imagination. Over the next few months, these literary sessions, often held off-campus, developed a regular cadence. Susanne was initially surprised by this growing rapport but was relieved to see her daughter happier and more settled. Gul never returned to Odense after that visit, spending his Christmas break in Oxford. Anne, in turn, did not express any desire to visit London to reconnect with Gul or other friends. Voice messages dwindled over the months, eventually giving way to emails that became less frequent. Susanne, having found her own joy after years of bereavement and retirement, appreciated Anne's connection with a like-minded colleague, recognizing that not all relationships needed to culminate in commitments.

At his alma mater, Gul's life grew busier. He secured grants and attracted postgraduate students, expanding his research focus to include workshops on non-irrigated regions in Punjab and Oman. He engaged in research visits and collaborations with subject specialists. His interactions with Baloch communities from both northern and southern regions broadened his understanding of their diversity, challenging the common perception of them as a monolithic group under the strong influence of tribal leaders. Unlike his native region, these areas had a burgeoning middle class where career ambitions and social mobility produced intriguing responses, often emphasizing religiosity over ethnic identity. Gul sent Anne a postcard from Muscat after attending a seminar at Sultan Qaboos University, where he met novelist Jokha Alharthi. She mentioned her next novel, centered around two Pakistani sisters and an Omani protagonist studying in Scotland and exploring cultural nostalgia. Gul recalled Anne's past interest in meeting Jokha, but that had been years earlier. Even after his return from Oman, he did not hear back from Anne. Time moved on, and past lovers, like the memories they carried, could not be held back.

Gul immersed himself in his work and took occasional walks through Tavistock Square, where the sight of Gandhi's statue evoked both smiles and pangs of regret as fleeting memories of Lisa and Anne surfaced, only to fade as the months went by. London absorbed him endlessly, acting as both a distraction and a remedy. Apart from infrequent conversations with Anjum and his parents, memories of Bristol, Bath, Exeter, Odense, the Peak District, and even Gwadar and Zhob retreated to a distant, obscure corner of his mind.

Anjum continued her career with the support of her husband, Nadeem, a civil servant, as they both held senior positions and decided to settle in the green, hilly environs of Islamabad. Bahram was briefly transferred to Lahore following a promotion but, along with Shireen, chose to remain in Karachi for easier access to

Turbat. They maintained their connections with Attock, and periodic visits ensured their sons stayed close to their grandparents on both sides. Zeenat, after a year at the Ministry of Foreign Affairs, was posted to Muscat as a second secretary until the opportunity arose for her to pursue a master's degree. This came at a time when Britain was slowly awakening to the pangs and anxieties of Brexit.

Gul had just returned from a meeting with a publisher in Bloomsbury Square, carrying a contract for his next book on Balochistan's political economy. He felt a mix of jubilation and introspection as he paused to pay his respects to the Mahatma Gandhi statue. His phone rang, and, with a sense of premonition, he sat down on one of the benches, bracing himself for potential bad news.

"How are you, Gul? I hope I'm not interrupting a class or meeting," Anjum's familiar, warm voice came through.

"No, I'm just in front of Gandhiji's statue in Tavistock Square on my way back to the office. Is everything okay with Ammi? I know she's been feeling a bit under the weather." Gul's voice held a hint of anxiety.

"Don't worry about Ammi and Abu; they're fine. They're visiting Bahram and Shireen for a few weeks, spending time with their grandsons. Nadeem, after resigning from his job, is now focusing on painting and plans to open a small gallery in Lahore or Islamabad."

"I always thought Nadeem was a misfit in civil service with his passion for art and his slightly otherworldly nature. His landscapes of Balochistan and Tirah are exceptional."

"Gul, I wanted to share some good news: Zeenat has earned a fellowship to pursue a master's in security studies at King's College. She should be arriving in London by late September. You'll need to help her settle in and adjust to her studies. Aunty Zahra insists on it, though we all know Zeenat is confident, outgoing, and independent."

"That's fantastic news! I'll do everything I can to help Zeenat, although she should probably stay in King's College

182

accommodations rather than renting a private place. Her accomplishments must already be inspiring many young people back in Makran and Karachi. I'm so pleased for Aunty Zahra and her family. Hard work really does pay off, Anjum, and it's all thanks to our parents for putting us on this path."

"Without getting too personal, have you heard anything from Anne in Odense?"

"Not really. Our relationship began to fizzle out after our return from Balochistan. It felt as if it had already reached its end. Anne's move to Denmark was partly due to job issues at Exeter and partly a search for her maternal roots, following a similar quest on her father's side. My own departure from Bath further cooled our closeness until it eventually faded into just a memory. It was a sad ending. It took me quite some time to regain my balance, and it must have been just as hard for Anne. I'm glad she has Willem, a Dutch colleague at SDU."

"Even from a distance, I could see you both drifting apart, though people in Turbat and even in Zhob remember her fondly. Mum confided in me that she was willing to accept Anne, even after you mentioned her surgery. Mum's feelings for Anne stemmed from genuine affection, her demeanor, and a motherly instinct for a near-perfect woman who couldn't be a mother herself."

"Anjum, we're so lucky to have parents whose sense of maturity and humanity surpasses conventional norms."

Gul walked into his office, buoyant on that September morning as the trees in Gordon Square began to take on a yellowish hue and the air felt fresh under the pale sunlight. It would be just two weeks until Zeenat arrived. He began to reminisce about their time together in Lyari, visiting cafés, bookshops, and street vendors, and recalled the gleam in her eyes after his university lecture when she expressed her desire to become a writer like him.

CHITRAL

While back in London, I continued reading appreciative reviews of Anne's *Blue Waters, Brown Horizons,* which praised her fusion of history and emotion, particularly her portrayal of the late Victorian era with Balochistan as the centerpiece. Her balanced depiction of the British Empire—neither wholly laudatory nor hastily dismissive—combined with her intimate understanding of locations and individuals in England and abroad, lent intrinsic validity to her narrative. The story seamlessly wove together themes of heroism and villainy, tradition and modernity, chivalry and modesty, all infused with romance and a subtle longing that never felt overbearing. Her diction exuded an effortless sense of confidence and spontaneity, the hallmark of accomplished writers whose works possess an enduring, independent life.

I reread her novel during a period when our communication had almost ceased, though without any bitterness. Anne had written me a detailed message about her growing relationship with Willem, which was not entirely unexpected. She had hinted at the possibility of their marriage, albeit with the caveat that Willem was adamantly opposed to raising a family. Similarly, Susanne and Nasser were practically living together, finding companionship more important than formalizing their union. Susanne, in fact, never lost touch with me, and our sporadic correspondence retained the warmth I cherished. Beyond some obligatory updates on Anne's well-being, we avoided discussions of nostalgia, loss, or other unwelcome topics.

My life, marked by a workaholic streak—professionally enriching yet socially isolated—began to feel monotonous until I decided to attend events beyond the academic realm. I started going to political rallies and public lectures by prominent dissenters like Noam Chomsky, Ken Livingstone, Jeremy Corbyn, and Tariq Ali. Topical issues such as refugees drowning in the Mediterranean, Brexit, the plight of the Rohingyas, drone strikes in Afghanistan and Pakistan, the war in Yemen, Israeli incursions in Gaza and the West Bank, and climate degradation transformed me into an academic activist. I began socializing with cosmopolitan, justice-driven individuals rather than remaining a passive observer or keyboard warrior. After lectures at SOAS and rallies in Trafalgar Square, some of us would gather in cafes and informal bars in Soho or Bloomsbury, debating global conflicts and the manipulative power elite.

At one of these gatherings, I noticed a woman in her late thirties, a Palestinian keffiyeh draped around her neck. She appeared more European than Middle Eastern, with green eyes and dark hair framing her slim, oval face, always lit up by a refreshing smile. Her interventions were fluent, delivered in a medium pitch, clear and succinct, often calming the fervent discourse, particularly among younger participants who were brimming with idealism and liberal ideas.

"Hello, I'm Gul from UCL. I've attended a few meetings recently and thought I'd introduce myself," I said.

"Oh, hello. I'm Esther. I'm currently between two countries and still undecided about where to pursue my doctorate," she replied.

"Well, I'm local, stationed here for quite some time. I teach and write but have been looking to break out of the mundane academic bubble."

"So, you're a professor, right?" she guessed.

"Yes, I dabble in sociology, politics, and some history, focusing on Southwest Asia, particularly Balochistan and the northern Indian Ocean."

"I taught at Hebrew University while working on my doctorate about Arab women in Israel, which places me in the field of sociology. I'd love to learn more about the Baloch people. They're academically overlooked, with most scholarship focused on Iranians, Arabs, and Pashtuns, which often centers on geopolitics," Esther said.

"You know how academic disciplines prioritize certain subjects. I know little about Arab-Israelis, especially women. They seem almost invisible, overshadowed by geopolitical narratives that frame Israel as a confessional state, where the outside world mostly hears about Palestinian Arabs as refugees or the besieged populations of the West Bank and Gaza."

"You're right. Under leaders like Ariel Sharon and Benjamin Netanyahu, Arab-Israelis became even more marginalized, and that suits the settlers just fine. That's partly why I left. And here I am, attending protests before I head to the U.S. for further studies. Reverse migration, Professor Gul!" she added with a smile.

"I'm sorry you felt the need to leave your home country. Populism is spreading across Europe and North America, exploiting issues like religion, immigration, race, and culture to marginalize people. Ironically, these same groups are essential for running vital sectors like healthcare, agriculture, transport, and services."

Our conversation continued as people began to trickle out of the café, heading their separate ways.

"I'm heading back to Gower Street to get back to work if you're walking that way, Esther," I offered.

"Sure, I'm planning to catch the tube from Euston station toward Finchley."

"I live in St. John's Wood, halfway to where you're headed, but I need to be back in my office for a tutorial. Let's meet again, maybe at another rally or sooner!" I suggested.

"I've heard about Jeremy Bentham's preserved presence at UCL; I'd love to take a stroll there sometime."

"Let me know when you're in the area, and I'll give you a tour." I shared my contact information with Esther.

As we parted near the college entrance, I stole a fleeting glance at Esther's profile. She was tall and athletic, as though growing up on a kibbutz and undergoing strict military training had contributed to her agility. I quickly felt awkward for lingering longer than was acceptable.

Summer is the time when academics often travel or engage in research, though those few weeks seem to pass too quickly. Aside from doctoral supervision and resits, I adhered to a strict routine of working on my ongoing research, spending almost every day in my office. I emerged only for brief breaks or when I needed to visit the British Library or SOAS to skim through some theses. Just two days after my conversation with Esther, she called to check my availability, and within an hour, we were meeting at the same spot where we had last parted. I led her through the labyrinthine corridors and staircases of the main building, pausing for a photo with the contemplative Jeremy Bentham at his relocated position, before heading to the library. There, a colleague briefed us on the archival holdings, particularly the collections on the slave trade and plantations in Mauritius and the West Indies. UCL's significant project on slavery had led to an expanding historiography and numerous dissertations, with high demand for digital access.

"Since I left Israel, I'm thinking about changing my research focus. I might study something related to the slave trade, especially since I plan to settle in the U.S. What do you think, Gul?" Esther asked.

"It makes sense, Esther. You could pursue both areas in parallel. Your work on Arab women could yield research papers, while a gender-focused examination of slavery-related archives could be your doctoral topic. Or you could do a comparative analysis using case studies. It depends on where you're institutionally based and how you develop your research focus. Let's grab some sandwiches, and we can continue this discussion in my office. Just a warning—it's a bit chaotic due to my disorganized nature."

"Sure, sandwiches sound great, as long as they're halal." She nudged my shoulder with a mischievous smile, and for a moment, I couldn't tear my eyes away from her lips, which, even without makeup, looked invitingly soft.

"I was actually considering a ham sandwich," I joked, nudging her upper arm in return.

"Go ahead, Professor. We'll just close our eyes and let the haram meat do its thing," she said with a playful grin.

We walked back to the quad, holding our warm paninis filled with Mediterranean vegetables, tuna, and corn.

"I have a kettle in my office unless you'd prefer to visit a café later," I said.

"That'll do for a cuppa. I don't want to take up too much of your time, Gul."

"Very considerate of you. I can spare some time for a fellow émigré academic."

"I like that term! But you're an émigré academic too. That makes two of us, although I'm still striving for a doctorate."

"You've got a brilliant mind and lovely, lush brown hair. I wish I could get back some of my hair—my doctorate took its toll," I joked.

Esther settled into a side chair, glancing at the wall hangings that featured maps, pictures from Turbat and Zhob, and a group photo of Joe and our class outside The Hawthorns in Bristol. She asked a few questions about the people and places, but her curiosity was polite and not overly intrusive.

"Turbat and Zhob have their parallels with some areas in Israel-Palestine, and your turbaned, bearded folk remind me of our traditional Talmudic elders, as if they'd just left Moses behind in the Sinai Desert to finish his conversation with the Almighty," she remarked.

"Yes, our Baloch and Pashtuns do get categorized in some intriguing ways. Even the Sikhs in Punjab resemble their Abrahamic counterparts. But in today's conflicted world, most of us focus more on differences. How do you take your tea, Esther?"

"Two spoons of sugar, no milk. Don't forget—I'm a Middle Easterner. No milk in my tea, please."

"I've got some McVitie's biscuits somewhere. I keep them around to appear hospitable to visitors. Ah, here they are. Sorry, the packaging's a bit crumpled—like me."

Our conversation meandered through her research and teaching in Jerusalem, the Bedouins, settlers, and the rise of the populist Right. I shared an overview of the qanat systems, demographic divisions of Balochistan, and the grim state of the humanities in the West. Esther expressed concern about the minimal interaction between Jews and Arabs in Israel and the shrinking civic spaces on both sides, weighed down by history and geopolitical tensions. We didn't linger on those topics for long, though humor and lightness soon returned to our discussion until it was time for her to leave. We planned to meet again over the weekend—her last in London.

Esther's ease was apparent from our first meeting at the café, and it was reaffirmed during her visit to my college. We spoke as if we'd known each other for years. Her independence was rooted in strong self-confidence and a humanist worldview, particularly in her support for the marginalized. She critiqued her homeland's policies but didn't absolve the Arab elite, who often oscillated between victimhood and self-righteousness. Her solidarity was with ordinary people whose struggles, especially in refugee camps, reminded her of the Jews in ghettos during the height of European fascism. Esther reminded me of Lisa with her warmth and authenticity, but in terms of mental acuity, she resembled Anne, possessing intellectual strength born of originality and instinctive wisdom. Our shared appreciation of food and wine was interspersed with lively discussions and a blend of seriousness and humor, ensuring that no moment was monotonous.

As I later discovered, Esther was in no rush to leave my apartment, having already informed her cousin of the possibility of spending the evening away. I came to realize I was speaking with a mature and astute academic, one who possessed a donnish aura yet remained natural and unpretentious. Despite being at least six years my junior, Esther held her ground with ease, exuding a joyful and daring energy that matched mine. Our moments of intense physical connection extended into endless serenades where gestures took precedence over words. Occasionally, we would drift to the kitchen for snacks, but sleep was a distant thought amid the electrified, nearly insatiable chemistry between us. The months I had spent isolated in archives, seminars, and lectures dissolved as I gazed into her deep green eyes, which accentuated the allure of her oblong face, now flushed with sweat and vitality.

"Gul, how did we rush into this intimacy so quickly?" she asked, a hint of wonder in her voice.

"Perhaps we were walking parallel, arid paths for so long that, when we finally met, our bodies and souls craved closeness, letting instinct take the lead while rationality and logic stepped aside."

"That's an apt way of putting it. My brief detour in London only quickened these urges, and I'm not complaining. I'm cherishing these moments."

"Thank you, Esther, for breaking the monotony and professional routine of my life."

"I know the grey English clouds will soon part for your lime sun, and I'll have to go. But I'll remember this time with laughter and warmth."

"I admire your honesty and courage, but I feel somewhat inadequate knowing I can't prolong your stay."

"Maybe it's best for both of us to continue on our separate paths, even if we revisit these moments in our solitary reflections with a smile. Hold me tighter for the rest of this special night, and let me run my fingers through your greying sideburns. But let's not talk too much."

I made sure Esther did not leave without a brunch as the morning light grew brighter. I stood by the window, watching her cab pull away toward Golders Green, replaying her parting words as she confidently walked to the door. "Travellers meet to part. Our paths may or may not cross again, but before we're Jewish, Muslim, or any other label, we are simply human—filled with intent, content, and dissent. The world can only be more peaceful if we keep talking to each other."

"Humans may look or sound different, Esther, but beneath it all, they share the same soul, yearning to break free from barriers. Farewell, traveler. Don't forget to send a line or two from your future home." After a long embrace, I stood at the open door, listening to her footsteps fade away, though her scent lingered in the air, refusing to leave my breath.

Esther was a breath of fresh air that reinvigorated me at a time when, without realizing it, I had become an escapist, using work as an alibi. To be honest, my work was monotonous, and the lack of socialization had dulled my enthusiasm. The separation from Anne, and even from Susanne and Bath, had left its marks during that taxing period. In my heart, I was grateful to Esther for reigniting my social instinct and vivacity, which had lain dormant, much like Bentham's lifeless effigy sitting in UCL, endlessly watching the corridors fill and empty until late at night when security staff came to lock the heavy wooden doors and ensure that loners like me had finally departed for home.

A newfound excitement stirred within me for the approaching academic year, and I wondered how Zeenat would find me after so many years apart. She had remained single, often engrossed in her job and travels, while also helping her brothers settle. Despite her commitments, she found time to mentor younger students in Lyari and Turbat during her visits south. According to Anjum, Zeenat had recently completed a short assignment at the UN, where she impressed her peers with her discipline, diligence, and eloquence. She often surprised African and Western diplomats when introducing herself as a Pakistani diplomat; her appearance and demeanor defied their preconceived notions of what a person from Pakistan looked like. To be fair, even within Pakistan, many were unaccustomed to seeing someone like her, especially since most traced their origins to Central or Western Asia or the Indus valleys, often unaware of the historical connections the southern regions had with distant lands. The waters of the Indus and Ganges may flow beyond Mauritius, but so too do the people and ideas, carried by the tides or driven by necessity. Slaves, pilgrims, indentured laborers, construction workers, and others bear the burdens of history across the Indian Ocean, which, like the Atlantic and the Mediterranean, hides the graves of countless bones and unfulfilled hopes within its irredeemable depths.

Activism, increased socialization, and reworked course modules revitalized me as Anjum informed me of Zeenat's upcoming arrival at Heathrow, requesting that I meet her in person. Naturally, I was eager and curious, having not seen her in quite some time. In my solitary moments, I thought of her, of Turbat, and of the Sheedis in Lyari, especially as reports of the disappearances of Baloch youths from their homes and universities at the hands of security agencies continued to surface.

Some never returned, and in a few tragic cases, their mutilated bodies were hastily buried in desolate places, only deepening the rift between the military and the people. I struggled to comprehend the rationale behind such heavy-handedness that alienated an entire generation, though I did not condone the armed actions of activists that targeted ordinary soldiers, Punjabi laborers, and office workers.

My parents had moved to Karachi, not far from Bahram and Shireen, who, along with Anjum, often voiced their frustration at the endless cycle of violence that left everyone feeling trapped. Some of my acquaintances had relocated to London and Switzerland, from where they occasionally made unrealistic demands for an independent Balochistan, as if partitioning three nations with pluralistic communities into separate enclaves would be an effortless endeavor. The reductive thinking on all sides only led to more bloodshed. Mutual negotiations, decentralization, and the empowerment of civic institutions, supported by development initiatives, seemed to me the only viable path forward.

Being a Baloch academic in London, amidst a diaspora with its own expectations, was a delicate balancing act. My approach of maintaining a detached stance—without appearing in different—helped me stay grounded. I attended seminars and intense discussions in West London and at the YMCA on Great Russell Street, but I carefully avoided providing financial or material support to militant groups. At these rallies, I often noticed non-Baloch attendees who preferred to remain silent, whispering only in the corridors with the organizers, as if these gatherings were peppered with agents with their own agendas, ample funds, and discreet recording devices.

Zeenat had lost none of her ebullience, though it was now tempered with the diplomatic finesse and vigilance that her position required. Yet, her physical charm remained undiminished; if anything, she appeared even more confident and youthful. In contrast, I felt somewhat worn down by the events since Anne's departure from England and my life. Esther had reawakened parts of my dormant self, but I was still trying to find my footing.

After settling into her spacious room in the college accommodation across the Thames and familiarizing herself with the neighborhood's shopping and transport connections, Zeenat started her semester in earnest. Her schedule quickly filled up with seminars, library visits, tutorials, and welcome events. I mostly let her explore the academic and social aspects of her program independently, joining her occasionally for lunch or coffee in the Strand or at the café in the LSE. Our walks across the Waterloo Bridge, past Bush House, and through Covent Garden often attracted curious glances, particularly at Zeenat. My Asian features were familiar and obvious, but her tall stature, olive complexion, almond eyes, wavy hair, and balanced figure exuded a distinct grace that made people wonder about her background.

"Gul, yesterday I attended a samosa-chai party organized by Pakistani students. I introduced myself as a newcomer from Islamabad, and many seemed unsure, as if they thought I had come from North America. When I spoke Urdu, they looked even more puzzled until a fellow from Karachi struck up a conversation. Tariq, in his unique way, explained how Pakistan's pluralism is often unknown even to its own people, with Karachi being the exception, where various ethnicities interact daily."

We stood by Lincoln's Inn Fields, unsure of where to go for lunch. This was just a few days after Zeenat's arrival in London, following her induction and orientation activities.

"Zeenat, your presence is a learning experience for many people, both here and back home. The more you engage with them, the more they'll learn. Even I encountered surprise at meetings in West London when Baloch dissidents realized that the Turbati author among them was also an academic."

"Yes, I enjoy seeing people try to place me into familiar categories, and that happened briefly at the Pakistani diplomatic mission in Lowndes Square. The receptionist seemed confused when matching my name with my appearance until he checked the message from a senior official allowing me in. With so few women in such positions, I don't hold it against them."

"That's why it's important for more women to pursue these roles and sustain them, even if they get married and have children. Sorry for sounding prescriptive!"

"I agree, although in my case, that chapter is either yet to come or has already passed. But I don't regret being single. Do you?"

"I can understand the pressure, but there's a balance between marriage and remaining single, if those are the only two options. Some people are happily married for decades, while others withdraw into themselves after minimal social interaction. There's a thin but significant difference between being a bachelor and being single, or between being celibate and otherwise."

"That's an interesting dichotomy. What do you mean by 'otherwise'?"

"I knew you'd ask that, Zeenat. Some people—both men and women—pursue intimate relationships without intending them to lead to marriage. They don't have to be voyeurs but can enjoy the connection fully, accepting any outcome, including separation. Yet, each relationship leaves its own wreckage that requires immense effort to recover from. That's why some people prefer to stay single—to avoid the fallout. But that shouldn't be a reason to avoid seeking closeness."

"It's sobering to hear, and it sounds like the perspective of someone who has experienced it. But what about those who never have intimate relationships, whether because they're too busy or because others feel inhibited around them?"

"I can't speak for such cases, where work, introversion, or fear of rejection holds people back. But on another note, we can pick up lunch on our way to UCL, if you'd like to explore my neighborhood in Bloomsbury."

Intentionally, I bought vegetarian baguettes from my favorite kiosk in Brunswick Centre before we settled on a bench in Tavistock Square after a brief namaste to Mahatma Gandhi.

"Now I see why you chose vegetarian lunch," Zeenat said. "We Baloch usually prefer meat, but this is in deference to Gandhiji, isn't it? You like making people happy, Gul, even though you keep a tough exterior. Is it a defense mechanism to avoid closeness?"

"Zeenat, I think you need to unlearn this candid approach with a Baloch man. But for Mahatma's sake, I'll let it slide before you start shouting about domestic abuse," I replied with a mischievous smile, unconsciously holding her left hand.

"Buying me lunch doesn't give you a free pass, Gul. I don't need Anglo-Saxon laws to protect me; my African and Baloch heritage is strong enough to fend off any offense." Zeenat pulled her hand away but then wrapped her arm around my back. I saw a rare blend of affection and friendship in her eyes, something I hadn't experienced in a long time. We stayed in that moment for a while before continuing our walk at a slower pace, reluctant to end the time too soon.

"I think that light lunch deserves a sweet treat to go with your coffee," I suggested, guiding Zeenat to George Farha Café on Gower Street, where she chose a slice of carrot cake while I opted for a Danish pastry. We both ordered Americanos. Navigating through the corridors and marble halls of the main building, we took the small elevator up to my office.

"I like the ambiance of your office with its marble walls, heavy wooden door, and solid furnishings. It suits your exterior, Gul. They must value your scholarship here. I'm sure it was just as good in Bath, though I understand you lived in a more working-class area in Bristol," Zeenat said.

"So, you've gathered all the details of my academic journey over the past two decades. Like Gandhi, I arrived at UCL first and spent some of my best years here. Now, they've brought me back. You could say it's loyalty on both sides!" I replied.

"It's been an enviable journey, Gul."

"Bristol, more than Bath, exposed me to a different side of England. I lived in a working-class neighborhood with a leftist historian as a housemate. John Gallagher practiced what he preached, and one of his books has been translated into twelve languages."

"Bristol is considered the gateway to the South-West but has a dark past linked to the slave trade. Still, it's a beautiful city, and I'd love for you to show me around sometime. It could help you relive your memories. I wouldn't mind visiting Bath either, with its Roman and Georgian heritage."

"You're already planning ahead, Zeenat. Sure, we can explore the West Country during your Christmas break. Bristol has moved on from its infamous past, though Bath is more picturesque yet less diverse."

"I should head back to my place and prepare for my classes and seminars starting next Monday."

"I can walk you to the tube station. Keep next Friday evening open for dinner. I could cook for you, but I'm afraid my skills might reveal my inexperience. We can eat out instead."

On Friday, I met Zeenat at the porters' lodge on Gower Street, and we strolled to the nearby pub where Jeremy Bentham's likeness—bearing an uncanny resemblance to Benjamin Franklin—watched over the patrons with a perpetual smile. The pub was filling up with students, faculty, medical staff, and familiar locals, though the queue at the bar wasn't too long. The bartender handed us two glasses of lemon soda.

"Zeenat, I'm not a teetotaler, so don't get the wrong idea. I just don' feel like drinking tonight," I said.

"I'm flexible, but not much of a drinker myself. Some of my colleagues back home made a show of their access to alcohol, which put me off a bit. This South Asian obsession with whiskey and vodka doesn't appeal to me."

"The lack of wine options is part of the reason behind the binge-drinking culture. Local beer isn't bad, especially in the summer, but it's pricey, and societal norms on abstinence play a role too."

"People here drowning in pints could be the flip side of the same phenomenon. For younger people, it's a way to socialize. The residence hall where I stay, which is mostly populated by postgraduates, has a visible wine culture—bottles clinking, corks popping, and bins filled with Italian, Chilean, and French labels."

"That reminds me of my own time in London and later in Bristol. Here, beer was king, while the West Country drew me into a wine culture. I still miss my lunch breaks and coffee sessions at The Hawthorns with Joe's class. He wasn't a conventional academic; his literature class expanded our perspectives far beyond Anglo-Saxon boundaries."

"Gul, I sense some nostalgia for Bristol in your voice, even though people often romanticize London, Oxford, and Cambridge—the so-called golden triangle. Was it just Joe and John, or was there more to it?" Zeenat's eyes sparkled with curiosity, framed by the warm glow of the pub's lights and the rows of ornate bottles behind the bar.

"Yes, I see where you're going with this, inquisitive diplomat! I met Annette Sandeman in Joe's class. She was from the West Country and had connections to Balochistan and Denmark. You can guess the rest. I'm not running from that past, but let's move on. I've booked a table at Shiraz by Lord's Cricket Ground for 7 p.m. I wanted you to meet Jeremy Bentham here since you've already paid your respects to the other notable figure in Tavistock Square."

The taxi ride to the Iranian restaurant was brief. The place was lively with diners, but Asghar, the manager, had reserved a quiet corner for us. He knew me from my regular visits and from his past academic tenure at UCL. On quieter nights, he would join me and recite Persian poetry, knowing my interest in Khayyam, Hafiz, Rumi, and Saadi—the classical poets. Our shared passion extended to Indian poets like Bedil, Ghalib, and Iqbal.

"Asghar, this is Zeenat from Turbat, my hometown in Balochistan. She's studying at King's College. Zeenat, meet Asghar, originally from Isfahan and a UCL alumnus. His hospitality and love of Persian poetry often bring me back here."

"Good to meet you, Zeenat. I wish I could learn Urdu and Brahui from the professor! *Khoosh Amdeed*—welcome to Shiraz!" Asghar said warmly.

"Thank you, Agha Asghar. You have a lovely place, and I'm sure the cuisine lives up to the spirit of Shiraz!" Zeenat replied with a smile.

"Asghar and Zeenat, the great poet Saadi often spoke of missing the dishes of Shiraz whenever he was away. When we were children, we imagined it to be an elaborate feast that Saadi yearned for so fondly. In reality, it was just naan with some kebab or vegetables. But let Agha get back to his work while we decide on our own *daawat-e-Shiraz.*"

With a slight bow, Asghar returned to his duties, and we chose to start with French Shiraz wine, accompanied by some tapas with Persian condiments. Zeenat made the selections, including a mix of salad, saffron rice, chalo kebabs, and a vegetable dish with naan bread.

"Aren't you being a bit modest, Madam Diplomat? Let the professor spoil us a bit," I teased.

"That's plenty, Gul, and we can always order more if needed."

"No wonder you take such good care of yourself—a perfect blend of exercise and balanced food."

"I try. Here, I can jog freely, and we have a small gym in the residence hall to stay active. I assume you visit the gym at least twice a week?"

"In Bristol and Bath, I cycled whenever I could, but I miss that here in London with all the traffic. I should be walking more; Regent's Park isn't too far from my place. I'd love to walk to your residence hall sometime."

"Last weekend, I explored the South Bank. It's full of cafés, book kiosks, and street musicians performing outside the exhibition halls. I'm glad it's pedestrianized along the Thames."

"That's my favorite part of London, though I've mostly explored it alone. I'm glad you're here, and we can roam together—minus the London Eye."

"Big cities like London often leave people feeling alone. Millions of people living, working, and walking in solitude, occasionally glancing at younger, cheerful groups that remind them of their own lost youth."

"True, Zeenat. Even smaller English villages can have lonely souls despite the romanticized image of country life. It's not always true for those who are old, alone, or shy."

"Cities like Karachi and Lahore, especially their newer areas, can be impersonal in their own way with the internal migration, but places like Quetta or smaller towns like Turbat still maintain a level of sociability that almost erases individual privacy."

"Quetta is a bit like Bristol: modern and traditional, imperial and diverse. I should tell you about Anne. Her ancestor, Robert Sandeman, partly inspired her visit to Balochistan, and we were quite close for a time. She came to Bristol fresh from Oxford, while I had just moved from UCL. Joe's reputation preceded him, and his seminars often turned into social events. That's where I got to know Anne better before she moved to her own studio apartment from Salford, a village between Bath and Bristol."

"But, Gul, weren't you both pursuing different paths?" Zeenat asked.

"Yes, exactly. She focused on literature, specifically creative writing and American authors, while I combined sociology and history with a touch of economics, which they started calling peasant studies. I joined Joe's class to explore African and Indian literature in English, far from my usual subjects. Perhaps it was fate that I met Anne. Her mother, Susanne, was Danish and met Anne's father, Terence, during a study visit to Scotland. Susanne became a librarian in Bath. After her doctorate, Anne secured a lectureship at Exeter, while I moved to Bath. Then we visited Balochistan together. Anne had undergone surgery in her late teens, which left her unable to have children—a fact she shared with me. It didn't affect our relationship, but it did put us in a difficult situation during our visit back home. On Anjum's advice, I told Ammi, and it shocked her because she had already considered Anne an ideal match for our family.

"Back in the UK, I discussed marriage with Anne, but she wasn't keen on it due to her inability to become a mother in the traditional sense. Her move to Odense, with Susanne already living there and a better job offer, marked the downturn of our relationship. Around the same time, UCL drew me back from Bath. Terence had passed away in Bath a few years earlier due to cancer, which partly explained Susanne's return to Denmark. She met Nasser, an Iraqi Kurd and academic, while Anne became close to Willem, a Dutch colleague at SDU. They now live together, though I've lost touch with her apart from the occasional message from Susanne. Susanne, traditional in many ways, reminds me of Ammi. Sorry for this long account of the past two decades of my life."

"That's quite a story. No wonder Bristol left such an indelible mark on your life. I'm sorry to hear about Anne's struggles and how you both went your separate ways. Your mother mentioned Anne a few times, and according to Bahram and Shireen, modern relationships are the new normal—partners can move on and drift apart."

"So my brother and his wife have turned post-modern, I see."

"Perhaps that's one way to put it. But back in Turbat, people adored Anne and thought she would come back as your bride. Some even assumed you were already married."

"I can imagine that. Our people often think every man-woman relationship must end in marriage. Your mother, though, knew we occupied separate rooms in our house. Aunt Zahra is one of the shrewdest people I know. I just hope she doesn't blame me for introducing her prized daughter to French wine!"

"Our people might seem old-fashioned, but they're pragmatic in their own way. Her main worry is that I'm still single, just like you. But while she's not concerned about you, she thinks I need to find a suitable match before it's too late."

"They're proud of your achievements, Zeenat. That's undeniable."

"Thank you, but I still dream of becoming an author someday." I looked into her thoughtful eyes as I refilled our glasses.

"Never mind. You're not driving, and this toast is to celebrate being together, away from prying eyes." I placed my right hand over her wrist, earning a spontaneous smile and a hint of color on her cheeks. "Tell me more about your life over the past decade."

"Well, aside from working at the foreign office, I served in Muscat, Geneva, and had a short stint at the UN mission in New York. Professional demands took most of my time, but regular exercise kept me grounded. If you're asking about my personal life, it hasn't been as eventful as yours, though I did have a brief connection with a colleague from Chitral. Aslam was well-spoken and, like me, belonged to a marginalized group—the Kalasha people. They're often mischaracterized as the descendants of ancient Greeks, holding animistic beliefs and awaiting Alexander's return. There are only a few thousand left, and while they aren't Muslims, they share cultural traits with the rest of Chitral's population. Aslam attended Major Langlands's school before going to Aitchison in Lahore. Unlike me, he joined the district management service and is now a divisional head in Mardan, with the potential to become a chief secretary."

"How did it go between you two, if I may ask?"

"It's fair to be curious, Gul, since you shared about Anne. Maybe there are more stories you haven't told me yet," Zeenat teased, pulling her hand away playfully. "Aslam was admired for his self-confidence, which made some colleagues envious. I visited Chitral and even the isolated Kalasha valleys with him. The Kalasha are polite and charming, akin to the Sheedis in the south—underprivileged and seen as outsiders for not following Islam, which invites fervent clerics funded by land mafias aiming to seize their lands for tourism and timber. My visit to Bamboriyat and other villages was eye-opening. Aslam's family welcomed me with garlands, though we kept things strictly platonic in public. Like in Turbat, the younger generation there urgently needs role models, and Aslam was trying his best."

"That sounds like a fascinating research topic—combining lower Balochistan with upper Chitral through the lens of political economy and sociology. By the way, Alexander did venture into Chitral and eventually made his way back through Pasni and

Gwadar before re-entering Persia. That's your historical context, though I appreciate your comparison of the Kalasha to the Sheedis. So, what happened between you two?"

"Aslam founded a small library in the main village, managed by Kalasha women volunteers. He also built a clinic and a water plant, overcoming significant challenges to secure funding. His team was hardworking and honest, with some members studying medicine in Peshawar and others becoming teachers and nurses. Like our Koh-i-Murad, they have a sacred site behind the village, a rocky structure called Malaush, where they make goat offerings during festivals. We met a few more times in Islamabad and once in Multan, where he was posted. We explored Sufi shrines and indulged in Multan's famous mangoes. Our relationship waned due to my overseas assignments and the increasing demands of work. We lost touch about three years ago, and I hear he's now married to a Kalasha doctor who practices nearby and offers free medical services. I admire his commitment and hope he writes about his people, who are often misunderstood as 'unbelievers.' The Kalasha women have slightly more rights than many women across the Indus, which was surprising."

"Is it true that Kalasha women are sent to an isolated place during their menstruation?"

"Yes, they go to *bashalini*, a place where they stay during their periods. It's where they bond and build camaraderie. I spent four days in *bashalini* during my extended stay in Bamboriyat and found it empowering. With no men around, we could socialize, laugh, and reflect. Some women read, crocheted, and composed poetry. We even had music and dance sessions in the evenings after our meals, which were simple but fresh."

"Is it true that Kalasha women are known for their beauty, or is that just an exotic myth?"

"In a way, it's true, especially given the emphasis on colorism. Kalasha, like Kashmiris and some Central Asians, tend to have lighter complexions. Their active, outdoor lifestyle contributes to their health, although poverty is widespread."

Asghar returned with a tray of desserts and a steaming teapot, grounding us back in London.

"Try these, Madam Diplomat, before you find yourself in a *bashalini* in St. John's Wood, with only one man for company—a man who admires intelligent women but often leaves them to their own devices," I joked.

"Well, now I'm intrigued about this abode and what I might find there."

"Zeenat, you should write about Kalasha women before their community fades or the pressure from both sides squeezes them out. They've preserved their unique beliefs and way of life for millennia, protected by the rugged Hindu Kush. You're in a perfect position to connect Turbat and Bamboriyat, much like the *Rig Veda* spoke of our ancestors."

"Well, collaborating on such themes sounds perfect, and involving Alexis could add a fascinating dimension. He spent significant time in the valleys, immersing himself in the culture until the region's growing militancy made him fear for his safety. He's back in Corinth now, surrounded by Kalash artifacts and his personal diaries and research notes. As a fellow academic, you'd find conversations with him enriching. During my time in the valley and later in Islamabad, Alexis was laid-back, almost Bohemian in his approach, but impressively articulate when discussing 'primordial' communities like the Kalasha."

"Zeenat, this is quite the revelation. You've opened up a whole new perspective for me and sparked an idea for comparative research that incorporates fieldwork. A trip to Chitral and beyond with a well-informed companion sound like an academic adventure worth undertaking."

AFRICAN BALOCHISTAN

Zeenat appreciated the way I maintained my apartment, with its minimalist furnishings contrasted by an extensive collection of books and music. The indoor plants and two paintings by Changez Sultan depicting the *Himalayan Odyssey* added a warm, vibrant touch. The apartment featured a small balcony overlooking a nearby square where I often sat with tea and a book or had lunch on bright weekends. Around the corner was High Street's shopping area, where Soutine's offered Parisian cuisine and a grocery-cum-delicatessen stocked with Mediterranean varieties, run by a cheerful manager who made everyone feel welcome, often greeting patrons with their newspapers and dogs.

We talked late into the night, pausing only briefly for coffee. Zeenat expressed an interest in investigating Balochistan's historical maritime connections with Oman and East Africa, sharing that her time in Muscat had been her most joyous posting. Oman, a society firmly rooted in its traditions yet progressing steadily, prided itself on shared cultural ties with the Arab world, Iran, Balochistan, and East Africa. The nostalgia for Zanzibar, which had once been the capital of the Sultanate of Muscat, was palpable. The legacies of the Portuguese, British, and Tanzanians had left lasting marks on the Omani expatriates, and Sultan Qaboos had taken steps to preserve this history. The Sultan had built a museum inside Fort Jesus, overlooking the Indian Ocean in Mombasa, dedicated to Omani textiles, handicrafts, and artifacts, and had restored the chambers where Omani elders and traders held their councils long before European incursions.

While serving in Muscat, Zeenat had visited Kenya and Tanzania, becoming well-acquainted with their histories, including the slave trade that Arabs, like the British slavers such as Edward Colston, had conducted. Zeenat was struck by the murals in Nairobi's National Museum depicting chained Africans being herded by their Arab captors. In Muscat, she had attended seminars and lectures where Oman's historical ties with Balochistan and Africa were occasionally mentioned, often met with reticence. The novelist Jokha Alharthi had touched on such themes in her work, but discussions about past slavery were still taboo in many parts of the Middle East and South Asia. Zeenat planned to delve into this overlooked subject through archival research in London and unpublished papers from Western universities, including UCL.

By dawn, we retired to our separate bedrooms. Despite the shared intimacy of the evening, we exercised restraint, avoiding the usual path where dates often culminate in shared beds and more. We lay apart, and though sleep evaded me, my mind raced. Did Zeenat feel she wasn't good enough for me? Was I simply weary from reaching the pivotal age of forty? Or was I waiting for Zeenat to guide us on this path? Should I even expect her to? As a modern woman, Zeenat was beyond the conventional definitions of liberation, yet she maintained decorum in personal situations. What would happen if we crossed that line? I chose to trust my instinct, believing it to be my most reliable guide.

When I brought her tea and toast—a morning ritual of mine—Zeenat was already awake. Mornings inspired me and were perfect for writing before the day's distractions began. In Turbat, the call of the muezzin and the birds' dawn serenades would stir us awake, though Ammi was always up earlier for her prayers, sometimes joined by Aunt Zahra.

"I didn't realize you woke up early, even on weekends, especially after such a late night!" Zeenat said, smiling.

"Old habits from Turbat die hard. Plus, I have special company and must be a good host."

"I enjoyed last night, but let me make us breakfast sometime."

"Next time, definitely. Today, I wouldn't want to disappoint Carlo, the manager at Soutine's. You'll like the place and the service."

"Ah, the joys and hiccups of being single, Gul!"

"I want to impress this guest, especially since she's a diplomat, and I claim a seven-year seniority over her."

"So, you've hit the fabulous forty?"

"Indeed, four decades filled with the pursuit of knowledge and friendships that have turned me into a true expatriate. It's time to act more responsibly."

Carlo, wearing his signature apron and an amiable expression, found us a table on the sidewalk, shielded by flowerpots and a vine-covered fence that offered a degree of privacy. The aroma of coffee, croissants, omelets, and roasted vegetables heightened our hunger, and we ordered hot beverages promptly.

"Zeenat, I'm sorry you couldn't go for your morning jog."

"I considered it before you brought in the tea and toast. Maybe we can substitute it with a walk around your neighborhood before I head back."

"Yes, we're close to Lord's, the Regent's Park Mosque, and the park itself. I'm looking forward to breakfast, especially since it's been a while since our Persian meal at Asghar's."

"Don't worry, I won't take my time with breakfast either. Perhaps next time, I could make parathas, omelets, and other desi dishes. Your choice, Gul."

"I wouldn't mind that at all. I've missed homemade desi food. But for that breakfast, we'd need to spend the night together—either at yours or mine. Are you ready for such boring company?"

"I like your humor—it's self-deprecating but still witty. I could jog here, and it wouldn't require an overnight stay. But it doesn't matter; you're decent company. The place and time don't count, Prof!"

While enjoying our platters, I continued probing Zeenat, who didn't mind my slightly acerbic humor:

"Our classical Persian poetry adores beautiful women like yourself, especially when accompanied by a bottle of full-bodied red wine and a musician playing the flute. Yet here we are, drinking French or Italian wine, even in an authentic eatery like Shiraz. I wonder if Khayyam, Hafiz, and the others lived in more tolerant times than ours. How can we deny these earthly pleasures to our poets and artists? They embody human instinct and earthly desires, which is why their works remain beloved centuries later."

"I agree. Life seemed easier for those sages, and even our own poets like Mir, Ghalib, and Bedil managed to write about wine, women, and pleasure with grace, never appearing scandalous. It's curious that neither Iran nor Pakistan, despite their temperate climates similar to Italy and Spain, produce quality wine. Our drinkers resort to hard liquor, and the ensuing intoxication only detracts from meaningful social interaction."

"The so-called heavenly delights are available here on earth, yet they must be enjoyed responsibly. No one has the right to coerce abstainers into drinking. But life, no matter where you are, has its share of charades and challenges. I hope they prepared the eggs and vegetables to your liking. I avoided ordering sausages for obvious reasons."

"It's perfect, Gul, especially paired with this delightful conversation about classical poets."

London's parks are never far away. After circling the mosque, we walked through Regent's Park until we found a spot by the pond to relax. After basking in the sun for a while, I walked Zeenat to Baker Street's tube station so she could head back to her hall.

"Thank you for your hospitality and support, Gul. I might need your help with my research, though I'm well-placed for now. Your writings could be invaluable during this initial phase."

"Keep next Friday evening open. We can explore Brick Lane, unless you have academic obligations. If so, we can plan for Saturday." Zeenat waved goodbye as she passed through the ticket barriers.

Teaching and administrative tasks kept me occupied during the week, which flew by. Zeenat messaged me to say she wasn't available on Friday due to a departmental event but was free for a Saturday outing. We planned to meet at the British Library for tea before heading east.

The library was bustling, its alcoves, cafés, and staircases filled with readers, students, and visitors—a scene starkly different from the hustle of Oxford Street or other parts of the city. After securing our tea and muffins, we found an empty table just as a couple vacated theirs. Zeenat seemed enthralled by the place, where serenity reigned despite the constant, quiet movement of people. We discussed her essay plans and recent commentary on West Asia in the newspapers, though Zeenat's focus was on scholarly articles, as she was already well-acquainted with the major works in her field.

The walk from the library to Brick Lane was pleasant on a dry day. We stopped at the central mosque, a building that had once been a Huguenot church and later a synagogue, showcasing the area's layered cultural history. The adjacent Jewish Museum offered insights into how this part of London had long been a haven for immigrants and refugees. In a nearby bookshop run by a Bangladeshi woman, I bought Zeenat *Salaam Brick Lane* by Tarquin Hall, a memoir of life in this diverse neighborhood, replete with stories of struggle and resilience.

"Zeenat, I knew you'd love these bagels. They're authentic and fresh, brought here by Eastern European Jews long before New York claimed bagel fame."

"They're delicious, especially with cream cheese and smoked salmon. And after that long walk, they're even more satisfying. But why do they spell it 'beigel' here?"

"For authenticity, I suppose! And they're budget-friendly, true to the area's character."

Our visit to Café 1001 was like stepping into another world, particularly at the back where modern-day hippies and solitary poets sat as if meditating, lost in their own musings.

"Does England have many of these Bohemian enclaves, or are they local Travelers?" Zeenat asked.

"Yes, cities like London, Liverpool, Glasgow, and Bristol have these groups who seem stuck in the 1960s. But Glastonbury is the epicenter. While I can't promise you the music festival, we could include Glastonbury in our West Country tour."

The academic year passed like weather systems over the North Atlantic, and before I knew it, Zeenat was preparing to return to her department, and I was planning a brief visit to Karachi. I was glad Zeenat had experienced the West Country, including a nostalgic visit to my old digs in Totterdown, breakfast in Easton, and a drive to Glastonbury for lunch at a local pub, before we headed to Bath for a weekend stay at the Francis Hotel in Queen Square. Our London outings to galleries, museums, and bookshops had only strengthened our bond. Despite holding hands and exchanging warm embraces, we never crossed the threshold of intimacy, restrained by an unspoken understanding until that night in Bath.

The West Country visit stirred memories of my decade in Bristol and Bath, with occasional trips to Salford and Exeter. Though they now felt like distant memories, the nostalgia mingled with a hint of longing. I would be lying if I said I didn't think of Anne while cycling through Bear Flat or during walks through the Two Tunnels. But Anne had moved on, building a life with Willem in Odense, and I, too, had reached a point where looking back felt unnecessary. Yet, dining at Bill's reminded me of Susanne, who had once joined me there for dinner. This time, other diners glanced discreetly at Zeenat, who walked with the poise of someone fully aware of her beauty and presence. Her black frilly dress and confident smile highlighted her elegance. She had taken the time to dress me in a way that matched her look: a casual combination with a cravat instead of a tie, fitting perfectly without appearing ostentatious.

Over dinner, I enjoyed a bourbon burger while Zeenat savored a ribeye, appreciating Bill's known reputation for meat dishes. The shelves lined with pickles, olive oils, and wines added to the informal yet cozy setting. I chose the restaurant subconsciously, perhaps drawn by memories of Susanne. Zeenat, however, seemed to enjoy the vibrant evening atmosphere. We took our time with a bottle of Chianti.

"Gul, I hope you don't mind me being so direct, but we've known each other for years, and in the months since I arrived in London, we still haven't shared a bed. Is it me, or is something holding you back?" Zeenat's question was forthright, yet gentle.

"I admire your honesty, Zeenat. I've cherished you since our walk in Lyari and have yearned for you over these months. But something held me back, perhaps my own desire for you to fully know me and my past. It was my way of being cautious, but I acknowledge that we could have taken this step sooner."

"I sensed that something was missing, though you've always been close to me."

"No, you're perfect. It was my hesitation, a mix of self-imposed decorum and my belief that I shouldn't misuse any position of influence. I wanted us to be equals, to move forward only when we both felt completely at ease."

"But I'm not the kind of woman who bows to traditional expectations or powerful men. I'm independent, which is why I'm asking, not out of need, but out of sincerity."

"You're my closest friend, Zeenat, and I'm grateful for your courage. You've lifted a burden I didn't even realize I was carrying. Here's to our friendship and your strength."

We clinked our glasses and ordered another bottle, lingering in the restaurant, content to let the evening stretch on.

Following a stroll in central Bath, starting with Pulteney Bridge and continuing along Paragon Street, the Circus, and past Jane Austen's former home, we finally returned to the Francis Hotel. The fresh, cool night air had proven to be a revitalizing tonic. Inside our room, with its traditional plush furnishings, Fleetwood Mac had never sounded more harmonious. Slowly, I wrapped my arms around Zeenat, meeting her half-closed eyes and sensing that, like me, she had lowered her guard. Her responsive lips, which I had longed to feel like a wandering bhikshu discovering forbidden pleasures, electrified my senses as our hands explored new, uncharted territories with inhibitions and doubts dissolved in Bath's misty air.

"You don't need to worry about consequences," Zeenat whispered, "I've been on the pill for quite some time. But judging by your moves, I don't think that's even on your mind."

"I can't think of anything else but traversing your divine figure, Zeenat, especially in this city where I left part of my past behind. I appreciate the precautions you take; it makes these moments even more joyous and enduring."

210

We must have overslept, as we missed the breakfast hour and ended up with coffee and croissants, planning the rest of the day before heading back to London. On Zeenat's request, I drove her to Bear Flat, my old neighborhood, recounting stories of Joe, Emma, and their family who lived nearby in Oldfield Park—a popular area for university students. Just as I was about to mention Ryan, my Irish neighbor, we saw a clean-shaven man in an orange robe walking toward the town center.

"That's Malinga, a Buddhist professor at the other university. I never met him while living here, but many Bathonian mothers seek his blessings for their babies," I said.

"Monks live austere lives and keep a distance from women. Their celibacy keeps them apart from the kind of connection we shared last night, Gul."

"I hope they don't see women as the cause of temptation. Too many religions obsess over this idea of original sin. I'm grateful that our poets and many Sufis don't spare the narrow prescriptions laid out by mullahs when it comes to relationships."

"Our 'sinful' night followed the sighting of a saint. Bath is full of surprises, and so are you. You abstain from intimacy for months, and then when you do engage, it's with boundless energy. But to be honest, the pleasure was mutual."

The single-story pub with the bear on its roof was gone, replaced by new flats over a convenience store. Standing outside, I recounted my memories of Ryan, my neighbor back then, but decided not to dwell on curiosity.

"Let me show you Newton St. Loe, a medieval village where history feels palpable."

"Why not, when I have the privilege of a guided tour from an academic who's retracing his own past in this heritage city?"

"Yes, the past is another country, and as immigrants, we can never fully disconnect from it."

Driving through Oldfield Park, I paused outside a stone house on a quiet street. "This is where Joe and Emma lived. Joe's classes broadened our minds, turning them into a kind of Athenian agora. He never received the tenure he deserved."

"So, how did Joe manage?" Zeenat asked.

"Well, Emma worked full-time, and this house was paid off. Joe was an Indophile, writing novels and travelogues about India, particularly Bengal and Chennai."

"Why are you speaking of him in the past tense?" Zeenat's tone was gentle but curious.

"Joe passed away a few years ago. He developed a rare infection that affected his sight, leading to the loss of vision in his right eye. Despite getting an implant and wearing dark glasses, his academic work suffered. He still updated us through social media and took his dogs for walks by the river. One day, he slipped and hit his head on the pavement. He never recovered from the concussion. Emma shared the news on Joe's page. The funeral was private, but some of us visited Emma afterward to offer condolences."

"That's so tragic, Gul! I hope his former students and colleagues honored his memory somehow."

"We held a memorial seminar at Bristol that ended at the Hawthorns, our usual gathering spot on campus. I dedicated a paper on *qanats* to Joe, and in another report, I acknowledged John Gallagher's work on the British Empire and peasantry."

"Why don't you knock on the door and see if Emma is home?" Zeenat suggested.

"This isn't Turbat, dear. You can't just show up unannounced. People here value their privacy. I came here to remember Joe and, as you said, relive a cherished past while sharing the present with you."

"Gul, you have a heart of gold. Remember that Neil Diamond song? You may be meticulous in your profession, but deep down, you're still a mellow, semi-tribal Baloch. Turbat's soil is in your veins."

We parked by the tiny corner shop in Newton St. Loe, facing an old tree. Walking around the stone houses, I felt the village's deep sense of history. Owned by the Duchy of Cornwall, with its headquarters in one of the larger mansions, the village contrasted sharply with Bath's liveliness, offering quiet stone houses that had sheltered generations of royalty and commoners. Few tourists knew of this secluded village nestled among trees and meadows, where horses, sheep, and bulls roamed freely. The new café and shop in a large barn sold Duchy products and served sandwiches, cakes, and tea. When I last visited with Anne, the village had only a small shop and post office in the square.

"Those buildings to the west belong to the university, enjoying this idyllic landscape. That's where John Gallagher, a renowned Trotskyite historian, taught until he retired. As I mentioned, John and I shared a flat in Bristol's working-class neighborhood that we passed through yesterday. His influence on me was significant, as you can see in my writing. If we take this narrow road, we can drive through the university and catch a glimpse of the two lakes designed by Capability Brown centuries ago."

"You gained so much from your West Country experience, Gul, but you also left a piece of your heart here."

"I would be lying if I said otherwise. These places are tied to specific people who helped me grow into a more cosmopolitan, mature person. It feels strange now to visit as an outsider."

Our tour, joyous as it was, left us even more famished since our breakfast had been light. I intentionally skipped suggesting a tea break, wanting Zeenat to experience the Globe Inn—halfway between Bath and Salford, just around the corner from Newton St. Loe. Despite the busy Sunday brunch hour, we managed to find a spot near the fireplace, eagerly awaiting our Sunday roast with Yorkshire pudding. Zeenat adored the country pub, especially its older, rustic sections. She initially considered ordering fish and chips, but at my insistence, opted for the traditional roast, accompanied by a glass of white wine, while I chose a local ale. Zeenat's ability to seamlessly blend into any environment never ceased to amaze me, embodying a rare blend of intellect and charisma. Momentarily, I was transported back to my meal here with the Sandemans, a distant memory that sent a faint ripple through my consciousness, though I didn't dwell on it for long.

"Did you come here often when you were based in Bath?" Zeenat asked.

"I did, but only on a few occasions and usually with colleagues and friends. The late Terence Sandeman, on leave from Dubai, once hosted a lunch for his family and me here at the Globe. That was years ago, and while the place hasn't changed much, it's now owned by a brewery instead of a family."

"How did Terence feel about his ancestral ties to Balochistan?"

"He had a strong connection, as did Anne. Unfortunately, Terence passed away too soon due to cancer. Anne's fiction captures her family's narrative, weaving together Scotland, Fort Sandeman, Las Bela, and Quetta, with mentions of Afghanistan. Like my own ties to the West Country, her connection to Balochistan was profound, though it might have softened over time after her move to Denmark."

"We're peculiar beings, aren't we? We move on, but our past never truly leaves us. It holds memories, both sweet and bitter. Elephants mourn their elders at the very place where they died, even after fighting for dominance. We humans carry our pasts in our minds, unless age steals it away with dementia."

"True. It would be dishonest to claim we're free of our past. We all carry an inner historian. Across the fields, there's a cycle path connecting Bath and Bristol, called the towpath, which runs parallel to the Avon River. It's lined with hedges and trees and is popular with cyclists. In my solitary moments, I miss it and the old train tunnels beneath Bath, which once connected the town to the southern coast. We should come back for a cycle safari sometime."

"Gul, life here feels slower than in London and the Southeast. I bet many people choose to retire here, while for you, it was the reverse."

"Sharp observation. Did you notice that from seeing older patrons here or at Bill's last night?"

"That's part of it, but also because younger professionals likely can't afford these Georgian homes. Bristol might be a different story."

"The Somerset countryside is a part of me, even during my busy London life. Beyond Bath and Bristol, which you've seen, places like Corsham, Lacock, and Castle Combe offer a glimpse of mythical rural England. Although the latter two villages are in Wiltshire, not Somerset, Salisbury is nearby, and Wiltshire has a high population of military families, a legacy of its colonial barracks and training grounds. It's like Pothowar in Pakistan, a region known for its martial tradition rooted in farming communities."

"Farmers fighting for land—theirs and others'—would be an interesting academic study. The British historically preferred Pothowari peasants and Jat Sikhs over Pashtuns, Tamils, Biharis, Bengalis, and Baloch, fitting each group into distinct categories."

"Military demographics are likely similar in today's India and Pakistan."

"I get the sense, Gul, that a part of you is always in Southwest Balochistan. Do you often feel alone?"

"I'd be lying if I said no. But I value the journey that brought me here. This cross-cultural experience has helped me grow, though I do feel a moral responsibility to contribute to education and mentorship in Turbat and beyond."

"That sounds like the best of both worlds, though balancing time and resources can be tough. Don't get me wrong, it's achievable and worth it."

"Bentham and Gandhi both inspire me to follow a path rooted in utilitarianism. I envision myself spending part of my career in Karachi, close to Lyari and Turbat, supporting local education initiatives. I want more Baloch youth to pursue technical education for better opportunities in the Gulf, while others prepare for civil and military services at home."

"That's a noble vision, Gul, but don't rush to leave your job and return home. Shireen and Bahram can lay the groundwork with Anjum's help. I'd be happy to collaborate."

"You wouldn't need to leave your job either, Zeenat. Your position is empowering for the community. You could contribute through workshops and other initiatives. But yes, let's keep talking about this."

Zeenat's remaining time in London until her graduation flew by like an eagle, and while our meetings were spontaneous and sporadic, they brought us closer than ever. Our excursions within the academic golden triangle, under the guise of seminars and workshops, were filled with joy and deepened our relationship. My siblings, especially Anjum, gradually became aware of our mutual affection and closeness. However, they respected our privacy and supported us without imposing their views. This subtle understanding, infused with love and support, renewed my instinctive desire to reconnect with Turbat.

When Zeenat left to resume her new position as a senior faculty member in her restructured training academy, I was left with a profound sense of emptiness. I missed her deeply and, at times, felt envious of her achievements. Yet, I fully appreciated that through her position in the corridors of power, she represented a triumph over the odds faced by many of us due to our ethnicity, gender, class, and complexion. Zeenat was a living testament to resilience—a Sheedi woman from a remote area, born into a humble family, now lecturing and leading those who often came from privileged backgrounds. To them, she must have been a shock, a powerful example that indomitable will and perseverance can lead to remarkable achievements.

Three months after Zeenat's departure, I boarded a flight to pursue a new dream. I took an extended leave from my job, a mix of sabbatical and self-financed time, and, with the assistance of Hamid Panjwani, a UCL colleague now working at a local university, I landed in Karachi. Shireen, Bahram, and Hamid helped coordinate my arrival. A week later, accompanied by my parents and Anjum, I flew to Turbat. Raheela, Anjum's classmate and a former air hostess, was not part of the crew; I learned from her successor that she had retired and was now living in Gwadar with her family, occasionally visiting Turbat and Karachi.

The four of us were returning to Turbat with a single-minded purpose. The excitement and energy in the air were palpable, especially from Ammi and Abu, who seemed to have found a renewed sense of purpose. I knew that this was more than just about my return.

After refreshing ourselves at home, we headed to Aunty Zahra's house. She was sitting in a corner, knitting in her newly built home, with framed pictures of her three children displayed on a pedestal. Zeenat's portrait, in her graduation gown and mortarboard, took the central spot, exuding grace and an elusive smile that seemed to search for me from within the frame. When we entered the room, I approached Aunty Zahra and touched her feet. She placed her hand on my head, then gently lifted me up, tears streaming down her cheeks. I stood there, rooted, as Ammi wrapped her arms around Aunty Zahra, whispering softly in her ear. The room was silent until Aunty Zahra's voice broke through, trembling but resolute:

"Zeenat is your daughter. She always was and always will be. And Gulbaz Khan Gichki is my son. He will make Zeenat the happiest person on earth. This is the proudest day of my life. Zeenat and Gulbaz make an ideal couple."

She had just finished speaking when Zeenat walked in, stopping in her tracks at the sight of us all gathered around her mother. Abu stepped forward and kissed her forehead, while Ammi and Anjum pulled her into a tight embrace.

"Even before I could lay claim to you, Zeenat, this trio has already taken you in," I said with a smile. "Welcome to the Gichki clan, you trailblazer!"

Both families decided to hold our wedding ceremonies in late December, during the winter holidays, to ensure that those of us working and living away from Turbat could attend. Before returning to Karachi and Zeenat flying back to Islamabad, we agreed to keep the ceremonies simple and traditional, focusing on Turbat without the grand feasts and extensive dowries typically associated with such events. Zeenat, after a long leave, would resume her job, while I planned to return to my teaching position at UCL once my sabbatical ended. This arrangement, with periodic leave, would continue for a short time until we decided where to settle together.

On December 15th, while in my university office in Karachi, I received a call from Susanne in Odense.

"Gul, thank you for the note you sent about your upcoming marriage to Zeenat. Congratulations! We're so happy for you," she said warmly.

"Oh, Susanne, that's so thoughtful of you. How is everyone over there?" I replied.

"Anne, Willem, and Nasser end their greetings and best wishes. Are you ready for a surprise?"

"Of course, Susanne. I'm eager to hear it."

"Gul, all four of us will be arriving in Karachi on the 20th to attend your wedding in Turbat."

"That's incredibly kind and such a wonderful surprise! The weather is perfect, and Balochistan will be delighted to welcome the Sandemans back."

Indeed, the past is not always just another country; sometimes, it reappears as the future!

ACKNOWLEDGMENTS

Without straying away from the genre of campus romance, my protagonists in this novel hail from less-traversed terrains often not found in such works, though their paths cross at cosmopolitan campuses such as UCL and Bristol. Balochistan and Totterdown, despite being thousands of miles apart, coalesce in multiple ways, inducting communities such as Sheedis—the African Asians—and Kalasha of Chitral. At the same time, our main characters partake in ethnic cuisines in Easton and break bread with Gandhi in Tavistock Square. My sustenance came from traveling across Makran, Muscat, and Chitral, whereas an almost three-decade-long teaching in Bath helped recap nooks and crannies in the West Country. While acknowledging support from my colleagues and students both in Bath and Oxford and certainly my immediate family, it would be remiss if I do not recognize a rich array of friends who accompanied a historian-turned-novelist on his journey from the Peak District to Oman, Iran, and Kenya. In Oxford, Liz Peretz, Bill MacKeith, Meena and Pritam Gill; in Lahore, Asghar Zaidi and Raheel Malik; in Karachi, Ameena Saiyid, Sarvat Hasin, Muneeza Shamsie, Aquila Ismail and Nadia Ghani; Vernon Hewitt in Bristol; Suhayl Saadi in Glasgow; Hamid Zaman in Boston; Karine Ancellin in Athens; Dur e Aziz in Ann Arbor; Osama Siddique in Lahore; Yasser Khan in Doha; Abbas Zaidi in Sydney, and at Amazon, Isaac Rich through his punctilious efficiency and Kate Mendes with her editorial diligence, helped in their own distinct ways to turn an abstraction into a reality. Brian Griffin, Gavin Cologne-Brookes, Amer Mukhtar, Elaine Chalus, Sheba Saeed, Tabish Khair, Rania Hafez, and Olivette Otele: my words can't match your creativity and humanity. My late friends, Nick Allen, and Joe Roberts, departed from this mundane world but not from cherished memories. My superb hosts in Turbat--and they are several, especially from among the writers and academics—and likewise colleagues and friends in Odense stood me in good stead whenever I feared losing my bearings.

GLOSSARY

Abu	Father
Ajrak	A traditional Sindhi cotton wrap-around with dark color patterns worn across the lower Indus lands.
Ammi	Mother
Bhikshu	A Buddhist monk
Burfi	A South Asian delicacy made of sugar, milk, pistachio and cardamom.
Cholay	Chickpeas
Couscous	Moroccan cuisine made of buck wheat.
Dukkha	Grief
Englistan	England
Firangi	Foreigner
Gulab Jamons	South Asian sweets made with flour, sugar and some other condiments, often served in a sweet syrup
Haandi	A meat dish cooked in an earthen pot, popular among the Punjabis
Habashi	Abyssinian/Ethiopian
Imambara	Lit: home of Imam; a mosque-like place of Shi'i Muslims
Lassi	Churned buttermilk

Mihrab	Prayer knave in a mosque facing towards Makkah
Muezzin	A worshipper who calls for prayer
Naashta	Breakfast
Nihari	Spicy, tender meat dish.
Pheeki	Sugar free
Pujari	A Hindu worshipper
Puris	Fried thin, waffle-like bread, consumed in breakfast.
Qahwa	Green tea
Sajji	Mutton leg grilled by open fire on swirling skewers. A traditional Baloch dish.
Sukha	Relief
Tamasha	Spectacle
Wilayati	British
Wisaal	Reunion

THE END